THE SCOUTS' BOOK OF HEROES

The Scouts' Book of Heroes

A RECORD OF SCOUTS' WORK IN
THE GREAT WAR

With Foreword by the Chief Scout
SIR ROBERT BADEN-POWELL, K.C.B.

WITH COLOURED FRONTISPIECE AND
EIGHT HALF-TONE ILLUSTRATIONS

The Naval & Military Press Ltd

Published by
The Naval & Military Press Ltd
Unit 10 Ridgewood Industrial Park,
Uckfield, East Sussex,
TN22 5QE England
Tel: +44 (0) 1825 749494
Fax: +44 (0) 1825 765701
www.naval-military-press.com
www.military-genealogy.com
www.militarymaproom.com

In reprinting in facsimile from the original, any imperfections are inevitably reproduced and the quality may fall short of modern type and cartographic standards.

CONTENTS

	PAGE
CHAPTER I	
1914	17
CHAPTER II	
FAMOUS SCOUTS IN THE WAR	21
CHAPTER III	
SCOUT HEROES OF THE ARMY	36
CHAPTER IV	
SCOUT HEROES OF THE NAVY	128
CHAPTER V	
HEROES OF THE AIR SERVICE	159
CHAPTER VI	
THE HEROES AT HOME	179
CHAPTER VII	
JUST—A SCOUT	203

CONTENTS

PAGE

CHAPTER VIII

CALLED TO HIGHER SERVICE 218

VICTORIA CROSS 257
C.M.G. 259
DISTINGUISHED SERVICE ORDER 259
MILITARY CROSS 260
DISTINGUISHED FLYING CROSS 274
DISTINGUISHED FLYING MEDAL 275
AIR MEDAL 276
DISTINGUISHED CONDUCT MEDAL 276
DISTINGUISHED SERVICE CROSS 283
MILITARY MEDAL 283
MERITORIOUS SERVICE MEDAL 313
MERITORIOUS CONDUCT MEDAL 314
DISTINGUISHED SERVICE MEDAL 314
ROYAL HUMANE SOCIETY MEDAL 315
PROMOTION IN THE FIELD 315
FOREIGN DECORATIONS 316

LIST OF ILLUSTRATIONS

	PAGE
Boy First Class. John Travers Cornwell, V.C. Colour Drawing by Sir Robert Baden Powell	*Frontispiece*
Four Famous Scouts in War	22
Slinging his pipes into position, Piper Laidlaw struck up the " Braes of Mar "	38
Putting spurs to his horse, the Chaplain galloped out into the open	64
One Fokker staggers for a moment, and pitches forward, a mass of flames	172
What the Sea Scouts did.	180
War Services of the Boy Scouts	190
War Services of the Boy Scouts	196
Called to Higher Service	238

FOREWORD BY THE CHIEF SCOUT

WHAT can we do to perpetuate the memory of those who, in the Great War, ennobled by their splendid self-sacrifice the otherwise brutish work of battle?

That is the question that has been much in the air. Pylons and shrines interest us in the present, but after all marble is cold and flowers fade. We want something that will live with us, something that will continue after us, something also that will help to make their sacrifice of self worth while.

Happily they left us that something of themselves which we can cherish and can pass on; it is their glorious *spirit*. This, through the recital of their brave deeds, we can at least keep alive, and fan to flame in the breasts of their successors, if we will.

That is our aim in the Scout Movement. That I take it is the aim of this book.

We have not to go beyond the ranks of our own fraternity to find a glorious record of gallantry.

FOREWORD

Those who were old enough to take their part in the fight for liberty and justice have given a noble heritage to their younger brother Scouts to take up. It is not one that is merely open to one class or another, it is not the dry historical record of deeds of heroes long dead and gone, it is the legacy equally of " cooks' sons and sons of belted earls," of Jack Cornwells and of Roland Philipps', lads of our own time and of our own breed and brotherhood

Their record, as the book shows, was not the result of military training or of drill. It was the outcome of the spirit that gives the essential self-discipline and " dare to do."

Military drill may give a surface discipline, but it is a veneer which experience shows will crack off under strain. Sound wood with a natural polish is what is needed ; sound discipline is from within and not from without. There is a breaking strain to discipline that is applied, there is none to *esprit de corps*. It is the spirit that tells, the spirit which it is the aim of Scout training to inculcate.

" Play the game " is the Scouts' motto. " Play in your place ; play all out to win ; play for your side and not for yourself."

That is the clarion call that these heroes of ours have sounded to us. It is one that all should hear.

ROBERT BADEN POWELL

PREFACE

IN presenting this *Scouts' Book of Heroes*, the Editor gratefully acknowledges the assistance and untiring energy of Miss Vera C. Barclay who has written a large portion of the work.

For the chapter on " Flying Heroes," the Editor is indebted to Mr. W. F. Waudby-Smith (late Lieut. R.A.F.).

Acknowledgments are also due to Lieut. W. R. Stanton for permission to reprint his article on " Sea Scouts " ; to *The Sphere* for permission to reproduce the picture of Piper Laidlaw, V.C. ; to Messrs. Hodder & Stoughton for permission to reprint certain portions of their book on *Jack Cornwell, V.C.* ; to Mr. H. G. Elwes, Editor of *The Headquarters Gazette*, for many helpful suggestions ; to the Editor of *The Scout* for permission to reproduce the picture of the Chaplain D.S.O. ; to Messrs. Humphrey Milford for permission to reprint extracts from Capt. McKean's book, *Scouting Thrills ;* the Editor of *The Daily Express* for permission to reprint the article on " Sir Julian Byng," and the numerous Parents and Secretaries

PREFACE

of Local Associations and Scoutmasters who have supplied information concerning the heroes.

From returns supplied by Headquarters, he has compiled a list of heroes, and these form a part of the book. It is doubtful whether this is absolutely complete, as some districts failed to render a return. Many arrived too late for insertion. The Editor would therefore be glad to receive additions and corrections, for use in further editions of the work.

The choice of the brave deeds to be described in this book has not been made with a view to representing the Scouts of the various districts, or of the various awards won. We are not out to compile an official record, but just to tell those stories which have appealed to us as being particularly stirring, or as illustrating especially well the true Scout spirit underlying the heroism of our boys. We have chosen and retold these stories that they may stir the hearts of the Scouts at home, and show them the heights to which the Scout ideals may attain.

There are hundreds of stories equally thrilling and equally noble which we have not been able to include, either for lack of space, or because it was impossible to collect sufficient detail. Many a glorious deed is recounted in the concise and uninspiring language of the official report, but try

PREFACE

as we would it was impossible to draw from the Scout concerned a single detail as to the incident. Others, less self-conscious perhaps, and knowing that true humility lies in simple and unaffected truth, have been willing to tell us the tale as simply as they might have told it to the Tenderfoots of the Troop, around the fire, some peaceful night in camp. They knew that all we wanted was to give the story to the Scouts of Britain, who long to know of the deeds of their brothers, and they gave what they had with a Scout's simple generosity. The humility and genuine selflessness of the way these stories were told was more typical of the Scout spirit than even the refusal to speak. Many a story begins or ends with such words as " I don't want to brag about it—anyone else in my position would have done the same " ; " My decoration ? Oh, it was served up with the rations." But perhaps the truest and the noblest words were those with which a gallant airman, holding a very high distinction, ended his account, in a letter to his father. " I have done my duty," he wrote, " and it was not in my own strength I did it, but in God's."

While a few of the stories told came to us in the words of the Scout himself, and were generously given, in spite of the natural shrinking to talk about self, there are a large number, the details of which we collected in other ways. We wish to take this opportunity of apologising to any of our brothers whom we may have displeased by giving their stories to the public. Certain stories we have retold, from the printed accounts which have appeared in the papers ; others, we have had from the Scout's relations, possibly unknown to him, or from members of his Troop.

To all we feel we must apologise for the inadequate expression we have given to deeds too noble to be expressed in our halting words.

F. HAYDN DIMMOCK,
Editor.

LONDON,
November, 1919.

AVE MORTUIS

Hail to the dead ! The heroes who have laid
    Freely their lives on freedom's altar-stone ;
    Who with their precious blood sought to atone
For the great wrong that other men had made.
Hail to the dead ! For we are not afraid
    Lest in those balances before the throne
    Of Him who judges righteously alone
Their lives be wanting, so their deaths be weighed.

They are not dead ; these dead can never die ;
    Death can do nought to those who died as they.
There is no death. Behold how gaunt and high
Stands up the Cross against that lurid sky ;
    There seems a dying, but on the third day,
    Lo ! death undone—the stone is rolled away.

                              C. H. Fox Harvey.

CHAPTER I

1914

IT is August. The fields of corn are falling to the reaping machines. The voices of the toilers float along on the gentle summer breeze. All is peace. Away on the hillside white tents gleam, and a little way off a column of blue smoke rises steadily in the morning sunlight.

Happy voices, joyous laughter fill the air, for happiness is always to be found in a Scout camp. The Scouts, clad only in shorts, move about the camp doing the many little jobs that have to be done.

Under a great oak we find the Scoutmaster, surrounded by his Patrol-leaders, planning the day's programme. It is a wonderful programme too. A hike across the fields to a neighbouring village, a tracking game back to the camp, tea, games, and then a singsong round the camp fire.

Suddenly the Scoutmaster espies a Scout running full speed towards the camp.

"What's up with Deerfoot?" he asks. "I've never seen him run quite so fast."

Deerfoot is the camp messenger. In another minute he is standing at the salute before his Scoutmaster, and gasping for breath, he jerks out that which had caused him to run so hard.

"Britain has declared war against Germany, sir."

For a moment there is dead silence, then the senior Patrol-leader jumps to his feet.

"Good old Britain," he cries. "Three cheers for our Country and our King."

Cheers rent the air. The camp is in an uproar. Everyone is excited. Hadn't their Scoutmaster, only the previous evening, told them what would be expected of them, if Britain declared war. They would guard bridges, telegraph wires, culverts, reservoirs.

The Scoutmaster calls his leaders together again. He had planned this little speech as he lay on his blankets last night, and he wonders, just a little anxiously, how his boys will take what he has to say to them.

"Well, you chaps," he says. "Do you know what this news means to us? It means that there is work for us to do. Most probably we shall have to break camp. It may mean, for some of us at any rate, that we shall not sleep in a proper bed for many nights. It is difficult to foresee what is in store for us."

The senior leader steps out.

" You can count on us to do anything we can, sir, can't he, you chaps ? "

" Yes, rather." The answer is unanimous.

" Very well then. I'll slip off to the town to report to the police. There may be something we can do almost at once."

And so the camp is broken up. The Scouts go off to guard bridges and reservoirs; to act as messengers to the public authorities; to assist at canteens, that sprung up like mushrooms in a night.

There is never a word of grumbling. Day after day, night after night they worked, cheerfully, eagerly, while our gallant Army marched to battle.

Then came the clarion call for men—and more men.

The Scoutmaster put his beloved uniform in the wardrobe, and sallied forth to battle, leaving his troop to his Patrol-leaders.

And they carried on splendidly. In many instances the Scoutmaster, battling at the front, was cheered and inspired by a single sentence in his leader's letter. " The troop is going on fine. Smith has just passed his First Class Tests."

The Scoutmaster knows Smith of old and he marvels because Smith was the biggest duffer in the troop.

As the leaders become old enough they went one by one, and Scouts too. They knew their country needed them and they answered the call as their Scoutmaster had done, and they were ready to sacrifice all.

Thus did the scout spirit go to battle.

And the Scout Spirit has come through the war unbroken. In the heat of the battle it stood the strain, and now that the war is over, it is stronger still. It lives in the heart of every Scout and Scout Worker, and those who read this book, be they Scout or not, cannot but feel this spirit underlying the magnificent deeds of devotion to duty and self-sacrifice that are here recorded.

CHAPTER II

Famous Scouts in the War
GENERAL SIR JULIAN BYNG ("BUNGO")
District Commissioner, County of Essex

THE FIGHTING CAREER OF GENERAL BYNG

SOMEWHERE near the fighting line of the steadfast and unbeaten Third Army in France during the war might have been seen a general officer's motor-car with the blue and red pennon, designating an Army commander, fluttering from its bonnet. In the car or near it you would have seen a tall, strongly knit figure, with a gold-visored cap pulled low over the forehead, hiding a pair of strong, honest, manly blue eyes which see everything.

General the Hon. Sir Julian Byng looks what he is—the apostle of efficiency. The strong, firmly set mouth, the scrubby moustache, the rugged face denoting a life spent in the open, the squared shoulders signifying strength, all make up a picture of a soldier as one would expect him to appear.

Soldiering is Byng's existence. He lives and dreams and thinks in terms of soldiers. For thirty-five years this cool-headed man of war has studied soldiering in every phase—in peace, in war, in camp, and at schools.

When he was twenty he became a subaltern in the aristocratic 10th Hussars. Here, instead of spending the usual golden hours in playing polo and dancing and racing, he improved his time perfecting himself in his profession. He learned his Clausewitz by heart; he assisted Colonel Henderson, on the battlefields of America, in the preparation of the classical Life of Stonewall Jackson; he commanded a column of South African Light Horse in the Boer War, and won the admiration of as fine a collection of cowboys, beachcombers, miners, vaqueros, Afrikanders, larrikins, remittance men, and heroic horsemen as ever got together in a single bunch.

The Hussar dandy with the swagger stick proved himself to be as tough a nut to crack in a rough-and-tumble affair as he was in an intellectual argument about the merits of Xerxes over Hannibal of Napoleon *versus* Prince Eugene.

When the Boer War was over Byng took command of the 10th Hussars in India. Then he came home, and was put in charge of the cavalry school at Netheravon. Next he became a cavalry brigade leader, and about ten years ago was made the youngest major-general in the Army—and promptly unemployed.

(1) *Photo, Russell.*
(2) *Photo, Vandyk.*
(3) *Photo, Canadian War Records.*
(4) *Photo, Russell.*

FOUR FAMOUS SCOUTS IN THE GREAT WAR.

[*To face page* 22

FAMOUS SCOUTS IN THE WAR 23

It was then that he interested himself in Boy Scouts. I remember seeing him and General Plumer at Hatfield some six or seven years ago putting a body of Boy Scouts through their paces. These boys have become the best soldiers of our Army, a fact which is readily testified to by both of the two men who were our most successful Army commanders in the West.

One of Kitchener's Men

A turn in command of the East Anglian Territorials completed General Byng's service at home in 1912, and then he was sent to Egypt to command the British troops. He was one of Kitchener's men, and Lord Kitchener always liked to have his men near him.

In the Great War he first commanded the 3rd Cavalry Division, which did so marvellously at Ypres; then an Army corps in France and at Suvla Bay, where he conducted the withdrawal without the loss of a man; then home again to command a corps. The Canadians wanted a new commander. They asked for Byng and got him.

If you want to rouse a Canadian soldier's ire say something derogatory as to General Byng's capacity as a soldier, and, by the same token, if you want to please him say something complimentary.

From the Vimy Ridge it wasn't much of a jump to an army command, and there he is.

Cambrai caused some people to ring joy-bells a bit ahead of time, but General Byng certainly deserved them, even though Cambrai did not come off entirely.

His intimates call him " Bungo." He is terribly in earnest about war, and equally simple and lovable and kindly-natured in mufti. He knows all about horses, being a cavalryman, can shoot straight at birds, having blue eyes, and his principal pastime when at home, which is not often, is to chop and saw wood, for exercise.

In *Mr. Britling Sees It Through* Mr. Wells pictures a Colonel Rendezvous, who is all for efficiency and national service and physical training and orderliness. " Even the flowers dress on parade as he passes by." That was meant for " Bungo " Byng, the man who in the war put all these theories to the test and—won out.

"THE SOUL OF ANZAC"

Chief Commissioner for India

ABOUT THE COMMANDER OF THE AUSTRALIANS AND NEW ZEALANDERS IN GALLIPOLI

" Lieut.-General Sir W. R. Birdwood has been the soul of Anzac. Not for one single day has he ever quitted his post. Cheery

FAMOUS SCOUTS IN THE WAR 25

and full of human sympathy, he has spent many hours of each twenty-four inspiring the defenders of the front trenches, and if he does not know every soldier in his force, at least, every soldier in the force believes he's known to his chief."

That was the great praise given by Sir Ian Hamilton to the commander of the Australians and New Zealanders in Gallipoli. It is rarely that such high praise is given in despatches, but in the case of Sir W. R. Birdwood it has been won in the midst of the most terrible fighting the world has ever seen.

General Birdwood is the man whose unconventional portrait was taken while swimming in the sea of Gallipoli, and was officially issued.

Like a good many more men who have come to the front in the war, he is one of Kitchener's men. He was, indeed, for several years Kitchener's right-hand man, for he was appointed his Military Secretary when in South Africa, and followed his chief to India in the same capacity.

To the Army, in fact, he was known as " Secretary Birdwood " until he was appointed to the command of the " dare-devil warriors from the South," to use the words of Sir Ian Hamilton.

And General Birdwood was just the man to lead them. Absolutely fearless, he has escaped death time and time again by a sheer miracle. Once during the Great War, for instance, his hat was struck from his head by a bullet, which ploughed a new parting through his hair, severely cutting his scalp and partially stunning him. Despite that, he refused to leave his post, nor did he leave it when his name appeared in the casualty list.

In the Boer War he was very severely wounded, and his high courage and magnificent fighting spirit were mentioned no fewer than five times in despatches. Before being wounded he had several narrow squeaks, his horse being shot under him in a skirmish near Pretoria among other things.

In all our Wars since 1883

In the Tirrah Campaign of 1897-98, just previous to the Boer War, he was also mentioned in despatches.

The now famous general has been through practically all our little wars since he joined the Royal Scots Fusiliers in 1883.

Most of his life has been spent in India. The Birdwoods, indeed, are famous out there, for generation after generation have served in building up our great Eastern Empire.

As Secretary to Lord Kitchener in India he helped his chief to re-organise the Indian Army and the whole of the military affairs generally, one

FAMOUS SCOUTS IN THE WAR 27

of the effects of which is now to be seen in the magnificent Indian Expeditionary Force.

General Sir W. R. Birdwood can speak a number of Oriental languages and dialects, and, in fact, he was interpreter to Lord Kitchener while in India.

Born in September, 1865, General Birdwood was knighted in 1918.

General Birdwood when asked to write something for this book, sent the following to the editor :—

Although some time has elapsed since I held the appointment of Chief Commissioner for Scouts in India, I have naturally retained a live interest in their welfare and progress of the Boy Scouts' Association. That this movement had great possibilities no one doubted, but I think few people, even among its most enthusiastic supporters, could foresee the success and prominence which it has achieved throughout the British Empire, to the most distant dominions, and particularly in the willing, loyal, and valuable service which our Boy Scouts have rendered to their country during the Great. War.

One cannot fail to realize the enormous value of this organization. We may indeed be proud of the past, of our glorious traditions, and of what our fighting forces have done for us : but it is on the coming generation that the future of our great Empire is to depend. In their hands is the preservation of those noble ideals for which the nation has willingly made the greatest sacrifices.

It is, however, the duty of the present generation to ensure that our boys are educated to the responsibilities that lie before them, and it is here that the Boy Scouts' organization is fulfilling a work of far-reaching national importance. One has only to see a parade of Boy Scouts to realise the effect of their training in the development of those qualities of keenness, practicability, alertness and chivalry, all of which are essential to both the soldier and the citizen : and it is a natural corollary that they should evince a real interest in life, and a determination to prepare themselves for the part they are destined to play in our national affairs of the future.

To the boys themselves I would commend the motto of their organization as one of their guiding principles in life. In this record of Boy Scouts and Scout workers the writers have made manifest the fine reputation which is in their keeping, and I am confident that it will be their resolution in life to maintain this high standard to the end.

(*Signed*) W. R. BIRDWOOD.

FAMOUS SCOUTS IN THE WAR

PLUMER THE POLITE
Member of the Headquarters Council

A GENERAL WHO MADE NO MISTAKES

SIR HERBERT PLUMER, who was recently made a Field-Marshal, is one of the most brilliant soldiers in the Army. He it was who took Messines Ridge, "the biggest bang" of the war, as it has been described.

His military record, in fact, has been one steady run of success. From his service in the Soudan in the early eighties, through the South African War to the day the Armistice was signed, he never made a mistake. In the hottest battle he keeps as cool and unruffled as if he were on parade.

In many quarters it was confidently expected at one time that he would take supreme command of the British forces in France. It would undoubtedly have been a very popular promotion.

A General who says " Please "

Plumer's politeness and extreme tidyness in dress have earned him the nickname of the " Dandy General." He wears a monocle which he is said not to take out of his eye even when he sleeps. His commands are always given with a " please," and he, unlike so many others in responsible positions, never forgets to give praise for any job done well.

During the advance of Mafeking a shell fell close to his horse, causing the animal to kick up a cloud of dust. Colonel Plumer, as he was then, calmly flicked his sleeve and said to his aide-de-camp, " Be so kind as to go to the officer in charge and ask him to be good enough to silence that gun ! "

Colonial troops swear by Plumer, for he has had considerable dealings with them. In fact, they rate him as highly as they do General Birdwood. His tact in dealing with Colonials is illustrated by the following story :

How he dealt with a " Drunk "

When in South Africa a particularly tough specimen of a Colonial trooper got hold of more liquor than was good for him and became mad drunk.

Wandering about the camp he spied Plumer, spick and span, standing before his tent, and he half rolled, half rushed up and struck the general a violent blow on the chest.

To strike an officer on active service is punishable with death, but all the general said to the soldiers who ran up was :

" Oh, take him away ! He is too drunk to know what he is doing ! "

FAMOUS SCOUTS IN THE WAR

And that was all the notice he ever took of the affair.

He has had some amusing experiences, and was once nearly killed for being a wizard.

In one of his early expeditions in Africa he was washing his teeth in the river and had used a few drops of eau-de-Cologne for the purpose. The scent made the water turn milky, and the natives, not knowing anything about eau-de-Cologne, accused him of poisoning the water by breathing on it!

BULL DOG BEATTY
Chief Sea Scout.

WHEN it was announced that Admiral Sir David Beatty, K.C.B., M.V.O., D.S.O., had accepted the position of Chief Sea Scout, Sea Scouts all over the Empire went wild with delight.

And little wonder, for Sir David has, during the Great War, proved beyond doubt that he is a sailor of the first water. His name has become a household word. To Scouts, perhaps, he is especially dear, because he it was who wrote the immortal despatch that told the world of the greatness and the bravery of Jack Cornwell.

Sir David went to sea when he was thirteen years of age, and his life since then has been full of adventures. He climbed the ladder of promotion and fame very rapidly. Looking at his record, we find that in 1910 when he was thirty-eight he was promoted to Rear-Admiral, and he was not only the youngest Rear-Admiral of his time, but the youngest in history, beating even Nelson's record of rapid promotion.

He is a man of extraordinary energy and resource, an expert seaman and a master of tactics, and a courageous fighter, as the men who have served under him testify. When he sails into battle it is with a feeling that he is going in to win, and he goes "all out." His audacity has held us spellbound.

It was in Soudan in 1896-7 that Sir David had his first experience of fighting.

He was second-in-command of the gunboat flotilla in Lord Kitchener's Nile Expedition, which went up the river and used its guns effectively on the Mahdists along the banks. Approaching the Dervish batteries at Hafir, Beatty was having an engagement with his little boat when Commander Colville was wounded.

Beatty then took command, and jammed his flotilla right up to the batteries, went at them, dismounted them and then proceeded towards Dongola. There he commanded alone, and dismounting the guns, cleared the way for the transports, and continued to hammer at the enemy.

For this piece of work he was awarded the D.S.O.

FAMOUS SCOUTS IN THE WAR 33

In the Boxer rising in 1900 he was given a chance of again distinguishing himself, curiously enough by the fact that his senior officer was again rendered *hors de combat*. Beatty stepped into the breach and led his men to victory. He was promoted after this to the rank of Captain.

Beatty's activities in the Great War are well known. Who can forget the Jutland Battle, Heligoland Bight, the Dogger Bank, etc.?

With what consummate skill was the battle of Jutland carried out, and had it not been for Nature's interference with fog, Beatty's audacious plan of destruction would have been a magnificent success. His cruiser squadron would have held the German Fleet at their mercy until Sir John Jellicoe's battleships had arrived. But the fog and the fading light enabled the enemy to sneak away to the safety of the Kiel Canal.

But the German Fleet was forced to come out at last. On the day of the memorable surrender Beatty, addressing his men, said: " I always told you they would come out—not on a piece of string, though."

Commenting on the surrender the Admiral said : " It was a pitiable sight—in fact, it was a horrible sight—to see these great ships following a British light cruiser and being shepherded like a flock of sheep by the Grand Fleet. We expected them to have the courage that we look for from those whose work lies upon great waters; we expected them to do something for the honour of their country; and I am sure that the sides of this gallant old ship, which have been well hammered in the past, must have ached, as I ached and as you ached, to give them another taste of what we had intended for them. But I will say this, that their humiliating end was a sure end and a proper end to an enemy who has proved himself so lacking in chivalry. At sea his strategy, his tactics, and his behaviour have been beneath contempt; his end is beneath contempt, and worthy of a nation which has waged war in the manner in which the enemy has waged war."

And now in conclusion I will add a story which is so typical of the great Admiral.

"On the second evening of the armistice conference on board the *Queen Elizabeth* the German Admiral, von Meurer, produced a parchment document in German caligraphy drawn up by the Kiel Naval Soviet, and asked Beatty to sign it. The latter, as always when addressed direct by the German Admiral, turned inquiringly to his interpreter, requesting him to translate the document. It ran:

" I, the undersigned, solemnly promise that

FAMOUS SCOUTS IN THE WAR 35

all German seamen of submarine or surface craft proceeding to British ports for internment will be immune from ill-treatment throughout their enforced sojourn."

" A space had been left at the bottom for Sir David to sign. ' Give me that ! ' he ordered, almost grabbing the parchment out of his interpreter's hand ; and then tearing it in half and throwing the pieces in the paper basket, ' Tell the Admiral, he continued in that biting, incisive way of his, 'that these men are coming to England. That's all there is to it.' "

Is it to be wondered then that Sea Scouts all over the Empire welcome Sir David as their chief ? And some day, perhaps, in the light of a camp fire or in the cabin of a ship, these boys will hear recounted the deeds of our Silent Navy in the greatest and most terrible of all wars by the great Admiral himself.

CHAPTER III

Scout Heroes of the Army

PIPER DAVID LAIDLAW, V.C.

(KING'S OWN SCOTTISH BORDERERS. ASSISTANT SCOUTMASTER, 1ST ALNWICK TROOP.)

Loos ! What thrilling stories does that name call up ! But perhaps none more thrilling and romantic than that of the brave Scottish piper, who knew how to stir the hearts of his fellow-countrymen and spur them on to victory.

The cloak of night had come down on the world. To the rest of mankind it was the hour for sleep and for repose. But to our boys it was the time when the order comes, " Stand to." Life began to buzz in the trenches. Working parties set to, repairing the parapets broken down during the day. Stealthy figures crept out to bring in the dead. Others marched off, shovel on shoulder, to dig a comrade's grave, and think, with every shovelful of earth, " To-morrow, perhaps, it will be my grave these chaps will be digging. I may have gone West where there are no fatigues."

There was movement in the German trenches, too. Parties were out carrying up rations, fetching

SCOUT HEROES OF THE ARMY

water, laying wire entanglements. They should not work in peace—our artillery was seeing to that! The shells from back behind the trenches hummed overhead, one after another, their sound growing quickly fainter, until the roar of their explosion rent the air and made the earth jump beneath your feet. The German guns thundered in return. And so the night went on.

At last the east began to pale. The grey light of dawn was creeping over the sky. The men were fagged out; but with day came the hope of a little rest. Moment by moment the light increased; it became possible to see the outline of the German trenches, once again. It was just as day had fairly dawned that our men saw a sight that filled them with horror. Over the dark line that showed the enemy's position, came floating a long, low cloud of greenish vapour.

"Gas." The word was whispered by one and another. All knew what it meant, though it was the first time they had experienced it. But happily the poisonous fumes had a fair distance to travel and had lost a good deal of their strength before they reached the British lines. Still, they had a marked effect on the men, for besides the usual smarting of eyes and nose, a strange feeling of stupefaction came over them; they stood about, unable to make an effort of any sort.

It was then that the order came to charge!

The men were too dazed to understand the command. No one moved. Then one man with a great effort roused himself from the effect of the fumes. He began to realise that somehow or other the men must be got over the top. This man was a Scout, and he had two characteristics of the true Scout—a habit of prompt obedience and no thought for his personal safety.

"Come on, you chaps," he shouted, and leapt up on the parapet. But no one followed—the effect of the gas had dazed them—they could not realise what was wanted of them.

For a moment Laidlaw stood irresolute. What should he do? It would be useless for one man to advance, alone. Must he get back into the trench? But with the resourcefulness of a true Scout he thought of a plan. He knew what would rouse these "Jocks" to action, and awaken in them the fighting spirit, once more. The skirl of the pipes has stirred the blood of Scots through countless generations.

Slinging his bagpipes into position, he started pacing up and down the top of the trench, and "The Braes of Mar" burst forth upon the air.

To the Huns, some 80 yards away, this pacing figure with swinging kilt and the strange, unfamiliar music of the pipes, must have seemed almost

Slinging his pipes into position, Piper Laidlaw struck up "The Braes of Mar."

[*To face page* 38.

SCOUT HEROES OF THE ARMY

uncanny. But in a moment fire was directed upon him. The bullets whizzed about, thick. Why he was not hit is beyond human comprehension. As he himself said, " Providence was on my side " ; God's protecting power is proof against the deadliest fire of German marksmen. This man's work was not yet done, and so he paced up and down on the top of the trench, in safety. Five minutes passed, and all the time the brave music went on and on, speaking to the heart of the Scotsmen in the trenches. Gradually, gradually they were awakening from their stupor. What did it mean, this music ? To what was it calling them ? To fight, of course, to fight ! To rush forward and turn the enemy out of his position with the relentless bayonet that he had learned to fear so greatly. One by one, heads appeared over the parapet, and then, with a rush, the men came over the top ! The pipes had done their work.

As his officer reached his side, the triumphant piper struck up " Blue Bonnets over the Border," and together they headed the charge.

He needed all his breath for running ; but it was the pipes that had rallied the men, and the pipes should help them to face the Hun at close quarters.

On, on went the wild music. The men were fairly roused to action, now. Over the parapet, and into the German trenches they poured. There was no mercy for the cowards who had sent over that cloud of green vapour. The clearing of the trench was quick work ; and then on they rushed. Still the inspiring music led them, until suddenly came a crash, a terrific explosion, and the brave pipes were still.

On rushed the battalion; the job must be finished well. The Huns should have no quarter.

The men who had been thrown to the ground by the exploding shell sat up, one by one, shaking the earth from off them. The gallant piper looked about him, and soon espied what he sought. His brave young officer, Lieut. Young, lay near him ; but alas, he had received a mortal wound. The piper tried to rise, but his shattered ankle made it impossible. Around him lay numbers of his comrades dead or dying. And his precious pipes, they, too, were shattered and useless.

In the distance he could see the fighting still in progress. With sudden horror the thought came over him. What if our men were pushed back, and the Hun came over the ground where he lay ? He shuddered at the thought.

The weary hours dragged on. It was late afternoon. Would assistance never come ? Then, at last, as grey dusk began to settle in, dark figures could be seen coming over from the British lines.

SCOUT HEROES OF THE ARMY

They were stretcher bearers! Oh, the relief of the sight! Before long he had been carried back to the dressing station.

* * * * *

It was as he lay in hospital, that the surprising news came to him that he had been recommended for the V.C.

On his return to England he received his reward at the hands of the King. This, and his precious pipes, are now his most treasured possessions.

Piper D. Laidlaw was the first Scout to receive the Victoria Cross, but he was not the last, as you will see.

SECOND-LIEUTENANT GEORGE EDWARD CATES, V.C.

(RIFLE BRIGADE. A.S.M. 2ND WIMBLEDON TROOP.)

The story of how this brave young officer earned his Cross is very short, but it comprises within itself all the heroism and self-sacrifice of which a man is capable, "*Greater love than this no man hath, that a man lay down his life for his friends.*" There was no exciting undertaking, no adventure, no call for skill, no chance of winning fame and glory. It was just the chance of doing a good turn for his men, that came his way, and, like a true Scout, he took it, knowing that it must cost him his life.

Lieut. Cates was in charge of a party of men engaged on deepening a captured trench. Like every good Scout he was ready to work himself, as well as to command. Thrusting his spade deep in, and throwing up an unusually large shovelful of earth, he disclosed to the horrified gaze of all present, a buried bomb, which immediately commenced to burn.

In another few seconds it would explode! There was no time to do anything, no time to get away. In that confined space the party would be blown to bits. His men must be saved—that was the one thought that flashed into the mind of this true Scout. Placing his foot on the bomb, he pressed it back into the loose earth at the bottom of the trench. It exploded, killing him, but doing no harm to those around. So passed a hero into the Presence of the One Who first set the example of supreme self-sacrifice.

SECOND-LIEUTENANT REGINALD HAINE, V.C.

(H.A.C. PATROL LEADER, PETERSHAM TROOP.)

THE story of how Lieut. Haine won the V.C. by achieving the apparently impossible reminds one of Marshal Foch's famous remark,

"*Une bataille gagnée, c'est une bataille dans laquelle on ne veut pas s'avouer vaincu.*

and of his philosophy of war, his belief that the

SCOUT HEROES OF THE ARMY 43

spirit of the leader can carry his men through almost anything, and often achieve the so-called impossible.

Our troops were occupying a pronounced salient, and the enemy were repeatedly counter-attacking. Our men were resisting the attacks splendidly, but it soon became plain that, should the enemy succeed in one of these, the garrison of the salient would be surrounded.

Lieut. Haine, realising that mere passive resistance could not succeed much longer, organised six bombing attacks, and led.them himself with utmost gallantry. These attacks were directed against a strong point which dangerously threatened our communication. Lieut. Haine succeeded in capturing this position, together with fifty prisoners and two machine guns.

Realising the importance of this daring move on the part of the British, the Germans decided to spare no effort to regain the position. Bringing up a battalion of the famous Guard, they counter-attacked, and succeeded. The position now appeared critical. Most men would have given up hope, but not so the indomitable Scout. Forming a block in his trench, he determined to resist to the end. Again and again, throughout that terrible night, the Huns attacked, but always to no purpose. At last day dawned, but the spirit of the exhausted little garrison was unbroken. It was then that Lieut. Haine inspired his men to attempt the apparently impossible. They would, themselves, attack Fritz, and at his strongest point!

Re-organising his men, he led them over the top, and towards the astonished Germans. Before long the strong position had been taken, and the enemy was on the run. Pressing the Germans back for several hundred yards, the gallant little party succeeded in relieving the situation.

Thus says an official statement:

> "Throughout these operations this officer's superb courage, quick decision and sound judgment were beyond praise, and it was his splendid personal example which inspired his men to continue their efforts during more than thirty hours of continuous fighting."

MAJOR A. M. TOYE, V.C. AND M.C.

(2ND MIDDLESEX REGT. PATROL LEADER, 2ND ALDERSHOT.)

"*Stick to it*" is one of the Scout's favourite mottoes, and 2nd-Lieut. Toye (as he was at the time of our story) showed the Huns what that motto can mean.

Lieut. Toye was in command of a post at a

SCOUT HEROES OF THE ARMY

bridgehead. The enemy, attacking in great force, managed to capture his trench. But Lieut. Toye had made up his mind to stick to that bridgehead, and before long he had re-established a post. This was also captured by the Bosche, but the persevering Scout established yet a third post, which fared in a like manner.

Ascertaining that his three posts were cut off, and that the bridge was in imminent danger of falling into the enemy's hands, Lieut. Toye made his last move. Fighting his way through the enemy, accompanied by one officer and six men, he was but just in time to find seventy men of the battalion on his left, retiring. These he collected, and, inspiring them with his own indomitable spirit and daring courage, counter-attacked.

It was too much for the Bosche. An enemy who could stick to it like that was more than they could deal with. Taking up his new line, Lieut. Toye determined to hold it until reinforcements arrived. This he was able to do. Without this action the defence of the bridge must have been turned.

Later it became necessary for the left flank of the battalion to retire. It was a retirement fraught with very great danger. By his extraordinary daring, however, Lieut. Toye made it possible. With a party of men from the battalion, he pressed through the enemy in the village, firing at them in the streets, thus covering the left flank of the battalion's retirement. He was twice wounded within ten days, but remained on duty.

PRIVATE R. E. CRUIKSHANK, V.C.
(LONDON SCOTTISH. SCOUT 53RD NORTH LONDON TROOP)

What does it mean to say a man is full of the "Scout spirit"? Well, it means that all through life, in the common, humdrum duties of the day he shows a chivalrous spirit in always wishing to be the one to do the dull, the difficult, the dangerous job, so that he may save others the trouble of doing it; and in doing it to show such cheerfulness and contentment that people imagine it must be the very job, of all jobs, that he likes doing best! If the job is long and irksome the man with Scout spirit shows patience; and if it is hard and well-nigh impossible, he shows courage and perseverance, though it may cost him much. Now, going through each commonplace day thus, he begins to acquire certain habits—and habits are the little seeds that grow and flower into character. A man's character is that which makes him act in this or that way on the instant, when there is no time to think and weigh consequences. The time to test a Scout is in moments of emergency.

Let us try to picture to ourselves the scene—

SCOUT HEROES OF THE ARMY 47

a ghastly scene—in which a man raised the Scout spirit to such glorious heights.

A platoon of the London Scottish finds itself in a bewildering, a terrifying position. From where, a moment before, all seemed quiet and still there suddenly breaks forth a sound like a burst of fiendish laughter. A machine gun rakes the lines so that men fall on their faces, one mass of bullet wounds. Almost as rapidly come rifle bullets. It is like standing in a swarm of angry wasps, but the sting brings you down, helpless; or means perhaps, a great darkness and silence, and the voice of a comrade saying, "He's gone West."

In this sudden storm of fire there was nothing for it but to make for the bottom of a wadi. Slipping, scrambling, the men descended the slope, many falling before they reached the bottom. Among the fallen was the officer in charge of the platoon. The sergeant who took over command sent a runner back to Company Headquarters, asking for support. But scarcely had he done so, when he fell, mortally wounded. The Corporal had been killed, and now the Lance-Corporal took over command.

Company Headquarters must be communicated with; the first messenger had been killed, he felt sure. He called for a volunteer to take the message back. It was a Scout who responded. Without a moment's hesitation he rushed up the slope. Swift came a bullet, and he found himself rolling back into the wadi bottom. But, thank God, he was not disabled; he could still attempt the job. Mustering all his strength he made a desperate attempt to reach the top, but another bullet brought him rolling down, dusty and blood-stained.

Shaken, bewildered, but impatient to be at it again, he waited while his field dressing was applied and then sprang up the slope once more. But a third time the German marksman got him, and this time he was badly hit. Managing to roll himself down into the wadi, he was obliged to lie still, and give up the enterprise. There was no cover to which he might be carried.

As he lay there a German sniper wounded him once more. But, Scout-like, he still smiled, and no word of fear or complaint escaped him. When at last help came, the wounded man was carried away, spent and weak in body, but with his Scout spirit unbroken.

SECOND-LIEUTENANT JOHN MANSON CRAIG, V. C.

(ROYAL SCOTS FUSILIERS. SCOUT, 5TH PERTHSHIRE TROOP.)

The Scout Spirit is a great and noble thing, even in the dull, plain duties of every day. But when, at last, a tremendous moment dawns, and in all

SCOUT HEROES OF THE ARMY

simplicity the Scout acts up to his Scout spirit, suddenly it becomes a glorious thing that all the world acclaims. To the Scout himself it is just the same old Scout spirit that has ruled his day ever since he took the Promise. He wonders that people make such a fuss about it now. He little knows that he has raised it to the sunlit heights of heroism; and that in recognition of it his King will hold out to him the highest of rewards, the great "V.C."

The story of how Lieut. Craig won the greatest of military distinctions is an example of this. His action began with that characteristic of the true Scout, prompt action in the carrying out of duty, regardless of personal danger or discomfort; and ended with that other and very human Scout characteristic, an intense desire to render assistance to those in need—the instinct of the "good turn" —cost what it may to self.

Lieut. Craig was the officer in charge of an advance post. Quite unexpectedly a large party of Germans rushed the post. A sharp fight ensued, during which a considerable number of our men were killed and wounded.

Hopeless as the case appeared, the young officer was undaunted. Rallying his remaining men he succeeded in pushing back the Germans, over broken country, to their trenches.

But Lieut. Craig's work was not done yet: a Scout's first thought, when duty has been accomplished, is for those who have suffered in the fight, and require help. With the assistance of his rescue party he set to work carrying in the wounded and the bodies of the killed. Many of the boys had fallen right out in the open, and as their brave rescuers reached them, the whistle and ping of rifle bullets sounded on every hand, with now and then the cruel hiss of a machine gun. That any of the rescuers escaped alive, was a marvel. Before long an N.C.O. had been hit. A medical officer went to his assistance, only to be severely wounded himself. Seeing what had happened Lieut. Craig at once went to them, and taking up the wounded N.C.O. hastened with him back to the poor cover of the trench.

Returning with all speed, he was preparing to perform the same service for his brother officer, when a German bullet got him. It was not, however, a fatal wound, and in spite of the pain and great inconvenience it caused him, he would not give up the job. With great perseverance he succeeded in rescuing the medical officer, also.

The enemy, meanwhile, were being equally persevering in doing everything in their power to harass the dauntless little party, as it rendered assistance to the fallen. To the rifle and machine

SCOUT HEROES OF THE ARMY

gun fire they added shrapnel and high explosive. It seemed as if the wounded must be killed where they lay. But while strength remained to him, Lieut. Craig determined not to spare himself, if even one man's life could be saved. With complete disregard of personal safety, under full observation of the enemy, and within close range, he scooped cover for the wounded. Thanks to this their lives were preserved, and their rescue, later, was able to be effected.

This was not the first time Lieut Craig had proved the worth of a true Scout. "On three previous occasions," runs the official report, "this officer has behaved in a conspicuously brave manner, and has shown an exceptional example of courage and resource."

Every Scout will feel glad and proud that one of their brothers has earned the "V.C." in a manner so truly befitting a member of the Great Brotherhood.

LIEUT.-COLONEL DIMMER, V.C., M.C.

Scout Worker, Southend

(ROYAL BERKSHIRE REGIMENT)

It was in those first terrible months of the war that Lieut.-Col. Dimmer (then, Lieut. Dimmer) won the Victoria Cross—the first to be awarded for service in Flanders. The story is one that will stir the heart of every Scout, and help him in difficult moments when the 8th Scout Law seems too hard to be obeyed, to grin, and carry on.

It was at Klein Zillbeke, on November 12th, 1914. The notorious Prussian Guard was throwing itself, rank after rank, against the English lines. The Germans were determined to break through. With shrieking rush the shells came over, crashing into our trenches, killing our men by the score.

Lieut. Dimmer was in command of four Maxim guns. His orders were to do all in his power to beat back the German advance. It was not long, however, before three of his guns had been dismantled. With his three remaining men he determined to use his fourth gun in a way the Germans would not forget!

Then it was that he received shrapnel full in the face. Staggering back, he must have fainted, had not his men supported him, and given him a drink from his flask of brandy.

Recovering himself, and paying no attention to the pain of his wounds, Lieut. Dimmer continued to give orders. The Germans were advancing in close order, and as the deadly fire of the Maxim was directed against them, it literally mowed them down in rows. They could not make way against this continuous fire, and yet, as one rank went down there was always another grim, grey rank to take

SCOUT HEROES OF THE ARMY 53

its place, with gleaming bayonet thrust forward, eager for British blood.

Then, a crash—flying earth, wood, pieces of metal. As it became possible to see once again, the officer found himself alone—his three brave men lay face downwards, dead.

Two more shrapnel bullets had wounded Lieut. Dimmer, this time in the shoulder. He had scarcely any strength left—it seemed to him that the end was very near. The one thing to do was to go on . . . go on. While his strength lasted he would continue to beat back those grim, persistent ranks.

Swallowing what was left of the brandy he staggered forward, and commenced to serve the Maxim. Three belts he emptied, of three hundred cartridges each, and then he fell, unconscious.

It had seemed to him the end; he had faced the bitterness of death. But that was not to be. The Germans did not succeed in breaking through. Lieut. Dimmer was taken up by the stretcher-bearers, and carried back to safety.

The brave " V.C.'s " promotion followed fast. By January, 1915, he had reached the rank of Brigade-Major. It was at this time that he spent some months at Southend, where he shared, with his fellow countrymen, the horrors of Zepp. raids!

Later he was given an appointment in the

Machine Gun Corps, and was then transferred to the 60th Rifles, and on being made Lieut.-Colonel was given a command in the Royal Berkshire Regiment.

Lieut.-Col. Dimmer's military career began long before the Great War. In 1902 he enlisted in the King's Royal Rifles, and was posted to South Africa. His career was full of brilliant success and heroic deeds. In 1906 he was sent to Belgium and Germany to study the military methods of these nations.

He received his Commission in 1908, and was specially selected by the Colonial Office for work in Africa, where he returned on leave, a few months before war broke out. He accompanied the first Expeditionary Force to France, and was mentioned in Lord French's first despatch.

Colonel Dimmer was a keen Scout, and did much to help the Scouts of Southend while in that town.

CAPTAIN G. B. McKEAN, V.C., M.C., M.M.

(SCOUTMASTER ROBERTSON PRESBYTERIAN TROOP, ALBERTA).

Captain George Burdon McKean, who wears the V.C., M.C., M.M., is a fine type of the English boy, Canadianized. He was born in a typical provincial town, Bishop Auckland, in Durham, and went to Canada as a youngster in 1902, to

SCOUT HEROES OF THE ARMY 55

join his brother who had preceded him. He settled in Edmonton, Alberta. When war broke out he was a student at the University of Alber a, in his third year Arts course with a view to entering the teaching profession. Those who knew him best could have predicted with certainty a brilliant career for him as a soldier. He was a Scoutmaster in charge of a Troop attached to Robertson Presbyterian Church ; played Soccer—inside left—with the University team ; and was keen on all outdoor sports.

He came over as a sergeant with the 51st Battalion in 1916, and went to France as a private in the 14th, early in June. When he won the M.M. at Bully-Grenay, near Lens, he had risen to the rank of Corporal, and he was recommended for a commission, which he obtained in April, 1917. The M.C. he won when in charge of a patrol engaged in scout duty, and on this occasion was wounded.

As to the winning of the V.C. we will let Capt. McKean himself recount the thrilling adventure which resulted in this honour, for he has done so in his book *Scouting Thrills*, recounting two years' Scouting at the Front.

It was in the critical days of 1918, in the country round Arras that the most hair-raising of Capt. McKean's " thrills " took place. The Bosche was attacking, but our authorities decided on a big raid. In preparation for this Capt. McKean had many an adventure, locating advanced posts, bombing blocks and machine gun posts, but it is what happened on the night of the advance that we are going to recount. His Scouts had been divided up, one going with each bombing party. McKean had chosen Pete—a born fighter, who had shared many an experience with him in the past. They had carefully led the men out to a large shell-hole and were waiting for the time.

A perfect stillness reigned, writes Capt. McKean, it was the time when the activities of opposing armies are at their lowest. But for an occasional flare-light, no one would have guessed that legions of armed men were facing each other across that narrow strip of land known as No-man's Land. It was chilly, and we shivered a little with cold. The boys lay there very quiet—scarcely breathing. I looked at my watch—it was time!

Suddenly and without warning, the eerie menacing stillness was violently broken with the screaming sounds of hundreds of shells. It was deafening, tremendous! Our bombardment had begun. Shrapnel was bursting low and just in front of us; we could hear the whang of the shrapnel bullets and the deafening roar of bursting high explosive. Myriads of coloured lights—all flashing back their messages—were sent up from the enemy lines, illuminating the sky. To the uninitiated it was terrifying, nerve racking. I knew some of the boys were new to this kind of thing so crawled round amongst them.

"Don't worry, boys, it's all our stuff. It won't half put the wind up him; he'll be scared stiff when he sees us piling in on top of him."

I then went over to Pete, who sat on the edge of a shell hole, his eyes shining in the darkness with excitement, his fingers nervously clasping his revolver.

"Is it time yet, sir?" he whispered.

"Not yet, Pete, another couple of minutes."

At last the luminous figures on my watch tell me the time is up.

"All right, Pete, get ready." Then turning to the boys behind, I called.

"Fire your rifle grenades!" They did. "Come on, Pete, I'm going with you! Come on boys!" I shouted. Pete and I sprang up together. We saw the Huns lined up waiting for us as we stumbled forward entangled in the wire. Suddenly there were several blinding explosions at our very feet, and we heard the wicked rasping noise of the machine gun in front of us.

Pete clutched my arm and cried:

"I'm hit, sir," and fell, mortally wounded. I reached down and grasped his hand.

"Hit badly, Pete, boy?" But he did not answer: he was already dead.

All about me there was a succession of blinding explosions, and men were crying out in pain. That mass of wire on each side of the block was proving to be an impenetrable barrier. I ran a little to the right. I braced myself up, ran forward and took a flying leap over the wire. I just cleared it, staggered forward a few steps, and then hurled myself, headfirst, on top of a Hun who was just levelling his rifle at me. I crashed to the bottom of a trench seven feet deep, with a startled Hun underneath me.

In crashing into the Hun my steel helmet came down bang on to my face, and took away the tip of my nose. At the same time I saw myriads of dancing lights. The strap of my helmet had been at the back of my head, so the helmet was now dangling in front of my face. I lay breathing heavily, with my right elbow sticking in the stomach of the Hun underneath me, who lay gasping—for I had knocked the wind clean out of him. I still retained a firm grip on my revolver, my finger on the trigger. I peeped over the rim of my dangling steel helmet and saw the figure of a big Hun gaily advancing upon me, the point of his bayonet about two feet from my throat. I promptly pulled the trigger; he gave a gurgling

SCOUT HEROES OF THE ARMY

sound and sank down in a heap, his rifle and bayonet clattering to the bottom of the trench.

The man underneath me, no doubt desperately startled by the exploding revolver, violently came to life and started throwing his arms around. It was no time for polite argument, so I pressed the muzzle of my revolver into him and pulled the trigger. I scrambled to my feet and adjusted my helmet just as another Hun came rushing along towards me. I let go with my revolver; he gave a howl of pain, turned around and ran. Being a great believer in the demoralizing effect of noise, I ran yelling after him. There were quite a few Huns in that trench, and soon the bombs began to fly about. I had a couple with me so let fly with mine. More bombs came over, and I had to back up a little to get out of range. I was beginning to feel a little lonely and worried—for that machine gun was still firing—when at last one of my men came up to me.

"Give me your bombs, quick," I said, "and go back for some more."

He handed me three bombs, I ran forward and threw them, forcing the Huns back along the trench. Back they came again with a mad rush towards me. I used my revolver with effect and they scampered back again, just as the man I had sent came rushing up with more bombs. I grabbed two—ran forward and threw them, following close up with my revolver. I ran into six Huns, shot two of them, when the remainder turned round and threw up their hands. A few yards beyond I saw them pulling down the machine gun. I called upon the man behind me to look after the prisoners, and pushed my way past them, in time to see the men with the machine gun disappear into a dug-out. I called back for a mobile charge and waited. It was two or three minutes before a man came staggering along with one—pulled the pin and threw it down the dug-out. A few seconds later the air was filled with flying debris. I leave to the imagination what happened to the Huns and the machine-gun.

Looking back, I saw the red flares—the recall signal—burning. I got back to find Pete's body had been carried into our trench. The next day, and for two succeeding days, I suffered from what is popularly known as " a stiff neck!" which will explain why it was the Hun lay winded underneath me.

Some weeks later the C.O. sent for me.

"McKean," he said, "I wish to congratulate you heartily on being awarded the Victoria Cross."

I felt rather staggered and bewildered.

"Thank you, sir," I replied—and that was all I could say.

SCOUT HEROES OF THE ARMY

LIEUTENANT DONALD JOHN DEAN, V.C.

(8TH BATT. ROYAL WEST KENT REGT.
SCOUT, 1ST SITTINGBOURNE.)

It was for "most conspicuous bravery, skilful command and devotion to duty" that this Scout gained the Victoria Cross. Lens was the scene of his marvellous success, which occurred during the period September 24th to 26th, 1918.

We had advanced and succeeded in capturing an enemy trench north-west of Lens. It was ill-prepared for defence and the left flank of the position was insecure. It was the unenviable job of holding this position that devolved on Donald Dean, that September night.

With the complete determination to succeed characteristic of the true Scout, Lt. Dean set to work, and soon had his men hard at it, consolidating the position. They had scarcely begun the job when the Huns tried to rush the position. Inspired by their officer's determination not to give way, the men held firm, and Jerry, surprised at his failure, in such an obviously weak spot, retired discouraged to collect a strong force, and ensure success next time. Turning his machine gun fire on the trench, he decided that at any rate he would make the work of consolidating the position impossible. He little knew with whom he was dealing.

Urging on his men and working with them unceasingly, Lt. Dean continued the fortification of the trench and was prepared to resist the determined attack which was made shortly after midnight. Day had dawned and it was broad daylight before the Hun was ready to repeat his attack. This time he was supported by a heavy shell and trench mortar fire, and he charged forward on the British position, feeling confident of success. But so skilfully did Lt. Dean handle his command that the Bosche found that not only was he held up by a dogged resistance, but that his own casualties were becoming so severe, that the only thing to do was to turn tail, and run.

All that day, and during the night, the enemy continued to shell that trench, and the brave boys under Lt. Dean continued to repair the damage as soon as it was done. Early on the morning of the 26th the Hun made one more desperate attempt. Putting over an intense artillery fire, he followed it up with a strong body of Infantry—only to be once again repulsed. How was it that the small party of British soldiers in so unfavourable a position had succeeded in holding it against five attacks, and an almost continuous fire ? It was due to the spirit of their leader, and his unwavering determination not to give in.

SCOUT HEROES OF THE ARMY 63
SECOND LIEUTENANT RUPERT PRICE HALLOWES, V.C.

4TH BATT. DUKE OF CAMBRIDGE'S OWN MIDDLESEX REGT. INSTRUCTOR, ST. PETER'S, PORT TALBOT)

" A Scout smiles under all difficulties," so says the 8th Scout Law. It was the heroic way Lieutenant Rupert Hallowes carried out the spirit of that Law, at Hooge, in the autumn of 1915, that gained for him the Victoria Cross.

They were terrible days. No sooner had one long and heavy bombardment died down than another commenced. It was enough to break the spirit of the bravest troops. To Rupert Hallowes all this was but an opportunity to put into practice the 8th Scout Law. His cheerfulness, courage, and untiring energy could not but serve as an inspiration to his men. On several occasions seeing that nothing but encouragement and a fresh impulse of confidence and courage would keep the men going, he climbed up on the parapet utterly regardless of danger, solely to put fresh heart into his men.

The Germans had captured and were holding several positions in our lines. It was necessary that reconnaissances should be made. These required daring courage. It was Lt. Hallowes who volunteered and undertook the dangerous job.

At the close quarters in which the battle was being carried on, bombs had become the chief means of defence and assault. So furious was the fighting, that the supply began to run perilously short. More bombs must be got up, but the bombardment was so terrific that leaving the trench looked like certain death. Undaunted, Rupert Hallowes set out and succeeded in bringing up a fresh supply. At last the brave Scout was hit. He knew that his wound was a mortal one, that he would never live to return home. No more fighting, no more reconnaissances, for him. But as he lay there, there was one thing left that he could do—he could keep up the spirits of the boys, until his own brave spirit should have sped away. Giving no thought to his pain and the weakness that was creeping upon him, he continued to cheer on those around, and even in his death, inspired his men with fresh courage.

THE REV. PERCY WYNDHAM GUINNESS, D.S.O.

(C.F. 3RD CAVALRY BRIGADE. SCOUTMASTER, 2ND CURRAGH TROOP.)

The Rev. P. W. Guinness was the first Scoutmaster to be honoured during the war.

It was at Kruistraat that he performed the two heroic "good turns" that earned for him the Distinguished Service Order.

Putting spurs to his horse, the Chaplain galloped out into the open.

[*To face page* 64.

SCOUT HEROES OF THE ARMY 65

Fierce fighting was in progress, and the 16th Lancers were suffering heavy losses. The ambulance workers and stretcher-bearers were overwhelmed by the number of casualties that must be attended to. In the front part of the line men were left to lie where they fell—it was impossible to carry them back to safety.

Suddenly word was passed from mouth to mouth, " the Major's hit." It was true, Major Dixon lay, mortally wounded, in the trench.

Who could be sent to fetch him in ? While the question was being decided, precious time was being lost ; the gallant officer was, perhaps, dying for want of help. A Scout acts without delay, and without thought for his personal safety. The Chaplain was a Scout. Quietly he set out, alone. Before long he had reached the spot. He saw, at once, that to tend the wounded man where he lay was out of the question. The bombardment was fierce. At any moment he might be hit, again. To get him back to the dressing station was the only hope. Picking him up, very gently, the Chaplain bore him back, facing gladly the danger to which he was exposing himself, that he might save the life of a fellow-man.

But a Scout does not limit himself to one good turn a day, even though that one may be the greatest he can perform—to risk his life for another.

Once again, that day, men were at a loss to know what to do in a sudden emergency, and once again it was the Chaplain that quietly took the job on himself.

It became necessary to send a despatch to Headquarters with all possible speed. There was no despatch rider at hand. Nor were there any horses—except just the Chaplain's mount.

The Chaplain was a Scout; he was ready not only to lend his horse, but to ride him himself, and bear the urgent message across that terrible open space where snipers' bullets whizzed with such deadly precision, and shells were rending the air.

Those in command hesitated to accept the offer. But the Chaplain was determined to carry through this perilous service for his country. He was given the despatch and, putting spurs to his horse, he galloped out into the open.

He drew the enemy's fire, of course. Bullets whistled past him, but not one hit either the brave man or his steed. Did he remember, perhaps, in those breathless moments the lines of the old hymn :

> "Cover my defenceless head
> With the shadow of Thy Wing"?

Triumphantly his horse's hoofs beat out a song of praise and gratitude to his unseen Protector,

SCOUT HEROES OF THE ARMY

as he flew over the last few yards of ground. He was in cover at last. The despatch was handed in. Just a good turn—a part of the day's work—so it seemed to the Chaplain. But to those in command it was a piece of heroism that did not go unrecognised.

CAPTAIN A. ILLINGWORTH BUTLER, M.C.

(ROYAL FIELD ARTILLERY. BLUE COAT SCHOOL (READING) TROOP.)

It was on March 21st, 1918, at Villiers Britonneux, that a Scout won the Military Cross in a way that we may say was unique, for he had the luck to engage German tanks, on the first occasion on which they were used, and the skill to put one out of action, so that in Sir Douglas Haig's Despatch of October 21st, 1918, he says: "A German tank was left derelict in our lines, and was salved subsequently."

We are not able to give as detailed a story as we know our readers would like of this deed of cool-headed courage, for the hero of the occasion, like most of his brother Scouts, has refused to talk about it, even to his parents. " I am one of the lucky ones," he says, " and my work came under notice. There are hundreds of others who deserve the Cross, but they were not seen."

The story, as far as we can collect it from various sources, is this:

The Huns had attacked in large numbers, pushing our men back. News came, however, that at one point they were being successfully held back. With a view to helping the men holding this part of the line so bravely, a single gun detachment was pushed forward. It was known that a German tank was advancing directly on the spot. Lieut. Illingworth Butler whose 18-pounder was concealed just below the crest of the hill, near a sunken road, determined on a daring course. He did not fire a single shot, but let the Hun tank come lumbering on, blissfully ignorant of its danger. Then, as it hove into sight over the crest of the hill, he opened fire.

On pushed the tank, followed up by the attacking party of Germans. It was a desperate situation, but the Scout meant to stick to it, and knock out that tank, before he should have to retire.

At last, when it was only 50 yards from him, he scored a direct hit that caused it to turn tail and make for home. Then, rallying the infantry, he held on until the last possible moment, and then carried out the retirement in good order, being obliged, however, to drive in a gun team himself.

The tank, thanks to Lieut. Butler's attentions,

SCOUT HEROES OF THE ARMY

did not succeed in "getting home." It was abandoned, and as, later in the day, Villiers Britonneux was regained, and completely in our possession, it was able to be salved.

A spirited little account of this deed comes into *Pushed and the Return Push,* by Quex (Blackwood & Sons).

The hero of the tank adventure is now Captain and Adjutant of his brigade, though only twenty-two years old.

LIEUTENANT LECHMERE C. THOMAS, M.C. and BAR

(EAST SURREY REGT. SCOUT, 1ST FARNHAM TROOP.)

Lieut. Thomas comes of a very distinguished Army family, with a remarkable fighting record. When he entered the Army at the age of eighteen, he had high traditions to uphold. Going back six hundred years, to the famous battle of Crecy, we find one of his ancestors acting as the Master of Artillery, when cannon was used for the first time! For his extreme valour and skill in this engagement King Edward I dubbed him on the field Knight Banneret, and also presented him with a diamond ring, which is still a valued treasure of the family.

Could this brave soldier of long ago have looked

ahead six hundred years, at the same fields of France, once more torn with artillery fire, and stained with the blood of Englishmen, he would have had cause to be proud of his young descendant, and of the way he was upholding the family traditions.

Arriving in France in 1915, Lieut. Thomas went straight to the trenches and remained in the fighting line from start to finish, with the exception of returning to rest camps or hospital, when necessary. He was in many actions and in his nineteenth year won the Military Cross for carrying out a very successful raid, in broad daylight, in the neighbourhood of Hulluck. A large number of Huns were killed in their trenches, Lieut. Thomas personally accounting for five, and taking three prisoners. He then skilfully withdrew his party, under heavy fire.

Performing a similar feat in December, 1917, he gained a bar to his Cross.

On March 21st, 1918, he was in the terrible battle of that date, when the East and West Surreys, with the Seaforths, were so terribly punished. On this date his C.O. was killed at his side and he himself shot through the foot, bones and nerves being completely shattered.

No sooner was he patched up again than he set out with another division, as Trench Mortar officer.

SCOUT HEROES OF THE ARMY 71

After being wounded a second time, he once more set out, in 1919, this time with high hopes of "marching into Germany."

SECOND-LIEUTENANT GEORGE MONRO McBEY, M.C.

(SEAFORTH HIGHLANDERS. SCOUT, ELGIN TROOP.)

It was at the fateful village of Beaumont Hamel, which changed hands so often, and saw so many tragic and glorious fights up and down its shell-torn streets, in ruined house and cellar, or in the air.

The battalion to which Lieut. McBey belonged, had taken part in the attack of November 13th, 1916. About two hundred of the battalion had fallen, no fewer than five of his brother officers being killed, and most of the others wounded.

Lieut. McBey's fighting blood was up, and he meant to lead his dauntless Scots in a fight that would be a severe punishment to Fritz for the havoc he had wrought in the battalion. Then it was that a German bullet wounded him in the chest. Severe as was the wound it could not deter the young Scotsman from his purpose. Regardless of the pain and the blood, he dashed forward. So brilliant was the move, and so unexpected, that before the Bosche knew where he was, a party numbering fifty had fallen prisoner into British hands ! It was a boy of nineteen who had accomplished this daring enterprise. He was awarded the Military Cross.

CAPTAIN H. P. SNOWDON, M.C.
(GLOUCESTER REGT. SCOUTMASTER, 4TH MALVERN LINK TROOP.)

The 1/5th Battalion of the Gloucester Regiment, though it had held trenches for many months, did not take part in serious fighting till July, 1916, when in the neighbourhood of Oliviers, it came in for the sort of fighting that means many casualties, and a series of thrilling night manœuvres, of intense importance to the men who take part in them, but of little outside interest.

It was during this series of local enterprises that Captain (then 2nd Lieutenant) Snowdon distinguished himself.

In each case there were limited objectives and one or two companies were employed. The bombing attacks were on a strong bombing block, in a communication trench, with a strongly held line just in rear of it. One of the night attacks was over country it was impossible to reconnoitre.

All went well, at first. The objective was gained with scarcely any losses from among our boys. Encouraged by this success the company pressed

SCOUT HEROES OF THE ARMY 73

on, and it was then that the Bosche began to give them hell.

There was nothing for it but to withdraw. The German fire was intense. The only thing to do was to make sure of one of the trenches, and consolidate this position. Furious fighting took place and two company commanders were killed. One after another the officers went down, until 2nd Lieut. Snowdon alone remained.

The entire responsibility of the very complicated position now devolved on him. The lives of many men depended upon him ; his own life seemed doomed, for, since all his brother officers had fallen, why should he, alone, escape ? But He in Whose hands are the lives of men, had work for this one to do ; his " call to higher service " had not come, yet. To-night's work was not to be wasted, and it was a Scout who was to weave final success out of what seemed failure and catastrophy.

Bewildering and terrifying as the position must have been, Lieut. Snowdon was as cool and collected as if he had been but commanding the night manœuvres of his troop on the Malvern Hills ! Gradually, by dint of courage and tenacity on the part of the men, and well-devised moves on the part of him who commanded them, the position was consolidated, and the remains of the battalion were able to settle down in the captured trench. Then came the difficult job of establishing communication with their former position, which, also, was successfully accomplished.

Who knows—perhaps it was those thrilling situations we all know so well in the great " game of Scouting" that had trained this man in the art of thinking quickly, acting decisively, leading and commanding skilfully, so that when his opportunity came, the young officer was able to pilot his men to safety, and win one hard-fought fight for Britain, in the Great War.

SECOND-LIEUTENANT ARTHUR H. LEE, M.C.

(Royal Fusiliers. Assistant Scoutmaster, 1st Eltham Troop.)

There had been a bombing raid on the German trenches, and many a brave chap who had gone out full of hope and determination had not come in. Among the officers whose men were missing was Lieut. Lee—a Scout. True to the instinct of the Scout, he set out, in the pitch darkness, stumbling over the rough and shell-torn ground, in case he might, perchance, find one of his boys.

He had not searched long before he came on a man shot through both legs. A swift investigation showed that one of them was badly broken. The man was not alone ; a comrade was trying to

SCOUT HEROES OF THE ARMY 75

get him back to safety. But even as the officer came up, this brave man was brought down, dead, by a stray shot from out of the darkness.

Trying every means he could devise, Lieut. Lee endeavoured to take the wounded man back to the trench, but it was a hopeless job. Noting his position carefully, the brave young officer made his way back to the trench, procured a flask of brandy, and, after obtaining the assistance of another man, returned to the wounded Tommy.

Between them they managed to carry him back to safety. For this deed of humanity and unselfish courage Lieut. Lee was awarded the Military Cross, and the soldier who assisted in the rescue the Military Medal.

Previous to going to France, Lieut. Lee had fought against the Turks in the first attack on the Canal. He also saw active service in Gallipoli.

SERGEANT-MAJOR J. H. W. HALL, M.M.

(SEAFORTH HIGHLANDERS. KINGSTON-ON-THAMES SEA SCOUTS.)

At the time of joining the Army in 1915, Harry Hall was a King's Scout with gold all-round cords, and five service stars. He played football all through the winter of 1913–1914 in the Kingston District Scout Team, which competed for, and won, the *Evening News*' Scout Challenge Cup,

Harry being the youngest player in the team. In 1917 his father wrote: "As far as I can judge from his cheery letters home he is 'still a Scout,' and I believe he is still an abstainer and a non-smoker."

To those who believe Scout training to be the best possible training for war as well as for peaceful citizenship, it must be of great interest to follow the military career of such a boy.

Though he was only a little over seventeen when he joined the Army, Harry Hall was promoted to the rank of Corporal, and to that of Sergeant after about six months.

On January 1st, 1917, he was promoted to the rank of Sergeant-Major, being at that time the youngest Sergeant-Major in the British Army (under nineteen).

On May 3rd, 1917, he was killed, "whilst (in the words of his C.O.) gallantly leading a section of the Black Watch into action," at Fampoux, near Arras.

But in those two years, what splendid service he did we will now try to relate. He was a real Scout all through, and his story should be an inspiration to all Scouts, even as Scouting was an inspiration to him in those terrible years.

The story of how he won the Military Medal is told by a friend of his, who was with him through most of his time in France.

SCOUT HEROES OF THE ARMY 77

" At Delville Wood on the Somme, on July 12th, 1916, Sergt. Harry Hall was in charge of the 26th Light Trench Mortar Battery, consisting of six ' Stokes ' guns, in six adjoining pits. The distance between our advanced front line and the Huns was about 75 yards.

" It was arranged that the 26th Brigade, 9th Division, were to attack at dawn (about 4 a.m.). The Black Watch were to lie in front of our lines, and near the German lines ; the Seaforths being in support, together with the Camerons and Argyles.

" The word was given for the main attack. The Black Watch and Seaforths suffered very heavily. And the Camerons and Argyles were cut off by the German counter-attack. Harry was working his six guns as many as nineteen rounds per minute, per gun. By this resort he saved the whole brigade, also the 27th and 28th Brigades, who were on the right and left flanks, respectively.

Out of the thirty-six men working the six guns, thirty-four were killed and wounded. Harry and one Corporal being the only two who came through unwounded. These two kept the six guns going by working right and left guns, and also the centre guns, so as to stop the German counter-attack. For this Harry (and also the Corporal) were recommended by the Commanding Officer of the Black Watch for the Military Medal."

He was also commended for blowing up two enemy machine guns that were doing terrible work at the end of a certain village. They were about 300 yards away when he got two of his mortars on them, and at the fourth shot hit one of them, and soon after got the other.

In November, 1916, he was awarded a bar to his M.M.

It was earned in the battle of Warlencourt. All lines of communication had been cut. The ration parties were making a brave attempt to reach the trenches, but the shelling was intense, and the roads almost impassable. The need for rations was becoming acute: something must be done. Then, Sergt. Harry Hall, with the true Scout's readiness to serve, volunteered to try and bring up the rations from Le Sars, which was under observation by the German artillery.

With those who had volunteered to assist him, he started off, over the open country. Four kilometres had to be traversed, but the gallant little party succeeded in the quest. To quote the words of his friend : " He got the rations up, made tea, and then went and carried on with his guns."

SCOUT HEROES OF THE ARMY 79

There is something very Scout like in this little statement.

He had not been back long, before his officer fell, severely wounded in the hip. Harry's Scout training came to his assistance, now. Skilfully he dressed the wound, and then, knowing that if his officer's life was to be saved he must receive further attention without loss of time, he set out to carry him the two kilometres to Warlencourt Abbey—a field dressing station. Progress was difficult and extremely dangerous, for the ground was chiefly open, and the crash of shells sounded on every side, and, what is perhaps harder still to stand—the ping of snipers' bullets. But, forgetful of all but his officer's need, he pressed bravely on, and at last reached the shelter of the Abbey.

Many another wounded man he carried in, but no one in this world will ever know those stories.

Six months after this he was called to higher service; he had "Done his bit," nay, more than his bit, and he went to receive the supreme reward of every "faithful servant."

CORPORAL AUSTIN R. JACKSON, M.M.

(RIFLE BRIGADE. A.S.M. 20TH WEST LONDON TROOP.)

It was in the attack on Cambrai, in November, 1917, that another Scout distinguished himself by a deliberate act of self-forgetfulness and voluntary service in his country's cause.

Corporal Jackson was in charge of the telephones, and in less than a quarter of an hour after our objective had been taken he had cut down a lot of the enemy's telephone wires, and used them to lay a wire to our own Headquarters. The wire ran along a little light railway, and as he lay between the rails, the German bullets pinged against them.

After a while the company was ordered to move to the right, and Jackson was recalled to Headquarters.

Some two hours after this a report came in to the effect that the company which was supposed to be holding the ridge was not there, and that the enemy was in possession. To verify the facts a visual signalling station was sent out, and told to try and reach the ridge and signal back information as to who really was holding it.

Before long, however, the party returned, saying it was impossible to pass the barrage which the enemy was putting up, halfway between Headquarters and the ridge. It was hard to know what to do, for the information must be obtained. Then a Scout came to the rescue. Corporal Jackson stepped forward, volunteered for the almost hopeless job, slung a telephone over his shoulder,

SCOUT HEROES OF THE ARMY

took a big drum of telephone wire, and started off.

Before long he had got into the enemy barrage. This consisted of gas shells and machine-gun fire. Almost miraculously he got through, unscathed, and reached the ridge. Very carefully he went up it, but could find no sign either of the Germans or of our own boys. Reaching the top, however, and taking a survey of the other side, he caught sight of our men, who were preparing to meet an enemy counter-attack—a very large one, outnumbering us easily.

Making his way quickly down the other side of the ridge Jackson reached our troops, fixed up his telephone, and got through to the artillery. But three times he had to go back into the barrage to mend his wires. Soon, however, British shells were falling thick and fast on the Germans, and Fritz was forced to make a hurried retreat.

The success of that day rests entirely with this Scout; but for his cool daring, the enemy's counter-attack must almost certainly have been successful. But the view he takes of it himself is just this : " It was only what I was there for, it was my duty, so why make all this fuss ? "

L/CPL. J. G. WELLS, M.M.

(R.A.M.C. P.L. 26TH GATESHEAD TROOP.)

St. George's Day, 1917 ; the Battle of Wancourt Tower. Scout J. G. Wells is facing the horror of battle for the first time. He is only sixteen and a half, and has been in France just three days, after six weeks' training in England. To every English boy in all ages " the din of battle " has presented romantic thoughts of chivalry, and fair adventure ; but Wells is finding little romance in this confused medley and deafening racket. The roar of shells ; clouds of low-hanging smoke ; blood and agony everywhere ; dead men ; shell-rent roads and fields ; the buzzing of aircraft overhead, and the strange sight of tanks, like great, relentless monsters crawling out towards the enemy's lines, to crush the life out of him. No, there is nothing romantic about war—war is vile.

And yet it is St. George's Day. After all, service of one's beloved land, the chance of giving one's life for one's friends, is romance of the highest ; and that which has been called " The Great Adventure " is a door which, however blood-stained and hideous on our side, is golden on the other, and leads into God's Presence. St. George discovered

SCOUT HEROES OF THE ARMY 83

that, and a Scout is one who strives to follow in the footsteps of St. George.

Suddenly, ahead, Wells sees a sight that fills him with horror. One of our tanks has stopped in its advance. Smoke is pouring from it. Now a tongue of flame shoots out. But there are men in that tank!

Heedless of the intense danger of thus exposing himself, Wells darts forward, running full speed across the intervening space. He has reached the tank and boarded it. The smoke and fumes are suffocating. He calls out, but there is no answer. Then he sees that every one of the crew is unconscious. The petrol tank is on fire.

There is no time to be lost. One by one he lifts the insensible men out of the poisoned air. As he emerges with the fifth, a bullet wounds him in the thigh and he falls helpless. But the job he has tackled must be finished; a Scout does not give in easily. Heedless of his own pain, he picks up his burden once more, and crawls over the broken ground, to a " Pill Box," then being used as a Regimental Aid Post. He has succeeded; the indomitable spirit of one more young St. George has raised human agony to the golden heights of heroism.

* * * * *

It was in the quiet wards of an English hospital that Wells learnt that the King had been pleased to recognise his courage. But like all true Scouts his modesty is apparent. "I was very much astonished," he says, "to learn that I had been awarded the Military Medal for my small deed of humanity to a very brave man."

SERGEANT W. B. McKAY, M.M.
(Scout, Elgin Troop.)

Perhaps one of the things most truly characteristic of a good Scout is the power of paying careful attention to all that is said to him ; of trying to make the most of any instructions or experience that may come his way ; and of carrying out whatever has been given him to do, to the very best of his ability, whether the job be pleasant or otherwise.

The story of how Sergt. McKay won his medal is an instance of this.

"By dint of hard work, and paying attention to all that was being said to me, I managed to reach the rank of Sergeant," he once wrote of himself.

He was known to be a man who could be trusted to do his duty carefully, coolly and without thought of self, and on the night of April 8th, 1917—the night of a great advance—he found himself in

SCOUT HEROES OF THE ARMY 85

charge of a platoon, the other platoons of the company each having an officer in charge. The time for the advance was drawing near. Then it was found that somehow the platoons had got mixed up, and the company was not in the proper order for an advance. Too much movement might have awakened the suspicions of Fritz, who was not far off. But quietly and calmly the Sergeant of No. 2 platoon straightened things out, and at 5.45 the company went over the top, following on under a terrific shower of shrapnel from our own guns.

In a few minutes the sergeant had been blown on his face by the concussion of a shell exploding near by, but he was up again in a moment, and was the first to reach the German line. Standing on the top of the trench, he was surprised to find it empty. Then, suddenly, the Bosches rushed out of their dug-outs. But one by one they were killed like rats, and our men took possession of the trench.

The next trench had now to be taken. But machine-gun fire was raking the intervening ground and making advance very dangerous and very difficult for our men. The only thing to do was to get that gun silenced.

It was Sergt. McKay to whom this dangerous and difficult job was entrusted by the Company Officer. Ready, as usual, to carry out his duty to the very best of his ability, this brave Scout set out. Armed with some bombs he crept up, making his way little by little towards the deadly weapon. At last, judging that he was near enough to reach it with a bomb, he took careful aim. "Take that, you lot of blighters," he cried, and sent a bomb hurtling through the air. It landed fair and square amongst them, and that gun gave no more trouble.

The next job entrusted to his care was the carrying out of a careful search for wounded.

Two days later snow began to fall. It made operations very difficult. Day and night the gallant sergeant worked, taking no time for sleep, through those three terrible days. But his untiring labours and quiet gallantry were not passing unnoticed. When, at last, the battalion came out of the trenches, he was awarded the Military Medal.

For two years and a half, in France, he "put his mind to his work," and did all he could to learn everything for himself. And so in 1917 he received a Commission.

RIFLEMAN A. J. WINGROVE, M.M.

(12TH COUNTY OF LONDON RIFLES. SCOUT, 6TH WIMBLEDON TROOP.)

In the British trenches near St. Julien, in the dark hours preceding dawn—the "Zero hour"—

SCOUT HEROES OF THE ARMY 87

of September 26th, 1917, our men talked in whispers; but their talk was not of the fact that at dawn they must face death; it consisted rather of the jokes and banter so typical of the British Tommy. And yet there was a feeling of intense excitement in the air, a confident feeling of success to come.

As the dawn began to break a deafening sound roared out from behind our lines, the drum-fire which preceded the attack.

Of all this waiting army, perhaps the most eager to be over the top and doing, was a Scout—A. J. Wingrove. His company had been given the particular job of clearing and holding the formidable block-houses—"Oliver House" and "Dear House." When the company went over, this Scout pressed forward, and, in his eagerness to be "at 'em," failed to keep touch with the rest of his platoon.

Before long he found himself at one of the two objectives—alone. A considerable number of Germans were holding the place, and little did they think one solitary Englishman, isolated from his company, was attacking them. Some six or eight turned out to show fight, but in a few seconds Wingrove had disposed of them. Then, fortunately for him, he was joined by a lance-corporal, and between them they took the remaining fifteen prisoners. The rest of the attack proved equally successful, and concrete emplacements which had meant to the enemy months of arduous labour, fell into British hands. This daring exploit won for Wingrove the Military Medal.

CORPORAL ERNEST SIMPSON, M.M.

(2/4TH K.O.Y.L.I. Scout, 1st Wakefield Troop.)

November 20th, 1917, at Havrincourt, our boys had been ordered to " follow the tanks," and gain a certain point. But following the tanks was no easy job, with great clouds of smoke every now and then obliterating the view, with shells bursting, and the bewildering rattle of the enemy machine guns. Besides, it was difficult ground.

Ploughing their way on, heeding nothing, waiting for nobody, our tanks proceeded, and the section under Corporal Simpson found itself hopelessly left behind. The men pressed on, however, making bravely for their objective; but soon it became evident that they were no longer in the wake of the tanks—a great unbroken mass of wire entanglements lay before them, and directly in line with the point they were making for.

"Well, here's a go," thought the Corporal to himself, "if we get on to that wire, we shall all go West."

So he told his chaps to lie down, and keep under cover till he should return. They did not

SCOUT HEROES OF THE ARMY 89

want to let him go, but he told them he was sure he could make a way for them to get through, and rush Fritz out of his holes.

Then, creeping cautiously up to the wire he began to cut it through. Bit by bit snapped beneath his clippers, but how slowly, slowly he seemed to be getting on! Hours seemed to be passing while he worked, with the knowledge that at any moment a German sniper might spot him, and send a sure, swift bullet his way. As it was, spent bullets, bits of shell, shrapnel, often went singing past him, or landed, with a ping and a splutter of earth, not far away.

At length he had come to the last bit of wire—and that seemed the toughest of the lot. But when that was through, and the way clear, he crept back to his men, over the broken ground. After a few minutes' rest, he led them back to the passage he had cut, and they scrambled through the loose ends of wire, expecting every minute to be hit, for the air seemed fairly alive. Once through the wire it was the matter of but a few minutes to reach the "holes" wherein Fritz was hiding, and of a little energetic bayonet work to turn him out.

When the job was done the brave young Corporal turned to see who was missing, and some distance away he saw his platoon officer, who had been hit, and was down. There was no cover, and the enemy fire was fierce, but heedless of his own safety, Corporal Simpson ran out to him. Kneeling down at his side he soon saw that he was badly hit. Then it was that he realised the great use of the ambulance work his Scoutmaster had taught him with such care, in the old Troop. Had it not been for that instruction and the constant practice, he would not, he felt sure, have known in the least what to do. But remembering what he had been taught he managed to arrest the bleeding, and to bandage the wounds.

This brave young Scout has since " gone home," but his deed will live in the memories of those who saw it, and of those who now read of it here, where for the first time it is recounted in detail. For Simpson never told the story to any one, until one day his Scoutmaster drew it from him.

> " I have reason to believe," writes his Scoutmaster, " that he never told any one else a tittle of what he related, under persuasion, to me—not even his parents. I promised him I would not relate his story, and I should not have done so now, but for the fact that he is dead, and the credit is his, and should be recorded as being worthy of a Scout and a man. . . . May he have his reward in God's Land of Peace."

SCOUT HEROES OF THE ARMY 91

PTE. D. PHILLIPS, M.M.
(4TH COY. 13TH ROYAL FUSILIERS. SCOUT, 2ND GOLDHANGER TROOP.)

It was in the big advance on August 23rd, 1918. The Division had had orders to capture Acheb le Grand. As the men went over the top as far as eye could see each way, troops were scrambling out of the trenches, simultaneously. The whole Division was in this stunt. The attack extended for miles.

There was no opposition for the first 100 yards ; our barrage had put the wind up Fritz, and he kept down under cover. But as British troops advanced, our barrage had to lift, and the German machine guns started. There was nothing for it but to dash up in a mad rush as close as possible to the German lines.

Phillips was in charge of a Lewis gun, and was determined to do some damage to the Germans ; but before he could turn his fire upon them a bullet had smashed his gun, and put it out of action. A Scout is not easily done out of a job he has decided to carry out. Phillips meant to use a Lewis gun on the Bosche, and as they had deprived him of his, he just set out to obtain another. This, of course, meant pinching one from Fritz. Before long, he had succeeded in doing this, and, turning the gun he had captured on the Germans, he showed them what a little British shooting, at close quarters, felt like. All day he kept it up until the Division was relieved at night. This daring piece of " cheek " was rewarded by a Military Medal.

But this was not Dick Phillips' only adventure with a Lewis gun. Not long after, he found himself in another advance, of a somewhat different nature. His company had been ordered to go up a sunken road. They had proceeded some way when they discovered that the Germans on their flank, and right behind, were enfilading them. Many men were getting hit, and it was hard to know what to do, for while the enemy fire continued it was impossible either to proceed or get back into cover. Then it was that the Scout with the Lewis gun came to the rescue. Working up, out of the road, he flanked the Germans.

Surprised by this unexpected fire they stopped off their own. Quickly the boys slipped back into cover, and, when his services were no longer needed, Dick Phillips crawled back after them, with his gun, concealing himself in the way every true Scout knows how to do. For this plucky piece of work, and truly Scout-like initiative, Dick Phillips was awarded a bar to his medal.

SCOUT HEROES OF THE ARMY 93

RIFLEMAN F. C. LAWRENCE, M.M.
(16TH KING'S ROYAL RIFLES. SCOUT, HIGH-CLERE TROOP.)

2 a.m. on a Sunday morning in the Hindenburg line. A heavy fog, like a great grey blanket, muffled the world. Over the slippery, sodden ground the regiment advanced towards Fontaine. An hour and a half's hard fighting, and our men were in the village—Fontaine was captured. But at three o'clock—only half an hour later—the Huns poured in, killing mercilessly, and Fontaine was lost again. But the Huns should not keep it—the gallant King's Royal Riflemen were determined on that point. At 5 a.m. the village was once more captured, and then, thank God, came another Division to help hold it.

A high brick building standing up in Fontaine had been a landmark, once. But when the grey dawn broke and it was possible to see a little, there was no longer a high building in Fontaine—only a pile of dilapidated bricks and mortar. A village, we called it, but daylight revealed a stretch of broken bricks and splintered wood, with desolate cats wandering about among the *débris*.

The regiments dug themselves in, and Fontaine became the front line. Battalion Headquarters were 1,500 yards back, across a great open space, torn and rent by shells. For two days these trenches were under enfilade fire, and shells were coming from all directions. It was during one of these terrible nights that a Scout won the Military Medal for his good work.

An urgent message had to be sent back to Battalion Headquarters, and the only possible way was to send a runner. It was Rifleman F. C. Lawrence's duty, and he set out without complaint.

It was dark and foggy. The guns thundered continuously, and shells burst with bewildering crashes that shook the very ground.

Climbing up, out of the shelter of the trench, Lawrence began to advance through the dense darkness. It would have been impossible to find his way save for his map and compass; and it was impossible to turn on his light, and look at the map, unless he was under cover. One glint from his electric torch and the snipers would have got him. Shell holes were the only possible cover; so, crawling into one, he managed to take a quick glance at his map, and then proceed a little further, to another, and then another, and so verify his direction.

Twice the concussion of a bursting shell, near at hand, threw him to the ground. The first time he lost his cap, and as it was drenching with rain, he wore a sand-bag in its place. At last he reached Headquarters.

SCOUT HEROES OF THE ARMY 95

The Divisional General was there, and the sight of this man, pale and shaken, drenched to the skin, and grotesque in his strange headgear, struck him very forcibly, and he complimented the Scout on his courage. The message being given, the return journey had to be made, and under the same difficulties, but Rifleman Lawrence regained his trench in safety.

A week later the regiment was relieved, and went out of the trenches. The men slept in little bivouacs—waterproof sheets over sticks. It was then that the General presented medals, and he did not forget the runner he had seen come in on that terrible night.

CORPORAL THOMAS JUGGINS, M.M.

(8TH GLOUCESTERS. PATROL LEADER, OAKLEY BISLEY AND EASTCOMBE TROOP, STROUD ASSOCIATION, GLOS.)

Nothing stops a Scout once he has got going and made up his mind to succeed. Corporal Juggins proved this one night, in the fateful Spring of 1918.

It was necessary to send rations and ammunition from the transport lines to the battalion at Kemmel. The only way was along the Reninghelst-Westoutre road. The enemy was shelling Westoutre. A journey along that road was not exactly inviting. But the stuff had to be got to the battalion, and Juggins, who was Transport Corporal, took on the job as part of the day's work.

The enemy was very busy with his guns, on that April evening, " and our job was to dodge him," as Corporal Juggins expressed the situation. So, at a brisk trot the little party set out along the road. All went well for some time. They managed to dodge Jerry most successfully.

It was as they neared Locre, and were between the village and the corner, known as Canada Corner, that mishaps began to occur. A shell burst not far off: the Corporal's pony started, staggered, and sank down. Blood was pouring from a gash across his shoulders! A glance showed that he was past help. Sadly the little cavalcade drew up, and a shot put the brave little beast out of pain.

Ahead, yellow tongues of flame were leaping up in the dusk, from among the ruins of black houses. The village was on fire in several places, and every few minutes another shell would fall with a tearing crash, throwing up a cloud of dust, bricks and splinters of wood.

The road was encumbered with upturned wagons and dead horses, and many a silent figure lay where he had fallen in the performance of his duty. Locre was a regular death-trap. The sooner

SCOUT HEROES OF THE ARMY

out of it the better, thought the little transport party. Whipping their horses to a gallop, they rattled down the village street. Not until they were past the houses on the further side of the village did they slow down to a walk; but they had halted too soon, for it was then that a ground-shrapnel shell burst, just ahead. The flying pieces of metal had hit the two drivers, and Corporal Juggins found himself alone, with three wagons and three teams.

Perhaps some people would have given up hope. But not so a Scout. Dismounting and quieting the frightened animals, he fastened the second team to the back of the front wagon, and the third team to the back of the second wagon; then, riding the foremost pair, he started on, along the road.

Over Kemmel Hill he trotted and down through the village. At last, at Rosignol Wood—once the "wood of the nightingales," now a very different place—he found the battalion, and reported that the rations had arrived.

But this was not the end of his adventures, for the return journey was still before this dauntless Scout! That nightmare village, Locre, where his two mates had fallen, was not an inviting prospect. With the resourcefulness of a Scout, who has naturally an eye to country, he devised

G

a means by which he could avoid it, and started off down a track.

He had gone some way when he found himself suddenly held up by a somewhat gruesome obstacle. Someone else had come that way, with transport wagons, and here he had been held up—for ever. A tangled heap of broken wagons and dead mules and horses barred the way. It was quite impossible to pass, and out of the question, of course, to clear the road.

Once more the situation seemed hopeless. But to a Scout there is a way out of every difficulty. Corporal Juggins (once Patrol Leader Juggins) decided that there was probably another track somewhere near, so he climbed over a barbed-wire fence, once erected by a farmer, and discovered one. He then demolished the farmer's fence, and before long the cavalcade was jolting along, over the new track. Fortunately this one was not encumbered by any very serious obstacles, and in the early hours of the morning, the Corporal trotted his teams up to the wagon lines.

It had just been his job, with an added spice of excitement, certainly, and the satisfactory feeling every Scout knows so well, of having found a way out of a tight corner. But his officers took a different view of the matter, and a Military Medal was the well-earned recognition awarded

SCOUT HEROES OF THE ARMY

to Corporal Juggins, " For conspicuous bravery and gallantry, especially on the night of April 15th, 1918."

PRIVATE R. L. DUCK, M.M.

(2/14TH LONDON REGT. LONDON SCOTTISH PATROL-LEADER, 4TH BANCROFT SCHOOL TROOP.)

It was a pitch dark night, and the final preparations had been made for an advance. Dranoutre Ridge, in the vicinity of Mt. Kemmel, was to be captured. A heavy ground-mist lay like a dim, grey curtain over the intervening country. Under its cover our men would be able to reach the ridge unseen by the enemy.

At 2.5 a.m. the barrage opened, and before long our men were over the top, and had reached their objective. And now the heavy cloak of mist became a hindrance, for it was very difficult to keep in touch, and to be certain of the direction.

The German outposts had discovered the British, creeping up like ghosts through the mist. The advanced machine-gun posts barked out their deathly challenge, and silently our men fell, riddled with bullets from the unseen foe. But fierce rifle fire and bombing swiftly silenced these guns, and turning, the Huns ran back in terror to give the alarm to the rear positions.

Among the men pushing forward in the darkness

was a Scout—Private R. L. Duck—and it is his adventure we will now follow, for it was this night's daring exploit that gained for him the Military Medal.

The platoon on his right—the end of his battalion—was almost completely wiped out, and of his section only he and the Corporal were left. It was very hard, under the circumstances, to know the direction in which to advance, and before long they found they were bearing too much to the right, as they had run into the left of the next battalion.

Starting off again, striking more to the left, they pushed on, listening intently for any sound of the enemy at hand. The Bosche had got the wind up badly, and was retreating as best he could, offering no fight.

Suddenly Duck found himself lying at the bottom of a shell hole, wondering how he had got there. The Corporal was close to him, enquiring in a low voice: " Are you hurt ? Where did he get you ? I think I got him all right." But Duck was not wounded—his " tin hat " had saved him. A bullet had struck this, making a dent in it about 2 inches wide. The blow had so stunned him that he had neither heard the report nor felt the concussion.

But the Corporal had seen the flash of the

rifle, and knew the direction from which the shot had come. Creeping to the edge of the shell hole the two men saw the Germans crawling out of their dug-out in the side of a bank. A few shots sent them scurrying like rabbits into the darkness. But the Scout and the Corporal were not content with shooting from their shelter. They knew of " a better ' ole " to go to—namely, the inside of that German dug-out! In a moment they were across the rough ground, and standing over the entrance. Then, with hands well raised, the Huns began to crawl out—great men 6 feet high, but without the pluck in them to offer resistance to these two daring Englishmen.

When eleven had emerged and the dug-out seemed empty, the Scout and his companion decided that the only thing to do was to take their prisoners back to our lines, for it was impossible to know for certain where the rest of our advancing troops were; and wandering about in the pitch dark with eleven hefty Germans was not good enough. The Bosches seemed quite to fall in with the plan, and the party started off along a path which led parallel to the front.

Before long, however, a German light went up, and a machine gun opened fire. Our two men came to the conclusion that it would be better to take a short cut back to the lines, and so turned their flock of Germans off the path, and led them over the rough ground, straight back towards our old position.

After a while they came upon a party of stretcher-bearers, badly in need of help. The prisoners were turned on to the job, the Corporal staying with them as guard, while the Scout, who was posted as runner, went back to try and find the remainder of the platoon.

Fortunately the other sections had not suffered so severely, and after about half an hour's wandering, he found them and was able to report to his officer. He then, once again, took on his job as runner, and was of great assistance in getting the remnants of the company dug in, before the enemy started his counter-attack.

A few days later, as Duck returned from a fatigue, he was sent for by his officer, and learnt that the Brigadier had sent him a message of congratulation on having gained the Military Medal.

"I have never had a bigger surprise in my life," he wrote back to his people. "The medal was given for the little shimozzle we had, that night, and it came to me as just as big a surprise as it will come to you all, at home." And that is the spirit in which our Scouts faced the "great adventure," and played the game of Scouting out in the shell-torn fields of France.

SCOUT HEROES OF THE ARMY 103

GNR. HERBERT HOLLAND, M.M.
(R.F.A. PATROL-LEADER, 20TH WEST LONDON TROOP.)

"Dick" Holland had had many a thrilling adventure before he performed the deed of heroic humanity prompted by the true Scout spirit, which won for him the Military Medal. Before recounting this deed we will describe one or two of his experiences, for Dick has "gone home," and will never be able to yarn, now, to the boys, about what happened "over there," in the first awful year of the war.

Dick was in some of the thickest of the fighting at Loos. His battery had to retire, leaving behind a large amount of high explosive ammunition. Volunteers were called for to go back and try to recover some of this. Dick was the first to volunteer. A party returned, and, arriving at the spot, set to work with all speed.

They had not succeeded in getting much, however, before the Germans spotted them. The only hope of getting out alive was to retire as fast as possible.

"Mount: Gallop!" shouted the sergeant-major. The order was promptly obeyed, for a hail of fire was being directed towards the spot. Dick, however, was still down in the dump. He crept along, under cover, for a while, and then made a dash for safety.

"You would be surprised how much metal they can send after a chap and miss him," he remarked, in telling the story of their hairbreadth adventure. Another time he had the unpleasant job of carrying despatches through a German gas shell barrage.

It was as he returned from one of his despatch-running expeditions that he performed the deed that won him official recognition. Making his way cautiously back to his battery, he saw, lying out in no-man's-land, what looked at first like a dead body. A slight movement, however, revealed the fact that the man was alive. A living man out in that place of indescribable danger awoke in Dick's heart all the feelings of chivalry and desire to help, that are part of a true Scout.

Heedless of his own safety, he crawled out over the rough ground, and at last reached the figure that had attracted his attention. The poor fellow was in a terrible state. Dick gave him some water, which the man drank thankfully, and then murmured:

"Leave me, chum; I'm done for."

"Didn't the stretcher-bearers find you?" said Dick.

SCOUT HEROES OF THE ARMY 105

"Yes," whispered back the man, "but I'm too bad—so they've left me."

"Well," said Dick, "*I* won't leave you!"

Telling the wounded man that he would not be long, he crawled back to the trenches to find something with which to make a litter to drag the man back on. There he met a chum of his, who agreed to return with him on this quest of mercy. Together they managed to get the man back in safety to the field dressing station.

Both Dick Holland and his friend were awarded the Military Medal. The man eventually recovered, and returned to the fighting line.

On October 5th, 1917, Dick Holland went out with despatches. On the 6th he was reported missing. A second party went out, and found him, on the 7th, badly wounded. They took him to a dressing station, where he died the following day. He is buried in the British Soldiers Cemetery, at Lyssenbroke, near Poperinge.

"I think his training as a Scout brought out all that was best in a good boy," wrote his father.

CORPORAL ROBERT HORN, M.M.

(THE BUFFS, ATT. SOMERSET LIGHT INFANTRY. PATROL LEADER, 1ST. CRANBROOK TROOP.)

It was very near the end of the war that Corporal Robert Horn got his chance of a little bit of

Scouting that must have appealed to him, as a Scout.

On the evening of November 1st, 1918, he was ordered to present himself at a Belgian farmhouse, then his Company's Headquarters. There he was told that the platoon that he had joined the previous day was to take an important part in a raid on Lectard, a village some distance away, and held by the enemy. The scheme was explained thus.

A barrage was to be put on the village at 1.55 a.m. on November 2nd. It would cease at 2, when the platoon would move forward and put a bridge of duckboards across a stream, and hold on until — Company (who should have entered the village from the other side) returned, over the bridge, which was then to be destroyed.

At two o'clock Horn's platoon left the "jumping-off place," and began to bridge the stream. But to their dismay they found the barrage was not being lifted, and that our own shells were falling very near at hand.

At length the bridge was completed, the work having been done under very difficult and dangerous conditions. The shells were still falling continuously, and it seemed folly to keep the platoon in danger of death, yet the bridge must be held. It was then that the Corporal, who, be it remembered, was a Scout, volunteered to cross the bridge with two men, and hold it, thus enabling the officer to withdraw the platoon to a spot not being swept by the barrage. His offer was accepted, and before long the three plucky men found themselves alone, in the darkness, on the outskirts of the village.

The moments crept slowly on. The shells continued to fall, bursting with violent explosions on either hand. Still no sound in the village— no bombing, no scuffles in the dark houses, no sound of — Company making for the bridge. What could it mean ? At length Horn decided to do a little Scouting on his own, and try to discover what was on.

Leaving the two men to guard the bridge, he crept softly into the village, and down the dark and empty streets. Looking into one house and another, as he went, he could find no trace of a Bosche, and yet the village was certainly in German hands. At last, by dint of creeping about very softly and listening intently, as every good Scout knows how to do, he discovered that the village was not deserted, as it seemed, but that the Bosches were all skulking in the cellars, for fear of our shells. Away, the other side of the village, the Germans seemed more lively, and beyond, their artillery seemed to be at work.

Creeping back to the bridge, Horn was just in time to see a line of black figures advancing towards it, from the other side. The three guards covered the advancing party with their rifles, and Horn challenged. To his surprise he learnt it was — Company. They had been unable to enter the village from the other end, and had sent up what they meant to be an S.O.S. signal, but which had been, in reality, an increased barrage signal ---hence the fact that our barrage had not lifted.

Horn reported what he had discovered about the village, and, as soon as the barrage lifted, he started out, as guide to the raiding party. Creeping into the village, and surrounding the houses shown them by the Scout as those whose cellars contained Germans, they proceeded to bomb Jerry out of his funk-holes. Besides some prisoners, a machine gun was captured, and an unopened mail bag.

The triumphant party then returned to the British lines, and were gratified to learn, later, that a great deal of useful information had been collected, as a result of the raid.

Horn's resourcefulness, initiative and courage were rewarded by a Military Medal.

SIGNALLER CECIL EDWARDS, M.M.

(ROYAL WELSH FUSILIERS. ASSISTANT SCOUT-MASTER, 1ST HOLYHEAD TROOP.)

It was in May, 1916, that Signaller Cecil Edwards performed his duty so faithfully, and with such cool-headed courage, that he earned the Military Medal. The bombardment was intense, and so many telegraph wires were smashed that the trench was cut off from communication with Battalion Headquarters. Edwards and another signaller sent urgent messages by means of a lamp, and then, risking their lives for duty's sake, proceeded out into the open, to repair the wires.

Full well they knew they would be a mark for German snipers, and that at any moment a shell might burst so near as to blow them to bits, or bury them alive, while a German attack was expected. Yet they worked on, steadily, at the difficult job of finding the ends of broken wire, discovering which fitted to which, and then joining them up. At last the work was rewarded, and they found themselves in communication with Battalion Headquarters once again. For this courageous performance of duty Edwards and his companions were awarded the Military Medal.

LANCE-CORPORAL R. MASSEY, D.C.M.

(MACHINE GUNNER, 6TH BATT. EAST LANCASHIRE REGT. SCOUT ST. PETER AND ST. PAUL TROOP. RISHTON, NR. BLACKBURN.)

Lance-Corporal Massey had been through some of the most thrilling episodes of the war before the night on which he won his well-deserved award. He was through the Gallipoli fighting, and was wounded in August, when our Force made their gallant and unsuccessful dash for the Narrows. After a few weeks at a hospital in Cairo, he returned to his battalion, then at Suvla Bay. Here he took part in the terrible experience of the evacuation ; and being a gunner, had the task of covering the retirement.

After a short stay at Port Said, the battalion was ordered to Mesopotamia, as a relief force to General Townsend. On May 4th, 1916, he took part in the advance of six miles, which brought them, after desperate fighting, to Sanniyut. After one day's rest, the battalion took part in another daring exploit.

At a very early hour the order came to go over the top. There was no bombardment from our artillery, and silently the men left the trench, and proceeded towards their objective, taking all possible cover. They had almost reached it,

SCOUT HEROES OF THE ARMY 111

when an enemy outpost discovered their approach. Our troops suffered a heavy repulse and the number of casualties was very great. The attempt to reach Kut this way was given up.

Massey's battalion was then removed to the right bank of the Tigris, and soon found itself attacked by both infantry and cavalry, but here our boys got a little of their own back, and caused the enemy to retire. It was, however, near Dejalia that Lance-Corporal Massey experienced the thrilling adventure that gained him his distinction.

He and a party of his comrades found themselves occupying a small piece of trench, with the Turks only thirty yards ahead, and on either flank. Their rifles proved to be of but little use, and machine guns and bombs became the chief means of defence. The enemy replied in the same manner, and their bombs almost annihilated the battalion.

But the main defence of the position rested with the machine gunners. Massey's gun was going strong, doing deadly work on the frontal position, and thinking he might be able to do further damage to the enemy, he left his own gun to those under him, and, taking another gun, proceeded to crawl forward into a sap. For some time he dared not open fire, for the bombs were coming over fast, and this would have attracted the attention of the enemy bombers. But before long, a raid from the Turks forced him to open fire, in self-defence. He had fired two belts consisting of 500 rounds, when a bomb hit his gun and put it out of action. There was nothing for it but to crawl back to his original position, and this he had to do over the bodies of many fallen comrades.

Reaching his own gun, he found it still going strong, and was just removing its position when the Turks began to pour over towards our lines. The only hope was to meet them face to face; and so, jumping up on to the parapet, Massey and his team raked the advancing enemy with machine-gun fire. But few minutes had passed before the entire team, with the exception of Massey and one other man, were hit. These stuck to their post, and resisted to the end. How they came through alive they never knew. Both were awarded the Distinguished Conduct Medal, and, later, the Serbian Silver Medal.

PRIVATE A. E. BENTLEY, D.C.M.

(1ST BEDS. SCOUT OF THE CHESHUNT TROOP.)

It was at Violaines, about eight miles from Ypres, that another Scout found an opportunity of raising the Scout spirit to the heights of heroism, and showed that a good turn, bravely and faith-

SCOUT HEROES OF THE ARMY

fully performed, can be the means of saving a comrade's life.

The Huns were giving our boys hell. Through the incessant rifle fire came, every few seconds, the roar of a shell, like a great, invisible express train, growing louder and louder as it approached, and ending with a crash that seemed to shake the very foundations of the earth. Men were falling on every hand. There was no time for sympathy or pity. Tending the wounded was out of the question—every fighting man must fight.

The 1st Beds were in the thick of things and among them was a Scout. To a Scout it goes against the grain to see men in need of help, to hear them crying aloud for assistance, and yet to be unable to give ear, to have to "carry on." Even a suffering animal is a friend who *must* be tended. But in war, stern duty comes first: it was this Scout's duty to use his rifle to hold back the enemy.

But before long the time came when his rifle lay forgotten in the mud, and he was free to turn his mind to saving life, instead of taking it.

A great piece of shell had inflicted a grievous wound in his thigh. It had seemed to him as if a sledge hammer had caught him with full force. The shock brought him to the ground, and for a while he lay, half-dazed and wondering what had happened.

Then he began to feel the hot blood soaking through his clothes and a strange burning that grew more and more fierce as the numbness caused by the first shock passed away.

To move at all increased the pain; the only thing to do seemed to be to lie still and hope that the Germans would not take that trench, and that the stretcher-bearers would come at last.

Muddy walls, a strip of grey sky—that was all he could see. Away, above him, sounded the crackle of rifle fire, the confused sound of orders, the crash of shells whose vibration seemed to rend his wound afresh. And then, through the noise of war, came another sound, quite close at hand; a sound that touched his Scout's heart, and made him forget his own pain. A man was groaning in his agony, and murmuring piteous appeals for the help that did not come. The pain was breaking his spirit, and his very lifeblood was flowing away, soaking into the earth.

It was more than Bentley could bear. Dragging himself up he saw the man. His Scout training told him that first aid promptly applied might be the saving of that life.

At first it seemed impossible to drag himself so far, to face the fierceness of his own pain. But the muffled sob of the boy who needed him touched his heart; and the memory of the great ideal of Service which he had made his own, kindled his spirit with brave determination. A good turn that costs one nothing is scarcely worth doing—every Scout knows that. Here, at last, was a supreme chance—a good turn that would cost him more pain than many a man has to bear in a lifetime; and might even cost him his life!

Painfully he dragged himself along the muddy floor of the trench. At last he was at the side of the wounded man. He was at no loss what to do. Much practice had made him familiar with the use of pad and bandage. Many a time, in the old club-room, he had pictured himself as tending a wounded man, and had applied a tourniquet or a sling to some brother Scout, in order that, if ever the time came, he might " Be Prepared."

At last the job was done and he lay back exhausted.

" Thank you, mate . . . thank you . . ." whispered the boy. He was a little easier now; and, better still, he was comforted, for a friend had tended him as gently as his mother could have done; he was no longer alone, forgotten, left to die with no one to care.

But Bentley's work was not done yet. The feeble moans of another fallen comrade reached his ears. Once again he nerved himself for the effort. Inch by inch he dragged his suffering body along the trench. With patient care he ministered to another man, to whom death was drawing very near. But still his task was not accomplished. A third man he dressed and comforted; and then falling back exhausted, he lay and waited for death.

But that was not to be. When eight weary hours had passed, relief came. The stretcher-bearers passed along the trench. They took him up and bore him away to safety. And they took up three other men, who, save for the skilful bandaging of their wounds, would have died hours before. And each of these three men told the same tale: how a comrade had crawled up and tended them, though he was, himself, wounded like them and in awful pain.

PRIVATE H. C. BULL. D.C.M.

(2/4TH LONDON REGT. SCOUT, THE BOSTALLS (2ND.) TROOP.)

"This man, a company stretcher-bearer, worked like a superman, absolutely regardless of any danger. He worked continuously for fourteen hours, and through two most intense

SCOUT HEROES OF THE ARMY 117

enemy barrages, and undoubtedly saved many lives. His devotion to duty was extraordinary, and he was the means of putting extreme confidence in all ranks of his company in a most difficult situation and anxious time."

(*Signed*) W. R. H. DANN, Lt.-Col.
2/4th LONDON REGT.

It was a Scout that was thus commended by his Colonel, and for his splendid courage he received the D.C.M. Inspiring as are the few lines we have quoted, we feel sure that other Scouts will like to hear the story in greater detail, and we give it here as it has been told to us.

It happened at St. Julien, east of Ypres, in September, 1917. The men had been told to prepare for an advance, at dawn. There was still five hours to wait—five hours of nothing to do but wonder how things would end. For many, these were their last five hours on earth. How splendid to spend one's last hours just waiting to go forward bravely, to serve one's own beloved country and one's King!

The rain was coming down in a ceaseless drizzle. The dark hours crept on, slowly. Then, as the chill grey light of dawn spread over the Eastern sky, a sound like the deep rumble of thunder began, behind our lines, and almost immediately voices shouting the long expected order—" Over the top, boys, and the best of luck to you " !

Scrambling up out of the trench the men found themselves looking at a strange view, hidden, before, by the parapet. It seemed almost as if a firework display were in progress on the ridge ahead. For everywhere was the strange light of bursting shells, and the frantic S.O.S. signals of the Germans. But soon the curious sight was forgotten, for our men were face to face with the Bosche.

Bull was regimental stretcher-bearer, and he saw that before long his work would have to begin. He was at his officer's side, when three Germans appeared immediately in front, their hands raised, in token of surrender. Our men went on towards them, but, suddenly, at twenty-five yards' range, the centre man produced a revolver, and shot the officer through the heart. In an instant Bull was on the ground at his side, but there was nothing to be done—he was dead.

Our men were falling on every side, for the German guns were answering our barrage. Within two minutes of going over eight stretcher-bearers had been killed. Bull, with those that remained, began his arduous task : within an hour and a half, he was left with only two others, to look after

SCOUT HEROES OF THE ARMY 119

the wounded of four companies and the machine gunners!

Here was a big problem to tackle, and it took all the wits, the energy, and the determination of a true Scout to face it, and all the true Scout's love of service and enthusiasm for saving life. But, besides this, it took the utmost courage, for machine-gun fire was raking the battlefield, and shells were bursting, incessantly.

Here is just one incident from the many experiences this brave Scout had, in those terrible fourteen hours.

Scouring the ground ahead, for signs of life among the many prostrate forms, he saw, away towards the German lines, a hand waving above a shell hole. Here was an S.O.S. signal that could not be ignored. Crawling forward on his stomach Bull managed to reach the shell hole. The man was badly wounded, and it took a little while to dress his wounds.

Whilst thus engaged Bull heard groans, near by, and so, having finished attending to his man, crawled on, to the next shell hole. In this lay a poor fellow with two broken legs. He was in terrible pain and there was little which could be done to ease him, but having arranged his legs in the most comfortable position, Bull crawled back to the other man, and, to his surprise, found him dead.

But it was not from the wounds he had so lately dressed that the man had died—he had been hit again in those five minutes since Bull had left him. Those groans, faintly heard through the booming of the guns, had called Bull away from almost certain death, and it came over him very forcibly that there was a Power watching over him and protecting him.

More and more men needed dressing, and, though tired out, Bull obeyed the old Scout motto, "Stick to it."

Hour after hour he toiled, thinking nothing of his own safety, taking no notice of his weariness. But at last he was, himself, wounded. He could not walk to the dressing station, but could only lie and wait. And even in his own pain his first thought was for others, for as wounded men crawled past he would not let them go without having their wounds dressed, and a drink of water. All night he lay helpless. It was not till twelve o'clock the following day that he reached the dressing station.

His wound meant a trip back to Blighty; and there he received his well-earned reward.

SCOUT HEROES OF THE ARMY

ROBERT GIDLEY, Croix de Guerre

(CROIX ROUGE FRANÇAIS. SECTION SANITAIRE ECOSSAISE NO. 20. SCOUT, 3RD CHISWICK TROOP.)

To all true Scouts the war brought an irresistible call to the service of King and Country. Those whom youth or ill-health prevented from " joining up " were bitterly disappointed, and many a story is told of the ways in which they tried to evade the authorities, and get out to do their bit. Perhaps few stories could equal that of Bob Gidley, for heroic perseverance.

" Bob Gidley had a remarkable career which was an example and inspiration to his brother Scouts. He joined the Chiswick Troop before he was twelve and remained a member of it throughout. He was a somewhat delicate and reserved boy, but his sterling worth was shown at the age of thirteen when he saved a child from drowning, at Strand-on-the-Green.

" In July, 1914, Bob was in Belgium with a party of Scouts, and was in that country when it was invaded by the Germans. Returning home he immediately volunteered for Scout war service, and served in the Foreign Office for several months. Before he was fifteen he joined the R.N.A.S. as motor despatch rider, and was transferred to the armoured car section. He was promoted to be

1st-class petty officer, and later on qualified as pilot's observer and made several ascents.

"After some fourteen months' service he was recommended for a commission in the Army and was sent to the Officers' Cadet Battalion at Oxford. He was there some six months, but the training was so severe that he broke down in health, and his age—then only sixteen years and ten months—was discovered. He was consequently discharged, but being determined to go to the Front, he immediately joined the French Red Cross, Convoy S.S.E. 20. He left for France on March 27th last, and to quote from a notice sent out by the French Red Cross, 'After only a few weeks' service his brilliant and self-sacrificing career was crowned by a most gallant death in the service of others.'

"Some people might call such an event a 'tragedy.' But Bob Gidley's one great desire had been *to serve*, as may be seen from his dauntless efforts, and, after all, to die for a cause is to render it supreme service, for the greatest of all Heroes has said, 'Greater love no man hath than this, that a man lay down his life for his friends.'"

The story of how this young hero laid down his life is short and simple—just one more example of a Scout, faithful to his duty, and forgetful of self.

As has already been said, Bob Gidley joined the Croix Rouge Français. " The work done by this ambulance column was necessarily of a hazardous character, only to be undertaken by those endowed with both nerve and pluck," as one of his officers says, in writing to his parents. Not the least dangerous and trying part of the work was that of driving the ambulance cars from the small town where the section was stationed, up to the front. The road was frequently shelled by the Germans, and, the journey once started, there was, of course, no means of taking cover.

One day, as Gidley, accompanied by one other man, was driving a car along this dangerous road, a fierce bombardment began. They put on their helmets and continued bravely to speed on towards the line. But the fire became so intense that they were obliged to halt, with a view to drawing back, a little, and trying to find some cover.

Gidley had just commenced to back the car, when, with a terrific explosion, a shell burst exactly in front of them and the glass wind-screen was blown into a hundred pieces. Gidley's companion, though shaken by the concussion, was unhurt, and thought, at first that his friend had not received any injuries, either, as he remained sitting in his place, and the car continued to back. But soon it became evident that the brave young driver was unconscious and that he had received some terrible wounds in the head and neck.

The shells were coming over every few seconds and the other ambulance man decided that the wisest thing to do was to try and back the car into a safer position. This he did for some sixty yards, when the back wheels collapsed, and the car came to a standstill. With the help of some French soldiers and another ambulance, the brave young Scout was taken back to the hospital, where half an hour afterwards he died.

"In this noble work of rescuing the fallen," wrote his chief, "your son has made the supreme sacrifice and we bow in homage to his memory."

PRIVATE FRANK G. HUGHES, M.M.
(ROYAL FUSILIERS. PATROL LEADER, ST. PETER'S, (114) MANCHESTER.)

It was during the operations south of Albert, on August 22nd, 1918, that a Manchester Patrol Leader showed the stuff Manchester Scouts are made of.

It was very early in the morning. Keeping carefully under cover a little party advanced towards a certain point on the Ancre. Every one in the party knew that the job they were on was not going to be what the Army calls a "cushy job," for it was to place a bridge across the

SCOUT HEROES OF THE ARMY 125

river that they had come, with the Huns not very far away.

It was not, however, until they reached their destination that our men realised quite what a terrible undertaking it was going to be. No sooner had they begun preparations for the work than, with a deafening rattle, machine-gun fire was opened upon them from the other side of the stream, and at very close range. It was impossible to get the bridge across without exposing themselves, and to expose themselves for the length of time it would take to put the bridge across, in the usual way, would mean almost certain death. It seemed impossible to know what to do, when the one member of the party who was a Scout, solved the problem, by jumping into the stream. Seizing the end of the bridge he waded across with it, every now and then disappearing in deep water, but sticking to his job like a true Scout.

Three machine guns were turned upon him, but it was as though an unseen hand protected him. At last he was across, and had got the end of the bridge into position. Then, still unhurt, he made his way back through the water, to his companions.

"Undoubtedly the prompt action of Pte. Hughes," says the official report, "had much to do with the success of his company in crossing the stream."

SAPPER SIDNEY J. KEMP, M.M.
(5/9TH LONDON FIELD COY., R.E. PATROL LEADER, 2ND ST. PANCRAS TROOP.)

It was in a raid on April 24th, 1917, that P.L. Kemp won the Military Medal by doing what he himself considered just part of the day's work. "I had no idea of making myself conspicuous in action," he wrote home, "I just did what was my duty." But carrying out of duty in this case meant a piece of self-sacrificing pluck that could not pass unnoticed.

Kemp formed one of the R.E. party which accompanied the Centre Infantry Detachment, and was in charge of the Bangalore Torpedoes. At first all went well, in the advance, but as the third belt of wire was reached it was found that this had not been cut. The R.E. party accordingly came up, and laid a Bangalore Torpedo against the enemy's wire. It was a dangerous job, for a hot fire at close range was turned upon them.

The little party retired, expecting at every minute to hear the torpedo explode. Something, however, had caused it to fail to do so. With

SCOUT HEROES OF THE ARMY

cool courage and complete disregard of his own safety, Kemp turned round, went back to the torpedo and relighted the fuse. This time the torpedo did explode, destroying the wire and enabling the detachment to rush the Hun trenches.

CHAPTER IV

Scout Heroes of the Navy.

BOY FIRST CLASS, JOHN TRAVERS CORNWELL, V.C.

H.M.S. CHESTER. SCOUT, ST. MARY'S MISSION (MANOR PARK TROOP.)

"Fear none of those things which thou shalt suffer. . . . Be thou faithful unto death."—Rev. ii. 10.

"Stick to it—Stick to it."—SCOUT MOTTO.

A VISION of the future! An inspection of Scouts by His Majesty the King. As he passes down the line carefully inspecting the Scouts, His Majesty suddenly reins in his horse and stopping, asks one of the Scouts, "What is the meaning of that Bronze 'C' on your breast, my lad?" The Scout, blushing with confusion, hardly knows how to answer the question, but fortunately the Chief is at hand. "The 'C' means, sir," he says, "that this boy is one of our 'Cornwell' Scouts. He has shown by his character that he has the making of a Jack Cornwell, the young hero of Horn Reef. Your Majesty may remember how that boy, when mortally

SCOUT HEROES OF THE NAVY

wounded, stuck alone to his post on the *Chester*. We felt this was an example for our scouts to follow, and so we instituted the Cornwell Badge."

Yes, Jack Cornwell was a Scout—a true Scout. He belonged to the St. Mary's Mission (Manor Park) Troop, and a jolly keen chap he was too. His mother says:

> "He was so attached to the Scouts, and so proud of his badges when he brought them home. I have often thought that what he learned with the Scouts helped him a lot in the Navy."

And the following letter from Scoutmaster J. F. Avery, of the 21st East Ham Troop:

> "I knew Cornwell very well, both as a Scout and in private life. He was always what I used to call a 'dare devil.' Nothing was too hard for him. He would attempt any task no matter how hard it was. He was just the sort of lad that would meet so glorious and brave an end. I don't think he knew what fear was. After passing his Tenderfoot he worked for the Second-class Badge, which he eventually won, and kept the pot boiling by working for and passing his "Missioner" Badge. This is as far as he got, as, at the outbreak of war, the officers

of his Troop enlisted and the Troop was dissolved.

"I also knew Cornwell as a working boy. He was always a good boy at work and carried out his duty with cheerfulness."

And that is exactly what was said of him later, when hearing his country's call he joined the Navy as a Boy—2nd Class, and came under the stern discipline of the senior service. His instructors spoke well of him—he was a good boy. There was no record of " crime " against his name.

Cornwell was trained at Keyham. Finishing his course there in April, 1916, he left as a Boy—1st Class with double his previous pay. He spent a few days at home with his mother, telling her of all his doings and of his hopes that before long he would "get into action and see the Germans beaten." He was ordered to join his ship, His Majesty's cruiser *Chester*, on Easter Monday. It seemed hard that he should have to leave on such a holiday, but when some one pitied him, he laughed and said, "It's just a matter of duty, you see. I should feel ashamed for ever if I got back late and had bad marks against my name."

There are some dates every one of us knows—

SCOUT HEROES OF THE NAVY 131

William the Conqueror 1066, William Rufus 1087, Battle of Trafalgar 1805, Battle of Waterloo 1815, and so on. There's another which we shall never forget—the 31st of May, 1916—the date of the Battle of Jutland, the first great naval action fought by the British Fleet for more than a hundred years.

In other books you will read of all that the sailors did in the Great War, and the full story of this tremendous fight when, after long months of waiting, the German fleet at last came out to give battle and was driven back to its safe harbour, broken and beaten by the glorious British Navy. I am going to write only of the part played in the Battle of Jutland by His Majesty's cruiser *Chester*, upon which Jack Cornwell had then served for just over a month.

Time and again during the war the British Grand Fleet under Admiral Sir John Jellicoe swept the North Sea in search of the German fleet, and on May 30th, 1916, it once more left its base in the far north of Scotland. The battle cruiser fleet, with Vice-Admiral Sir David Beatty (as he was then) in command, was further south scouting for the bigger vessels. On May 31st, the German fleet under the command of Admiral von Scheer had also put to sea, and steamed northwards with a large force of battle cruisers and light cruisers and destroyers in advance as a screen in front of the battle fleet. Great was the joy on board the British battle cruisers when at half-past two on that memorable day news came that the enemy was in sight. Full steam ahead was ordered, and the ships dashed through the water to try and cut off the German cruisers, who, when they discovered the British were there in force, turned back to join their Battle Fleet. At a quarter to four both sides opened fire. At the beginning of the battle fortune favoured the Germans, who fought well and bravely. In less than half an hour two of our finest ships had been hit and sunk, but in spite of these losses Sir David Beatty still pursued and pounded the German cruisers until, at five o'clock, the whole German battle fleet arrived on the scene. Now the British Admiral changed his tactics. He determined to draw the German fleet northwards towards the British Grand Fleet, which he knew was coming up behind him as fast as it could steam, so he turned north again with the Germans in hot pursuit.

In advance of Sir John Jellicoe's giant ships, now heaving through the waves to meet Sir David Beatty's cruisers, was the third battle cruiser squadron under Rear-Admiral Hood—they are

SCOUT HEROES OF THE NAVY 133

names to remember, these—and he was ordered to join Sir David Beatty with all speed and help to hold the enemy till the heavy battleships could get into action. The *Chester* belonged to this third squadron. At half-past five Admiral Hood saw flashes of gunfire and heard the sound of guns in the distance. He sent *Chester* forward to find out what was happening and report to him.

His Majesty's ship *Chester* is a fast light cruiser. She had not been built very long, and the Battle of Jutland was her first fight. When the order came from Admiral Hood, every officer, every man, every boy on board the *Chester* knew that at last their great hour had come, the hour for which they had worked and trained so hard. It was just after half-past five, and although at that time the light was fairly good, mist was rising in the distance, and out of that haze the German fleet was coming towards them. That mist meant very much in the Battle of Jutland, for you will understand at once that while it is easy to shoot from the edge of the mist at a ship outlined by the sun in the western sky, it is very difficult to hit a target when firing from the light into the distant haze as the *Chester* would have to do.

On board the *Chester* there was that tense silence

which always comes before the storm of action. The decks had been cleared, all the officers, men and boys were at their posts, just as they had been hundreds of times before when they had practised—but this day it was the real thing, and no make-believe. Everything, everybody was—Ready.

At the left-hand side of the shield of the forward six-inch gun, almost touching it, stood Jack Cornwell—ready. Fixed right across his head and over his ears was what is called a telepad. You may have seen people wearing them in telephone exchanges—instead of putting one receiver to your ear this double receiver is clamped over each ear so that you can have both hands free. A wire went from the telepad straight to the gunnery officer of the *Chester*, and through that wire would come the most important of all messages for the gun crew, the officer's orders as to when and how to fire. Now you can see why such pains are given to the training of boys like Jack Cornwell, now you can see where discipline comes in. You hadn't realised, few of us indeed yet realise, that a small boy of his age can and does play such a big part in the great game of life and death on board a ship in action.

Jack Cornwell was sight-setter to this forward gun on the *Chester*. Whether that gun would

SCOUT HEROES OF THE NAVY 135

hit or miss the enemy depended largely upon the coolness and quickness in carrying out the telephoned orders he received. In front of him was a brass disc, pinned through the centre and moving like a wheel. A touch, a turn, of this disc, and the muzzle of the gun was raised or lowered— that is why Jack Cornwell's hands had to be free, and why the telepad was across his head. For *he* had to turn that disc. The gunnery officer in the centre of the ship orders, let us say, to set the gun for hitting at 10,000 yards. The disc is turned until the notch on its edge marked "10,000" is straight with the arrow on the brass plate below it. "Up 300!" comes the command, and before you can say it, or even think what it means, the disc is turned until the arrow points to 10,300 yards. "Down 400!" —another twist and it points to 9,900 yards. It doesn't sound very difficult, does it? It isn't —if you are so trained and ready that every order is carried out without a single second's wait. But you have to be very quick, very accurate, very attentive and obedient to the voice at the other end of the wire. Suppose you were to say to yourself "What? *Up* three hundred? He really means *down* three hundred, I expect. We have been lowering the gun every time lately. I'll put it *down* three hundred instead." And then the order comes to fire. A miss! And your fault, too, for the gunnery officer can see and you can't, and the enemy was steering away and your shot fell short. ·Your fault! And perhaps that was the last chance of hitting, and perhaps as a result of that wrong move your ship is hit instead, and very precious lives are lost and a grand ship sunk. It may mean the loss of the battle itself, and the loss of that battle may even mean the loss of the war. Who can tell?

It is not so very difficult in practice if you are willing to forget all about yourself and give your whole heart and soul and body to the work of carrying out each order as it comes through—but it's not so easy when the real thing comes.

The *Chester* was in action for about twenty minutes. What minutes they were! A quarter of an hour after she left the third battle squadron she was in the thick of the fight with three or four enemy cruisers. It was at least three to one, you see, but the *Chester* never wavered. She fought all three, beat them off, and twenty minutes later—at about five minutes past six that evening—she rejoined the battle cruiser squadron, her work nobly and successfully done.

I wish I could picture for you those twenty minutes. But no one can. Even those who fought through them and lived to tell the tale

SCOUT HEROES OF THE NAVY

cannot do it. The noise, the shock, the strain are so tremendous that the memory of the fight is dimmed and all confused. Every man is so intent upon what he himself has to do that he has neither time nor wish to think of, or to see, what is happening to any one else or even to the ship herself. There are no spectators, no onlookers on board a ship in action, no one to keep the score, no umpire, no reporter. From Captain Lawson on the bridge to the stoker by the furnaces down below, to Jack Cornwell standing by his gun, every one on board had his tremendous duty to perform, and when after that twenty minutes the *Chester* returned to the squadron, still in fighting trim, it was because they all had forgotten themselves and thought only of that duty.

The forward gun turret of the *Chester* received, the minute the battle began, the full force of the enemy's fire. What that force is none who have not been through such a fight can even imagine. Tons of metal flying through the air at the rate of 3,000 feet a second explode under the deck, thud upon the armour that protects the gun. The noise almost splits the ears, the flashes blind the eyes, and the smell of burnt cordite and of burning paint choke the breath.

Jack Cornwell stands by his gun, his hand on the disc. There is a crash that almost flings him off his feet. A man falls at his side, cut in pieces by the splinters of an enemy shell—dead; another flings up his arms and tumbles, horribly maimed, across the deck, then another, then another. A fragment of shell rips across his body, piercing, stabbing, tearing his flesh. The gun's crew, the crew of *his* gun, are being killed one by one, two by two. In a few minutes there are only three left of the nine who stood by him as they went into action. Then a shell bursts right over the gun and—two only are left and they are under cover. Jack Cornwell is standing all alone, with nothing to shelter him against the shot and shell, and he has been terribly wounded. Alone. Around him the dead and dying; himself torn, bleeding, very faint from pain and the horror of the sights and sounds of battle. For war is very, very horrible.

Jack Cornwell's job was done. There was no one left to fire the gun. No orders were coming through the wire to him; there was no one to carry them out if they had come. He could lie down with the others—it would ease the pain a little, perhaps. He could creep away below deck where the wounded were being looked after— there were doctors there who would help him

SCOUT HEROES OF THE NAVY 139

and give him something to stop the pain. He had done his job. No one could blame him if he thought of himself now.

Then there came to his mind, from the memory of his Keyham days, the old Navy order that a gun must be kept firing so long as there is one man left who is able to crawl. No! `no! no! his job was not done. He might still be needed. There might still be work for him to do. His duty was to stand by the gun and wait for any orders that might come through, stand until he was relieved, stand in the hope that others might take the place of those who had fallen, to *stand* by his gun until he dropped. And he *wouldn't* drop. He clenched his teeth, clenched his hands, almost forgot the pain as he strained to hear if a voice called at the other end of the wire, his hand still stretched out towards the disc to carry out the order if it came. All alone—listening, watching, Jack Cornwell stood by his gun—" awaiting orders." And so he stood until the fight was over and the *Chester* steamed back to the fleet battered, bruised and splintered, but still ready for another fight.

Chester had played her part well. She returned with what was left of her crew and her guns to the third battle cruiser squadron, which at once came into action. Our losses were heavy; splendid ships and splendid men had been sunk, for let us never forget that, as Admiral Jellicoe himself said, the Germans fought gallantly. But they already knew they were beaten, for their losses were heavier still, and when, later, the British Battle Fleet joined in the fight, the remnants of the German High Seas Fleet turned and fled to port under cover of the night. The Battle of Jutland was indeed a glorious victory.

When the fight was over and the wounded were carried below, the doctors saw that there was little hope for Jack Cornwell. As soon as it was possible, he was taken ashore and placed in a hospital at Grimsby. He could still talk a little, and though in great pain and nearly too weak to speak, his quiet cheerfulness never left him. The matron asked him how the battle had gone and he replied in simple sailor-like fashion, "*Oh—we carried on all right!*" These were almost his last words. His mother had received a telegram from the Admiralty and was on her way to her boy. At the end, just before he died, he said, "Give mother my love. I know she is coming."

And now I want you to read what the captain of the *Chester* wrote to the boy's mother, because

SCOUT HEROES OF THE NAVY

it tells, in words which are already a part of British history, the story of Jack Cornwell's heroism

"I know you would wish to hear of the splendid fortitude and courage shown by your son during the action of May 31. His devotion to duty was an example for all of us. The wounds which resulted in his death within a short time were received in the first few minutes of the action. He remained steady at his most exposed post at the gun, waiting for orders. His gun would not bear on the enemy: all but two of the ten crew were killed or wounded, and he was the only one who was in such an exposed position. But he felt he might be needed, and, indeed, he might have been; so he stayed there, standing and waiting, under heavy fire, with just his own brave heart and God's help to support him.

"I cannot express to you my admiration of the son you have lost from this world. No other comfort would I attempt to give to the mother of so brave a lad, but to assure her of what he was and what he did, and what an example he gave.

"I hope to place in the boys' mess a plate

with his name on and the date and the words 'Faithful unto death.' I hope some day you may be able to come and see it there. I have not failed to bring his name prominently before my Admiral."

And when, afterwards Admiral Jellicoe wrote his official report of the Battle of Jutland, he added these words:

"A report from the Commanding Officer of *Chester* gives a splendid instance of devotion to duty. Boy (1st Class) John Travers Cornwell, of *Chester*, was mortally wounded early in the action. He nevertheless remained standing alone at a most exposed post, quietly awaiting orders till the end of the action, with the gun's crew dead and wounded all round him. His age was under sixteen and a half years. I regret that he has since died, but I recommend his case for special recognition in justice to his memory, and as an acknowledgment of the high example set by him."

Wonderful, thrilling words these, but so that you may never forget that, as I have said, Jack Cornwell, hero, was a boy like other boys, I am

SCOUT HEROES OF THE NAVY 143

going to copy the last letter his father received from him, not many days before the battle. You'll like to read it because it's such an ordinary boyish letter :

" DEAR DAD,—

" Just a few lines in answer to your most welcome letter, which we received on Monday —first post for a week. That is why you have not had a letter for a long while. Thanks for the stamps you sent me. We are up in the —— somewhere, and they have just put me as sight-setter at a gun. Dear Dad, I have just had to start in pencil, as I have run short of ink, but still, I suppose you don't mind so long as you get a letter, and I am sorry to tell you that poor old A. L. is dead, and I dare say by the time you get this letter she will be buried. I have got a lot of letters to send home and about, so I can't afford much more, and we are just about to close up at the gun, so this is all for now : have more next time.

" I remain, your ever-loving son,
" JACK.

" *P.S.—Cheer up, Buller me lad, we're not dead yet!* "

The funeral took place on July 29th at Manor Park Cemetery. Scouts lined the route, and a large number under the command of the District Commissioner, Mr. Frank Hamlett, joined in the procession.

The coffin, covered with the White Ensign, rested on a gun-carriage, drawn by a team of boys from the Crystal Palace Naval Depôt. The carriages which followed contained amongst others, Dr. T. J. Macnamara, Financial Secretary to the Admiralty; the Bishop of Barking, the Mayor of East Ham, Sir John Bethell, M.P. for the Romford Division; and members of the East Ham Borough Council.

Six boys from his Majesty's ship *Chester*, all of whom were in the battle with their late comrade, were in the procession, and carried the floral tributes from the ship. Many other wreaths included one from the Lord Mayor of London, and one from Admiral Beatty, bearing the simple inscription, "With deep respect."

The coffin was removed from the gun-carriage and carried to the grave by a bearer-party of bluejackets. Sailors, soldiers and civilians bared their heads, and sang " Eternal Father Strong to Save," with its familiar and stirring cry, " For Those in Peril on the Sea." The special burial

SCOUT HEROES OF THE NAVY 145

service arranged for the occasion was conducted by the Bishop of Barking.

After the committal service Dr. Macnamara stepped forward and said: " I come to pay my tribute of respect to the memory of a hero, and to lay at this grave in the name of the Royal Navy a wreath of tender, loving thoughts. John Travers Cornwell went forth with his fellows in the sacred cause to which the Allied nations stand committed. The hopes and aspirations of early youth, the expectations of vigorous manhood, the dreams of life, its affections, its adventures, and its opportunities—he laid all these upon the altar of duty. He died inscribing his name imperishably upon the roll of British honour. It has been written that what good men do is oft interred with them. Not so here ! This grave shall be the birthplace of heroes. From it shall spring inspiration that shall make hearts more brave, spirits more dauntless, and purpose more noble amongst generations of British subjects yet unborn. Boy Cornwell will be enshrined in British hearts as long as faithful, unflinching devotion to duty shall be esteemed a virtue amongst us. Think of him ! Seek to emulate him ! For by his sacrifice and that of the goodly company of heroes to whom he belongs—heroes of land, and sea, and air ; heroes who sleep

K

beneath the waves, on the plains of Flanders, amid the rugged slopes of Gallipoli, by the banks of the Tigris, away far on the African veldt, and in the valley of the Somme—will the British ideal of freedom be maintained and flourish, and not perish in our midst. For freedom they went forth to fight and die. By freedom shall their sacrifice be justified."

* * * * *

The Chief Scout has awarded the Bronze Cross, our highest decoration for heroism, which it is hoped will become a treasured heirloom of the Cornwell family.

MIDSHIPMAN DONALD A. GYLES, D.S.C., R.N.R.

(LATE PATROL LEADER, 1ST MUSWELL HILL TROOP OF BOY SCOUTS.)

The Scout movement is particularly proud of the brilliantly plucky deed of Midshipman Donald A. Gyles, of H.M. destroyer *Broke*, who formerly was a member of the 1st Muswell Hill Troop.

This is how it happened.

Somewhere off Dover, two British destroyers, the *Broke* and the *Swift*, on night patrol in the Channel, were proceeding on a westerly course, when at 12.40 a.m. the *Swift* sighted an enemy flotilla of six destroyers on her port bow.

The *Swift*, without hesitation, swung round

SCOUT HEROES OF THE NAVY

and ran straight for the line of enemy destroyers, trying to ram one. Unfortunately, she missed, but pluckily returned to the attack, torpedoed one of the Germans, and raced off after another.

When the enemy were first sighted the *Broke* was steaming astern of the *Swift*. The *Broke* launched a torpedo at the second boat in the German line and hit her and then opened fire with all her guns.

A Hand-to-Hand Fight

The six enemy craft were now going top speed for home and emitted a dull glow from every funnel which enabled the captain of the *Broke* to decide on his tactics. He swung the *Broke* round to port and rammed the third boat at full speed.

Locked together thus, they fought in the hand-to-hand style of Nelson's days. The *Broke* swept the enemy's decks at point blank range. In the meanwhile, however, the remaining two German destroyers poured in a destructive fire on the gallant vessel. The foremost guns' crews were reduced from eighteen men to six, and Midshipman Donald A. Gyles, though wounded above the right eye and in the leg and arm, kept all the foremost guns in action, himself assisting to load.

While he was thus pluckily employed, a number

of frenzied Germans swarmed up over the *Broke's* forecastle from the rammed destroyer.

Amid the dead and wounded of the guns' crews, half-blinded by blood from his head-wound, the heroic Midshipman met the rush single-handed with an automatic pistol.

A great German grappled with him and attempted to wrest his smoking weapon from him, but the Hun was bayoneted by Able-Seaman Ingleson.

The remainder of the boarding Germans, with the exception of two who lay down and feigned death, were driven over the side—the two "shammers" being made prisoners.

A few minutes after ramming the destroyer, the *Broke* managed to wrench herself free from the sinking Hun and turned to ram the last boat in the line. She missed in the ram, but hit the other boat with a torpedo.

This is the heroic middy's own modest story:

"I was asleep when we first sighted the enemy, and all hands were called to action stations, and I went to my post forward. The first shells from the enemy hit the superstructure of the bridge, taking away one side completely, and killing and wounding several of our crew. Some men who manned the port gun No. 2 below were also killed and wounded.

"I myself was struck in my right eye by a

SCOUT HEROES OF THE NAVY 149

fragment of shrapnel, which is still there—and they intend leaving it there.

"My eye bled profusely, and I mopped away the blood as best I could with my coat-sleeves and my handkerchief. I was momentarily stunned and floored by the concussion of the explosion and I was also wounded in my right leg and right arm; in fact, I was struck all down the right side.

" Picking myself up as best I could, I ran down to the guns below where the first gun is, our own gun having been put out of action. Finding the lower gun also out of action, I ran to the forecastle—all this, mark you, in the short space of two minutes—where I found only five men alive out of all the entire crew who were capable of manning the gun.

" Then Able-Seaman Ingleson, whose gun was also out of action, came forward to where we were to see if he could help. Ingleson loaded the port gun to fire, while I myself loaded the starboard gun.

When the Germans Boarded

" As we were loading and serving the guns Germans boarded us, yelling like mad for mercy, and saying things we could not understand. But once on deck they attempted to attack us, rushing in our direction.

"Pointing my revolver at them, I ordered them forward. One burly German, a regular giant, made a lunge at me. I evaded the thrust, but he managed to reach my hand and grabbed at my revolver.

"Determined not to be outdone by a German, big as he was, I forced my wrist away, and he was coming at me again when Petty Officer Woodfield, who was close by, let out his right arm and fetched him one full in the face.

"Then he tried to escape round the gun to attack me in the rear. He meant finishing me if possible, but Able-Seaman Ingleson got in a timely thrust from his cutlass, putting it clean through the German. Then we tumbled him over the side.

"After that we cleared the decks of all the Germans we could see, killing all those who intercepted us and making the rest prisoners. We found two Germans skulking and kneeling forward in an attempt to hide themselves.

"We torpedoed one destroyer and rammed another. Then we were unfortunate enough to get hit in the boiler-room, which prevented us from manœuvring successfully. Later we drifted down on to the vessel which we had previously torpedoed, and her crew, who were left on board, were all crying out for mercy.

SCOUT HEROES OF THE NAVY 151

" Steering as best we could, we got closer: and then the Germans fired upon us. But we instantly replied with several quick rounds, which finished them.

" By this time the action had finished, and I could see two German destroyers sinking, although I had only one eye. If I had been able to see with the other, I might have seen, two more sunk. We were by this time helpless, and tugs came out and towed us into port."

Donald Gyles felt the lure of Scouting directly it was started, in 1908, and he joined the 1st Muswell Hill Troop in that year. A glance round the rooms of his home in Muswell Hill reveals at once how keen a Scout he became, for everywhere there are snapshots of his Scout life in camp on various expeditions. A more enthusiastic follower of the Trail than Donald Gyles would have been hard to find.

The Scouting instinct is in the family, for his elder brother also figures in the " snaps."

His brother, who, when serving at Salonica, wrote home to say that his training as a Scout, especially the training for the Cook's badge, had come in very useful, as the men of his regiment were roughing it and had to cook and shift for themselves generally.

Donald worked hard for badges and altogether

had the true Scout spirit in him. His fine aptitude brought him before the notice of the Commissioner of his district, and Donald often accompanied him in his work. The Movement was in its infancy and so the hero middy was quite " one of the old school " of Scouting.

He reached the rank of Patrol Leader and continued to take an active part in troop work until four years ago, when he made up his mind to go to sea, and went as a cadet in the White Star Line. Amongst the photographs is one of Donald as a cadet on board the training ship *Mersey*.

On the *Mersey* he was trained as an officer and travelled round the world.

Just before war broke out came his .chance and he was nominated as a midshipman to H.M.S. *London*.

The news of the way in which the heroic young officer had distinguished himself did not come as a great surprise to those who knew Donald Gyles. Just as he had been so tremendously keen and energetic as a Scout, so he had flamed up with the same spirit when he came face to face with the more grim business of war.

One of his most cherished possessions is a telegram from the Chief Scout congratulating him on his pluck.

SCOUT HEROES OF THE NAVY 153

The Dover battle was not his first smell of powder. The beginning of the war found him in the Mediterranean on a battleship. Then he went all through the Dardanelles adventure and helped to land some of the first Australians at Gaba Tepe under the terrible fire of the Turkish land guns.

Twice he was wounded, though fortunately not seriously, and when he came back from the Mediterranean last November he was appointed to the *Broke*, on which he has served ever since.

At his home is now a treasured ribbon from the cap of the German sailor whom Seaman Ingleson cut down only just in time.

On the ribbon is inscribed " VI Halb flotilla VI." The cap belonging to it the gallant ex-Scout has given to Ingleson, his rescuer. All that Midshipman Gyles regrets is the loss of his revolver, which he prized highly. " I know how to use that revolver," he says cheerfully.

ERIC WILLIAM GARDINER
(WIRELESS OPERATOR. SEA SCOUT, EDINBURGH.)

A Brave Wireless Operator

Scouts everywhere will cherish the memory of the brave Scottish Scout Eric William Gardiner.

Gardiner was killed in a fight between a liner and a U-boat, and his sticking to his post as a

154 THE SCOUTS' BOOK OF HEROES

wireless operator was the means of saving the ship. While the ship was being shelled by the U-boat Gardiner stuck to his post, sending messages for help and eventually got in touch with a British destroyer, and when the Captain advised him to take cover, he replied that he was in touch with an American cruiser which was nearer, and would stay to finish the message. A few minutes later the submarine hit the cabin with a direct shot, killing Gardiner as he had almost completed the message from the American ship.

The ship managed to hold out till the arrival of the American cruiser, but could not have done so except for Gardiner's plucky action in continuing the message.

In his work and play Gardiner had always shown the true Scouting spirit, and his death adds another name to the list of Scout Heroes of the War.

PATROL LEADER EDWARD IRELAND
(22ND LIVERPOOL TROOP)

The Cornwell Badge of Courage which is the highest award in the Scout Movement, has been awarded to Patrol Leader Edward Ireland of the 22nd Liverpool Troop.

When the large White Star Liner *Britannic*, engaged as a hospital ship, was sunk off Greece, there were sixteen Boy Scouts on board employed as signallers, messengers, and lift boys.

SCOUT HEROES OF THE NAVY 155

The following report was received from Colonel H. Concannon, Deputy County Commissioner for South-West Lancashire and joint manager of the White Star Line:

"These boys were fortunately saved, and all of them, I believe, did uncommonly well, but one of them, named Ireland, is reported to have displayed special courage in remaining by the commander on the bridge until he was taken away by a quartermaster who was ordered away to save himself just as the ship was sinking. I hope the Chief Scout will be pleased to award Ireland whatever decoration may be applicable to the case."

Captain Charles A. Bartlett, who was in command of the *Britannic*, wrote:

"Without exception all the boys behaved splendidly throughout, but I have specially to commend Scout E. Ireland, of the Liverpool Scouts. He was attached to the bridge at the time of the explosion, and he remained at his post until I sent him away finally with the quartermaster (who left the wheel to save his life), although on several occasions I told him to go to the boats. He was of great service in telephoning my orders, and I have great admiration for the pluck that he showed in standing by with a prospect in front of him of eventually going down with the ship. I hope that in this connection some action may be taken by the Scouts' Association, which will be valued by the boy for ever."

The following is an extract from the *Liverpool Courier* :

"In an interview with Master-at-Arms Coe it was learned that when the disaster overtook the vessel he ran to the bottom of the ship where the boys' quarters were. The Scouts' quarters had been blown in, but fortunately none of the boys were there. On the alarm being given the boys took up their posts of duty. Some of the Scouts were attending to the lifts, which brought up a thousand people to the upper deck from below. The boys were accustomed to boat drill, and knew their duties perfectly.

"Ireland, one of the Scouts mentioned above, was on the bridge with the Captain, and Price, another Scout, accompanied the chief officer, shouting the orders through a megaphone. When the order was given to abandon ship the nurses took to the boats, and they expected the boys would follow.

SCOUT HEROES OF THE NAVY

Not so, however. The Scouts refused to leave the vessel, and the boats had to leave without the boys.

"The Scouts had to slide down a 50-foot rope, and the friction took the skin off their hands. Two of the boys had to swim to safety. He could not speak too highly of the boys' courage and calmness. Everyone was surprised at their perfect demeanour and thorough absence of fear. The boys had no wish to leave the ship, and had to be ordered to go."

The idea of the Scouts being expected to leave with the nurses! Women and *children* first is always the order, but clearly the Scouts felt "the post of danger is the post of honour," and they stuck to their post until almost driven away: in fact, Colonel Concannon says: "Ireland had literally to be forced from the bridge when the ship was sinking."

It is also stated that the ship's officers were "amazed at the boys' courage." They reported: "The conduct of the boys in such a trying time was exemplary, and calls for high commendation."

The Chief Scout at once decided that the recommendation of Captain Bartlett as to Scout Ireland's courage should be accepted as sufficient and satisfactory qualification for the first test for the Cornwell Badge.

Then the papers were referred to the Cornwell Sub-Committee to see that the boy was qualified on the other necessary points, for it will be remembered this badge is not awarded to every Scout who shows a courageous character. He must be a thorough all-round Scout holding a First-class and certain badges of proficiency, and with a Scout-like character for industry, smartness, and reliability.

Needless to say the Sub-Committee were delighted to find that all reports of Ireland were satisfactory; he was a First-class Scout and held the Missioner, Signalling and Swimming Badges; while the independent reports of his character were entirely satisfactory.

CHAPTER V

Heroes of the Air Service

PERHAPS no branch of His Majesty's Services appealed to the Scout more than the Air Service, and because the Scout lives a clean, healthy, outdoor life, it was not surprising that the authorities encouraged Scouts of the right age to enlist with a view to becoming pilots and observers.

And they proved that their training as Scouts had not been in vain. They were quick to grasp what was expected of them, and when the time came to test them in actual warfare they were not found wanting, either in physical courage or technical ability.

In the following stories you will read of the wonderful adventures and escapes of Scouts who sailed the air, fighting sometimes against terrible odds, but always with that determination which is the hall-mark of a true Scout.

LIEUTENANT MOSBY, D.S.O.

(A.S.M. 1ST NORWICH TROOP)

The old Scout motto of " Stick it " can hardly

ever have been more splendidly illustrated than in the case of Lieut. Mosby, D.S.O.

He was engaged in what is known as "artillery patrol"—a tedious occupation at times, but with the always present possibility of the tedium being unpleasantly relieved by what may be termed with literal accuracy "a bolt from the blue."

In this patrol work the observer is allotted a portion of the enemy's lines; he has to watch it carefully and spot the fall of shot upon it from a special battery and report to them by wireless how their shots are falling. The machine he is in patrols slowly up and down his allotted section, trailing below itself a long line of copper wire which makes it exceedingly difficult to manœuvre quickly even if safety so desires: certainly some protection is afforded by a patrol of Scout machines some thousands of feet above, but this protection is sometimes eluded or destroyed by the watching foe.

On one such occasion Lieut. Mosby was acting as observer in the spotting machine and had not long been at his work of watching the shots fall and signalling back their position and effect when three hostile machines swooped down from aloft, two of them in front and one seeking the deadly position on the tail of his plane.

Quickly discarding his wireless tapper for a Lewis

HEROES OF THE AIR SERVICE 161

gun Lieut. Mosby engaged the one behind. A stream of tracer bullets shot from his gun, found their mark, and flames burst from the enemy plane, which dropped out of action and reduced the odds against him. Rapidly he swung his gun round to assist the pilot, but the two planes in front had been able to get their blows in first, one bullet striking him and wounding him severely, whilst another killed the pilot in front of him instantaneously. With the weight of the pilot's dead body the joy-stick was pushed forward and the machine fell into a steep nose-dive. Lieut. Mosby was almost thrown out, but grasped convulsively at the side, and then in spite of the sickening pain from his wound, with a great effort he fitted the dual control system of the machine, thereby securing the management of it and succeeded in pulling the machine out of the nose dive.

In spite of falling 2,000 feet he had the machine again under control and the prospect for a moment seemed to be brighter. But only for a moment did this relief last. The Huns following down the crippled plane to make sure of their victory observed the recovery and dived rapidly to complete their work. Fighting and manœuvring to the utmost of his ability Lieut. Mosby beat them off again and again until he was once more hit in the body. Then faintness from pain and loss of blood began to supervene and his control of the machine relaxed, allowing it to spin towards the earth.

With a truly superhuman effort of the dogged will he forced control upon his reeling brain and straightened out his spinning machine. Controlling the machine with one hand he operated the Lewis gun with the other, his nerves strung taut with the desperate determination to reach his own lines some fifteen miles away. At last he approached them and the disappointed Huns drew off from their invincible foe.

Into a fierce driving hailstorm he rushed, and over his vision crept a blinding red mist, but through it he saw, below, his home hangars and dived towards them. Still his iron will gripped the situation, though his body was racked with pain and his strength flowing swiftly from him. He descended steadily in a long glide, flattened out as deliberately as though in an exhibition flight and landed safely. Careful hands lifted him from the machine and placed him in an ambulance.

Lying there he made his report in gasped-out sentences, and then having stuck it out to the end he drifted into unconsciousness as the hospital was reached.

When writing to his father he said : " It was

HEROES OF THE AIR SERVICE 163

not in my own strength I did it, but in God's."
Extract from paper

" Whilst on an artillery patrol he was attacked by the enemy machines, two from the front and one from the rear. He engaged and drove off the latter, but was hit in the abdomen, and when he turned to engage the others his pilot was hit and instantly killed. Although his machine fell out of control from a height of 3,000 feet to 1,000 feet, he continued to engage them and was again hit in the abdomen. But he succeeded in driving them off, and though his machine again became out of control he righted it and safely landed it at his aerodrome. He showed indomitable pluck, both during an unequal contest and in determining to land his machine without injury, although nearly unconscious through loss of blood."

SERGEANT MIDDLETON D.F.M.

(R.N.A.S. SCOUTMASTER, 2ND EPPING FOREST. TROOP.)

" Died like a Scout, fighting and smiling."

Who could desire a more noble epitaph than this ? First as a Scout, and then as a Scoutmaster of his Troop, Sergeant Middleton had learned and taught how to smile whilst fighting.

Then in the war—baffled again and again in his efforts to take some really active share in the defence of his country, he was at last successful, and in 1917 got to France as aerial gunner and observer.

The *London Gazette* of September 21st, 1918, noted him as follows: "He has taken part in sixty-seven raids and has shown conspicuous gallantry and skill in bombing enemy lines of communications, dumps and aerodromes. On one occasion he obtained six direct hits, despite intense anti-aircraft fire."

Daylight bombing has the great advantage that your target is visible to you, but it has the great disadvantage that you form a target for anti-aircraft guns, which can be most disconcerting to your accuracy of aim, quite apart from other considerations. Furthermore you are eagerly sought for by patrols of enemy machines, who with superiority of numbers and singleness of purpose have very considerable chances of ending your career.

Sergeant Middleton on one such occasion wrenched not only his safety but also the Distinguished Flying Medal from an encounter with the most famous of all German patrols, that of Richtoffen's Circus.

Five British bombing machines, in one of which

HEROES OF THE AIR SERVICE 165

was Sergeant Middleton, had left their aerodrome and reached their goal. In spite of the fiercest possible anti-aircraft opposition, bomb after bomb fell into the appointed quarter until the flight had no more left. It was now time for home and the Richtoffen Circus arrived to hurry them off: thirty German planes against five British. Quite safe odds, thought the Germans, but the British thought so also, and turned from flight to fight. A veritable dogfight followed. Planes dashing in all directions, banking, side-slipping, turning, zooming, tail-sliding; only a quick eye and a cool brain can tell in the hustle and excitement which is friend and which is foe.

A volley of bullets flies at a foe—in vain, for he has shot up out of sight. Pitching and swaying from side to side in his ever-twisting machine, Sergeant Middleton took every chance he got, and his gun peeped and spat out messages of defiance in one direction after another. Plane after plane goes down, not British but German. Above him a plane is diving towards him with ruthless determination. It gives him his chance. He fires and the plane continues to dive, but now no longer in his direction. Uncontrolled, after his deadly salvo, the machine reels past him; it staggers, turns over, and goes fluttering downwards flames bursting from it.

Richtoffen's Circus have had enough. Eight planes destroyed! This is too discouraging and the odds are now too heavy against them. Why! They have only twenty-two machines against five British. This is no task for them and off they go with noses down, and the five British machines return home in triumph.

This was merely one of his adventures. Sergeant Middleton sought out every opportunity of fighting and made the best of it when found —always a smiling fighter.

Once he led the squadron to bomb the Somme bridges, and on his triumphant return received the personal congratulations of General Salmond. Once he was left behind when the British were compelled to retreat, in order that he might fire and destroy the aerodrome, so preventing it being of use to the Germans. Fearlessly and thoroughly he carried out his task even though the enemy rapidly drew near. Just in the nick of time a British cavalry patrol rescued him. Almost every day saw him raiding relentlessly the enemy, his smiling courage apparently conferring on him a charmed life, and stimulating and encouraging his comrades.

His last fight was against the usual odds. Whilst on reconnaissance duty over the German lines he was attacked by four German planes at

HEROES OF THE AIR SERVICE 167

once. With his old skill and courage he faced them till the fatal bullet struck him and he could fight no more. Back to the aerodrome his pilot brought him, and he faced one last fight for his life.

In this he could not win success, so, smiling— he died.

LIEUTENANT. A. A. TUTTE, D.F.C.

(SCOUT, 19TH (ST. MARK'S) PORTSMOUTH TROOP.)

Night bombing is an operation full of thrills at all times.

There are what may be termed the ordinary kinds, such as the blinding glare of the enemy's searchlights marking out the target for the anti-aircraft guns. Traps can be laid in the air to catch and destroy planes. Strings of balls of light, flaming onions as they are called, may appear pretty if watched from a distance, but a deadly bonfire results if one touches your machine; just as effective in the same way are the streams of incendiary bullets.

All these may be expected to occur as a matter of course, but there are others that can hardly be foreseen, and yet will call for a very high degree of cool thought and firmness of courage.

One such occasion, encountered and mastered,

won for Lieut. Tutte the Distinguished Flying Cross, which in the Royal Air Force is the most honoured and coveted reward after the V.C. The F.E.B.2 type of aeroplane is what is called a "pusher machine," that is to say, the propeller is behind and pushes the machine along. The observer sits in the front cockpit and is in charge of the bomb-dropping apparatus, as he alone has an uninterrupted view of the objective. Behind him in another cockpit sits the pilot, who has a dual bomb-releasing gear, so that he also can have some of the fun of bombing. Behind the pilot is fitted the engine and propeller.

It was in such a machine as this that Lieut. Tutte set out to bomb Seglin, and it was only his fifth time over the lines. As he and his pilot approached the goal, searchlights shot up their beams, and in spite of the twisting and turning of the machine held it in their all-illuminating grasp, whilst bullets whistled round them and shells burst near.

Down through the heavy barrage of flaming onions they glided until they were about 1,000 feet above the ground, Lieut. Tutte eagerly looking out for his target and in the meanwhile standing up and putting in some good shooting at the searchlights with his machine gun.

More and more the machine rocked under the

HEROES OF THE AIR SERVICE 169

concussion of the exploding shells, and its progress became increasingly erratic. Lieut. Tutte attributed the extraordinary zig-zag course to the pilot's efforts to dodge the enemy's fire, until as the objective came into view and range he called through the telephone to the pilot and then heard that he had been wounded.

The bombs began to drop, the pilot insisting on doing his share at first, but later weakness and exhaustion overcame him, and so Lieut. Tutte dropped the remaining ones.

Now the situation became very perilous. They are several miles over the enemy's country, the pilot, severely wounded, is losing strength, searchlights grip them relentlessly and flaming death again and again only just misses them, whilst not far off enemy planes are waiting for a chance to dash in and destroy them. The pilot had hardly headed for home when he fainted and the machine began to go down.

Through a gale of some eighty miles an hour, Lieut. Tutte, hampered as he was by flying gear and heavy boots, climbed out of his seat and clambered on to the cowling between stays and struts. A single false step would have sent him hurtling several hundreds of feet to the earth below. Even in a machine stationary on the ground this feat is by no means easy; to accomplish it in the air, on a machine no longer under control, is a performance surely miraculous.

He made no slip but reached the pilot's cockpit, and leaning over the side of it grasped the joy-stick and gained control of the machine. Then pulling his brandy flask from his pocket, Lieut. Tutte set himself to revive the pilot and succeeded temporarily, but his wound had so exhausted him that it was beyond his power to make the machine climb out of range of the enemy's guns. On they sped therefore through a perfect tornado of shrapnel and bullets whistling through the planes, but none fortunately striking a vital part, nor any being of the inflammable variety.

Three times the pilot fainted and three times was he restored by Lieut. Tutte. At last the enemy's lines are left behind and the British lines are reached. Now is the time to signal the secret code for the day on the lights attached to the wing-tips. The switch being on the far side of the cockpit Lieut. Tutte cannot reach it. The pilot tries, but so racked with pain is he, that he can only send a muddled signal, likely to arouse the gravest suspicion in the British batteries, as to the nationality of the plane above them.

Hurriedly pulling out a Very's pistol Lieut. Tutte fires over the side a red light, turning after a time to white, the special signal for the day,

HEROES OF THE AIR SERVICE 171

but to his horror the plane is now so low, that the red light reaches the ground before it has had time to turn to white.

Desperate now and expecting every moment to hear the roar of bursting British shells about him, Lieut. Tutte risks all on one last venture and once more clambering forward fires another, Very's light upwards. If the light falls back on the machine, then all is lost. It misses, and falls downwards towards the earth, the red flame changes to white flame, and answering signals flash out from below.

Now back to the pilot again, but the end is in sight. Down they glide and the none too easy task of landing is accomplished. The pilot is quickly taken to hospital and his life is saved. When the plane is examined the marks of bullets are seen all over it. Several bullets have passed through the seat in Lieut. Tutte's cockpit, and had he been there instead of clinging to the outside of the machine he would surely have been killed.

LIEUTENANT. J. W. WARNER, D.F.C.

(Assistant Scoutmaster, 10th Harrogate Troop.)

On October 4th, 1918, Lieut. Warner in charge of his flight took the air for the last time, though he knew it not, and led the way for an offensive.

He was only nineteen years of age and yet his fame was already spreading. His initiative and courage had been generally observed and his fitness for the honour and responsibilities of a Flight Commander was evident. He had been in many a previous offensive patrol; sometimes flying low he had bombed the enemy with the great accuracy gained at terrible risk.

A born fighter, he carried out all his adventures in the true offensive spirit, that revels in the keen joy of the attack regardless of personal safety. On such an occasion as this, his last patrol, his responsibility weighed with him but not on him, and he never confused rashness with courage nor led his flight into avoidable dangers.

Once in the air the machines picked up their formation as they rose over the aerodrome and then headed away to search for the foe. It was not until they reached the enemy's lines that the Hun machines came into view, flying at about 7,000 feet, but keeping well within their own country.

The old British Naval Motto, "Seek out the enemy and destroy him," is the motto of the Air Force also, so off they speed, opening their throttles, their noses down, chasing after the Huns. They overhauled them at last and Lieut. Warner gave the signal to attack.

e Fokker staggers for a moment, pitches violently forward, a mass of flames bursts from her, and down she plunges to her doom. (*A thrilling incident on page* 173).

[*To face page* 172.

HEROES OF THE AIR SERVICE 173

At full speed, something like 120 knots, they charged into the enemy formation and broke it up, but hardly had they done so when more Huns swooped to the rescue of their comrades and heavily outnumbered the British.

Lieut. Warner tackled three of them at once, and now diving upon them, now side-slipping away, now hoicking up, and now circling round them, he skirmished grimly, until at last he obtained the position of vantage that he sought. Tap, tap, tap, his machine gun speaks out, and leaden messengers of Death speed on their way. One Fokker staggers for a moment, pitches violently forward, a mass of flames bursts from her, and down she plunges to her doom. Lieut. Warner has no time to rejoice ; the air is thick with Hun machines.

Hotter and hotter waxes the fight as the conflicting planes crowd together till friend and foe are indistinguishable. Here in one direction flames burst from a machine, but no one knows if it is a gain or a loss for us—here again another plane disappears from the fight, hurtling down in that last sickening spin. Tired muscles and brain find the task of manœuvring the rocking plane getting stiffer and stiffer, but there is no chance for a rest. Flying boots and leather jacket seem to grow heavier somehow and restrict the activities of the exhausted body.

At last the fight is broken off and the combatants retire to count their losses. Three British officers from this patrol, one of them Lieut. Warner, failed to return.

Somewhere in the whirling confusion of the fight the fatal blow had been struck. Unknown is the moment when his flying steed no longer answered to his controlling touch. Downward to earth it fluttered to crash into ruin, whilst the pilot passed to enter the Valhalla of heroes.

CYRIL RUPERT DEELEY, D.F.M.

(R.A.F. Scout, Birmingham Association.)

That the possession of Scoutcraft is a valuable asset was clearly shown when Deeley was one of the six successful candidates out of fifty-eight applicants for admission into the R.N.A.S. as Boy Mechanic in the Wireless Section. Furthermore, as he was already proficient as an electrician, signaller, swimmer, and in physical drill, knot-tying and musketry, promotion came his way within five weeks from his entry.

He carried with him throughout his service the attributes of a Scout, and so it is not surprising that a year later he was awarded the Distinguished Flying Medal, the highest award apart from the V.C. that a rating in the R.A.F. can win.

HEROES OF THE AIR SERVICE 175

Needless to say he had many adventures and many narrow escapes whilst serving as wireless operator in a seaplane squadron, patrolling for submarines, etc.

On one occasion the aeroplane engines gave out after an hour's flying and the machine began to sink down towards the sea. A wireless message was sent out, and then he had only just time to scribble a hasty note of their position and fasten it to a carrier pigeon before the machine sank, leaving the pilot and himself swimming in the North Sea, miles from land.

For three hours he was in the water, his swimming powers now tested, and found adequate, until at last a trawler, summoned thanks to the carrier pigeon, came into sight and rescued them both, almost unconscious, but still fighting for life.

After only a few days he was back again with his patrol, but was shortly transferred to a large flying boat, and his patrol work extended as far as the Frisian Islands, Holland, and the German island of Borkum.

Now adventure crowded upon adventure, but one outstanding one demands special reference.

One beautiful summer morning five flying boats, each armed with five machine guns, set out with the definite intention of finding and fighting the enemy somewhere. Definite orders had previously been given to report position by wireless every fifteen minutes, so it was obvious that the German wireless stations would be able to pick up the signals and arrange a suitable reception.

The squadron had arrived within ten miles of the northern end of Terschelling when one of the boats developed engine trouble and had to descend on the sea. The remainder circled round their defenceless colleague exchanging signals on the flash-lamp. Meantime there came into view five large Hun seaplanes who, however, disliked the idea of fighting with so small a superiority and made off in haste.

The four disappointed British machines returned to the damaged one, and found that quick repair was impossible. A larger squadron of German planes was in the distance, so orders were given that the defenceless machine should " taxi " to the Dutch island, the crew saving themselves after burning the machine so that none of our secrets should fall into the hands of outsiders.

The remaining four now turned their attention to the enemy who were seen to be ten seaplanes in battle formation. Then a second British machine developed engine trouble and so increased the odds to ten to three. Quite undaunted the British gave battle. Deeley's duties were twofold ; he had to keep in communication with his base

HEROES OF THE AIR SERVICE 177

by wireless and also when possible to plug the enemy with the tail machine gun outside his wireless cabin.

For thirty-five minutes the battle raged, countless bullets whizzed round the flying boats, one crashed through the wireless cabin whilst Deeley was working the gun, fortunately for him.

The next time he returned to the cabin after another spell at his gun he found that another shot had carried away half of his wireless aerial. He calmly effected the necessary repairs, tuned up and was soon again in touch with his base 140 miles away.

Meanwhile British bullets were also doing their work, and first one and then another German plane fell, riddled with bullets, into the sea, one of them bursting into flames just before it reached the water. This was too much for the enemy, so they drew off hurriedly and raced for home. Much as they would have liked to chase them and exact a further toll, the British machines could not do so for petrol was running short and more engine trouble was beginning. They therefore turned homewards in the evening "at the end of a more or less perfect day," with ninety-seven bullet wounds in Deeley's plane.

His achievement of sending and receiving signals over a distance of 140 miles under these exciting conditions was described officially as being " particularly fine," and he well merited the D.F.M. and the distinction of being the first Birmingham man to win it.

CHAPTER VI
The Heroes at Home

IN the foregoing pages we have read of gallant deeds cheerfully done under shot and shell and extremely trying conditions, which even those who have passed through the ordeal, find difficult to describe.

But these are not the only heroes the war has produced from the Scout Movement. Like their elder brothers on the battlefields of France and Flanders, on the deserts of Egypt, or those who went through the horror of the Gallipoli campaign, many of the Scouts who were forced to stay at home performed great deeds, which, if omitted from this book, would render the work incomplete.

Perhaps the most outstanding service done by Scouts during the war was that of coast watching.

Handy, resourceful, versed in the signs of the skies and the changing moods of wind and weather, the Sea-Scout was on guard in his hundreds along the coasts of Britain,

> " Whose rocky walls beat back the envious siege
>   Of watery Neptune . . . . ."

He fended for himself, cooked for himself, acted as his own housekeeper, housemaid and gardener, and was never at a loss when confronted with the knottiest problem.

In his coast-watching duties the most severe demands were made upon the individual responsibility and resourcefulness of the Sea-Scout. At many stations there were no coastguards or local Naval Officers, and the boys, organised under their patrol leaders, were in sole charge, receiving only occasional visits of inspection from the coast-watching Commissioner or Coastguard Officer. When the Movement was initiated, it was regarded with amusement not unmixed with hostility by the regular coast-watching service. The boys have now established themselves firmly in the respect and affection of all who have come into contact with them, and they are recognised as being as essential a part of the national organisation as the fully-fledged soldier or sailor.

They lived for the most part in two or three-roomed cottages, which they managed and controlled themselves. The leader kept the ration account and the daily log. A selection of entries in these logs gives a vivid idea of the varied activities of the coast-watching Scouts.

nalling. 2. Look-out Duty. 3. Reporting to Station Officer. 4. Challenging a Photographer. 5. Chauffeur to the Coast-watching Officer. 6. Life Saving.

WHAT THE SEA SCOUTS DID IN THE WAR.

THE HEROES AT HOME 181

" Warned a destroyer off the rocks in a fog." " Sighted and reported airship going S.S.E. five miles distant." " Provided night guard over damaged seaplane which was towed ashore by drifter." " Lights shown near —— at 3.15 a.m. for seven minutes, and again from apparently the same spot at 4.35 a.m." " Trawler No. ——came ashore. Permits all in order except J—— M——, who had none. Took his name and address to Police Superintendent at ——." " Floating mine reported by fishing boat No.——. Proceeded with the Patrol boat, which located and blew up the mine." " Provided guard over wreck and stores three days and nights in—— Bay."

When one details the duties which have been performed by these lads one is amazed by the pluck, endurance and readiness of mind which they showed. The boys had to patrol the beach, three miles out and three miles back in all weathers. Rain and sun, hail, storm and snow were all alike to them, and clad in their sou'westers and overalls, they might challenge comparison with the most seasoned mariner. They had to watch out for fishing boats that worked by unauthorised hours at night and to examine all boats that came in to the shore to see that the men's permits were in order. No easy task, this for a lad of twelve or fourteen, who knew that he was likely to be received with disdain as a presumptuous and meddlesome whipper-snapper. The Scouts had to answer all Naval calls on the telephone, and report all vessels passing up and down; they had to patrol the beach or telephone lines, to salve wreckage and to give assistance to any vessel in distress. A vivid word picture, painted by a Sea-Scout Commissioner after a visit to "somewhere on the South Coast," may here be quoted:

"In the dark hours of the morning the station was awakened—not that all were asleep—by the booming of the rockets betokening a ship in distress in the Bay in front.

"'Turn out, the Scouts off to the Cliff.'

"There, while the wind and rain howled over the storm-tossed seas, they waited; watching to see if they could be of assistance to their fellow men out on the helpless vessel which was being buffeted by the heavy seas as they roared up the beach.

"At last the day broke, and there could be seen the outline of a 3,000-ton steamer, driven high up on the shore, whose steering-gear had broken down, leaving her helpless and at the mercy of the seas. Knowing the shore as he did, the officer in charge on

THE HEROES AT HOME 183

the cliff called to a Scout to signal out to the crew to wait until the tide fell, as by then they would be able to walk dryshod to the shore.

" Promptly the order was carried out, and the signal duly acknowledged. But in spite of this the crew, at the risk of their lives, leapt into the sea and, with the help of willing hands, struggled ashore. Such are the incidents that relieved the monotony of our brothers who took the place of the coastguards who were called away to more dangerous and arduous duties."

Nor is this record of the Sea-Scout's duties yet complete. Despatch carrying was one of the most essential and arduous of his tasks. He had to pass on from hand to hand the daily log kept by his own patrol and by the patrol next to him, until it reached the Naval Base Commander. Every night during the war these lads carried their despatches along the coast, in foul weather as well as fair, through storm and snow-drift, until their duty was accomplished.

Such were some of the Sea-Scout's activities in war-time. Many more pages might be written, if space permitted, of his grit, his courage, his resourcefulness in emergency. But the story which has already been told is sufficient to prove that the work which these lads did was as heroic, in its own field, as that of the soldier or the sailor, and that it was no less essential to the defence of the country to whose call they so readily responded. They were entrusted with responsibilities beyond their years, and, in a favourite phrase of the Scout, they " played the game." They have learned to endure hardships gladly and have proved that " boys can be men." In the years to come it will be their proud joy to know that they stood by their country in her hour of direst peril and faithfully played their part to the utmost of their ability in the great battle for the liberation of the world.

HOW THE GERMANS SHELLED ME

My Experiences Under Fire.

By King's Scout ROB MILLER, *who lost one of his legs through being hit by shell splinters during the Bombardment of Whitby on December 16th*, 1914.

The watches at the coastguard station change every four hours, and I relieved the 4 to 8 early morning watch at 8.

My work at the station consisted entirely of messenger work, and, to help you to understand better, I should tell you that the actual signal station was a two-storied building shaped like a

THE HEROES AT HOME

tower on the cliff edge. Next to it was a flagstaff, and a footpath ran backward to the houses where the coastguards lived.

At about nine o'clock on the morning of December 16th, I was standing with a Territorial in front of the watch-house, when two cruisers suddenly hove in sight, coming up from the south and travelling at great speed.

"Go and fetch your glass, Rob," said my companion. "Let's see what they are."

I ran into one of the houses for my telescope and watched the cruisers approach.

At first glance we thought they belonged to our own Fleet, though, of course, we couldn't make out why they were in such a hurry.

Just then the operator came out of the house with an ensign, which he told me to haul up.

I had no sooner done this than there was a terrific bang, and a great bit of the cliff fell down. We didn't need any more telling that it was the Germans out at sea, and we didn't wait for the next shell.

The Territorial and I then ran towards the houses down the passage. Just as we passed the door of the watch-house, I was hit by shell splinters in both legs, but managed to keep on through the yards to the coastguards' houses. These yards were choked with fallen masonry, but we both managed to get into shelter, where we stopped until some other Territorials came up.

When they saw that I had been hit, a sergeant very kindly bandaged my legs.

Meanwhile the firing had stopped, and a Territorial carried me down towards the town. Halfway down the ambulance met us, and I was taken to the Cottage Hospital. Gangrene set in immediately, and my right leg had to be amputated on the following day.

I didn't feel scared in the least by the bombardment, probably because it was so unexpected. If I had known it was coming I should have been scared out of my life. I wouldn't believe they were German boats until they opened fire.

I hadn't time to think which was the best way to go, as I was just in front of the lookout station, but I followed the others. It was like a thunderstorm, very near, and we could see the shells bursting. When I ran through the yard it was full of bricks and slates.

The worst part was when we were lying down in shelter behind the houses, as we could only lie still and listen to the bursting shells, wondering whether we should get hit again. I, of course, was quite helpless and couldn't have moved, whatever had happened.

* * * * *

THE HEROES AT HOME 187

King's Scout Miller tells his story in a simple way, and although he did not get an opportunity to do much to help, he showed that a Scout can bear pain cheerfully. And we who have felt shell splinters know that it is hard to grin and bear it.

WALMER SEA SCOUTS TO THE RESCUE

It was at 12.15 p.m. on November 11th, 1914, that H.M.S. Gunboat *Niger* was torpedoed by a German submarine. The *Niger* was stationed in the town opposite Deal as a guardship.

The chief officer at the Deal coastguard station immediately ordered the coastguard boat to be launched. This was speedily accomplished by seven sea-Scouts attached to the station, and with these boys as crew he put off to the assistance of the sinking ship.

Several more boats had set out on the same errand of mercy, but the one containing the Sea-Scouts was the only one proceeding under oars. The sea was very rough, and this no doubt assisted to the success of the submarine. To add to the difficulty half a gale was blowing.

The boat encountered very rough seas, made worse by the number of ships of all description racing by. It narrowly escaped collision and came near to being capsized on more than one occasion. The chief officer in his report stated it was only through the discipline and coolness of the boys that the boat was saved from disaster on two or three occasions.

They had no opportunity of saving life, as there were many ships near the spot which were able to save the *Niger's* survivors.

They were, however able to render useful service by passing signals from destroyers, etc.

Their return proved a difficult matter. Owing to the strong tide and the fact that the boys showed signs of exhaustion, the chief officer could not bring the boat back to Deal. He would probably have had to make for Ramsgate (10 miles off) had not the Kingsdown lifeboat hailed them and offered them a tow into Deal.

The Scouts were afloat for about three hours. They arrived back in an exhausted and soaked condition—one scout had partially collapsed in the boat through cold ; but from first to last they proved themselves real sailors and showed great pluck, coolness and discipline.

The boys were all members of the Walmer Sea-Scout Troop, and they were awarded Certificates of Merit.

Their names are Donald Rose, P.L. ; Fred Arnold, 2nd ; Stanley D. Stokes ; Albert Foam ; Walter Bullen ; Alfred Bushell, and Bertie Beal.

THE HEROES AT HOME

LAND SCOUTS

Pages could be filled with the doings of Land Scouts during the war.

From the outbreak of hostilities until long after the Armistice was signed, they assisted wherever their help was needed. They guarded bridges in the early days ; acted as messengers ; assisted at canteens ; collected waste paper for charity ; blew the all clear ; rendered first aid during air raids ; in fact they were to be found everywhere where help was needed.

The following account was written by Marcus Woodward (Hon. Sec. the South Downs Association) in August, 1914, and gives a vivid account of the work done by Scouts in guarding bridges :—

I am writing under a bridge of the London, Brighton, and South Coast Railway at dead of night, to tell a stirring story of how the Boy Scouts of this part of Sussex sprang as one man to the call of duty when the War of the Nations broke out.

They are peace Scouts ; and very peaceful at the moment are the majority of the members of the troop with which I have thrown in my lot. In fact, they are fast asleep in their tent.

But eight of them are wide awake, guarding the railway line.

These eight, taking their spell of night duty, are peace scouting. True, the outbreak of war has given them their present job. In a way, each Scout now on duty is fighting.

Yet he is fighting strictly in accordance with the spirit of the Scout movement. The Scouts about me to-night are doing a good turn to the country.

They are doing their best to see that no harm comes to passengers travelling on an important railway line connecting London with the coast.

The Night Watch

We are out to-night on the most interesting kind of peace scouting we have ever known. Guarding this railway bridge in this lonely forest is the best scouting game we have played.

We realise why we are Scouts—not simply in order to have a good time, but to make ourselves into good citizens, and do good turns to the country.

It is very quiet in the forest, except when the trains with passengers and troops go roaring overhead.

The only sound otherwise is the churring of the nightjar.

And now and then I hear the soft footfalls of the two Scouts who are doing their two hours' spell of marching up and down between the two bridges under our charge.

Harvesting.   2 Despatch Riding.   3. Farm Work.   4. Allotment Work.   5. Guarding Bridge.   6. Canteen Work.   7. Dairy Work.   8. First-Aid Work.   9. Building Huts for the War Office.

WAR SERVICES OF THE BOY SCOUTS

THE HEROES AT HOME

On or about each bridge two other Scouts keep watch and ward. They hardly expect a German spy to appear, armed with revolver, gunpowder, and dynamite ; but, if he should appear, they are ready for him.

Some Territorials, with bayonets fixed and bullets in their rifles, are near at hand. Yesterday we were doing duty along with a ganger and a policeman.

How we were Called Out

At eleven o'clock the other night a motor-car stopped before my house, in a village under the South Downs in Sussex, and the County Secretary of the Sussex Boy Scouts' Association sprang out, handing orders for me, marked " Very Urgent," then sped away to pass on the orders to our District Scoutmaster.

By five o'clock next morning the District Scoutmaster was out on his bicycle, passing on the orders to Scoutmasters.

Some he found at home in bed ; some were in bed in camp ; others were about to go out on the day's business.

He cycled forty miles that morning before most people had thought of beginning the day. Our district is a large one, and there were more than 200 Scouts to be brought together.

How the Scouts Rallied

One example will show how these Scouts of Sussex responded to a sudden emergency call:

Their Scoutmaster was roused from bed at 6 a.m. He lives in a country place, where the Scouts are scattered. By 11 a.m. every member of the troop, thirty-four strong, had reached the meeting place, an important railway junction, a good five miles from headquarters.

The mobilization complete, the Scouts marched off in small detachments to the various bridges and culverts on a long length of line lying between Three Bridges and Lewes.

Their orders were simply these: They are to guard the bridges against spies.

They were advised that their services might be needed for an indefinite time, so that they should use their best wits to make themselves comfortable.

Tents were brought up in the course of the day, bedding, food, and camp kitchens.

Bridges, culverts, embankments, and points were examined carefully, and the best ways of guarding them decided upon.

Then the night duty was arranged, and each Scout was given his special job.

The usual arrangement is that from two to four Scouts guard each bridge or culvert together for

THE HEROES AT HOME

two hours at a spell. Two other Scouts patrol the line, taking good heed of the trains.

The remainder, at night, sleep till their turn comes.

That first day of calling out the Scouts, drafting them to their posts, bringing up tents and supplies, and inspecting the line under our care was indeed a strenuous one. It seemed to me by the end of that day that I had walked hundreds of miles and ridden thousands.

By eventide every bridge and culvert on that long stretch of line was properly guarded by Boy Scouts, who were thoroughly provisioned and equipped for a night's work under the stars.

How the Scouts do their Job

I must say the Scouts are magnificent.

There has been no hesitation in turning out at a moment's notice. There is no grumbling at the job. Many are making heavy sacrifices to answer the call of duty. But each feels here is a real chance to do old England a good turn.

The Scouts' parents are magnificent, too. And so are their employers, who let them off their work, wherever possible. The parents are proud that their sons should serve.

Their boy friends, not Scouts, are a little envious. The boys who are not Scouts wish they were.

Where the Scouts best show their self-reliance is in the confident way they are prepared to tackle any emergency.

Their orders, as I have said, are simply to guard the bridges.

But what, some people ask, could unarmed Scouts do if the line were attacked by armed and desperate spies?

The Scouts have no doubt about this. When I asked two of them what action they would take if a spy should come, they answered:

"We should give him a good fright, sir. We shall raise the alarm, depend on't."

And that is just what the Scouts can do.

If any spy comes along, they can raise the alarm, and no doubt can frighten him away. A large bridge cannot be blown up, either by dynamite from above or gunpowder from below, in the twinkling of an eye; half an hour's work might be needed to do the job.

If any outrage or accident happens on the line, the Scouts can spread the news to police, soldiers, and railwaymen, and by their lamps and flags they can stop trains from rushing to disaster.

AIR RAID HEROES

In all parts of London where bombs fell, Scouts were quickly on the spot, eager to assist the

THE HEROES AT HOME 195

injured or to help extinguish fires, or act in any useful way.

The St. Mary-le-Strand Troop was holding a parade of the elder boys, one night in October 1915, when bombs fell within a few yards of their headquarters. This was before the warning system had been organized. In the words of the Scoutmaster : —

" We at once made for the basement until the bombing had stopped, when we turned out with the Troop's stretcher, etc., to see what help we could render. As this raid was one of the earliest of the London raids, and the Ambulance Services had not then reached the high state of efficiency that they did later, we found ample opportunity to render help, and conveyed a number of injured people to hospital on the Troop's stretcher and trek-cart.

" The behaviour of the lads was splendid, in face of the very unpleasant sights that they were called on to witness.

" Unfortunately one of the junior members of the Troop, who was not on parade that night, was killed by a bomb in Aldwych, and one of the senior lads who had been helping with the first aid work, arrived home late at night, only to find that his father was among the killed.

"After this raid, the troop kept an Ambulance Squad in readiness on nights when raids were likely or expected, for a considerable time, in fact until their headquarters were taken over by the Government, but fortunately the services of the boys were not again needed. Ultimately for various reasons the Raid Squad had to be abandoned, chiefly owing to the elder lads who had formed it joining H.M. Forces."

BRAVE SCOUTS OF BETHNAL GREEN

There were signs of a raid and all the necessary precautions were being taken. The Scouts of the St. Matthias', Bethnal Green, Troop had reported to " J " Special Constabulary. The first duty assigned to the boys was to deliver about ninety warning cards to the houses of the Special Constables, and this was successfully accomplished before the maroons sounded, and the anticipated raid became a real thing.

Were these boys nervous ? Not they. They were Scouts and they were keen to carry out the important work given them to do. They had no thought of themselves, but for those who were weaker—the women and children.

The boys were divided into two parties, one half going to the Bethnal Green Police Station as " All

king. 2. Helping the Wounded. 3. Rabbit Trapping. 4. Sounding "All Clear:" or the Wounded. 6. Flax Harvesting. 7. Poultry Work. 8. Stretcher Work. 9. Orderly Duty for the King. 10. Waste Paper Collectors.

WAR SERVICES OF THE BOY SCOUTS.

[*To face page 196.*

THE HEROES AT HOME 197

Clear " boys, the remaining half taking shelter at the railway station.

Bombs were dropping now and the whizz and explosions of the shells from the anti-aircraft guns was sufficient to make even the bravest soldier feel uncomfortable. But these Scouts never complained, and before daylight dawned again they were to see sights such as they had never seen before, and, please God, they may never see again —sights that can hardly be described.

It was at 11.50 that a bomb fell on a chemical factory in the near vicinity, followed in quick succession by others which found their mark on some tenement buildings.

Help was needed to rescue the victims, and as there were but few Special Constables on reserve, a call for volunteers was made among the Scouts. It doesn't surprise us that every lad came forward, for they were true Scouts and prepared to help others even at grave risk to themselves.

Stretchers and first aid outfits were quickly procured, and two minutes after the bombs had dropped the gallant party were on the spot, despite the fact that the raid was still at its height and there was every possibility of a bomb falling among them as they worked.

Bravely the Scouts rendered first aid to the injured, and many were the exciting rescues successfully accomplished by these boys amid the ruins.

They also assisted the firemen to run out hose, and numerous small fires were extinguished by the boys themselves.

They were repeatedly warned by R.A.F. officers and falling shrapnel to " take cover," but they kept going until 5 o'clock in the morning, when they were dismissed and thanked by the Inspector of Police. They were back again at 8 a.m. and remained on duty all day until eleven o'clock at night.

Throughout the whole of the sad work, the boys carried on with great pluck and cheerfulness.

Three letters from the Police, Ambulance men, and also the Fire Brigade were received, praising the Scouts for their pluck and assistance. Later the Commissioner presented fifteen boys with Gilt Crosses at the People's Palace, Mile End Road.

Many brave deeds were done by Scouts during air raids, but perhaps the most astounding individual effort was the plucky act of Assistant Scoutmaster, Arthur S. Nice.

When a house was smashed down by a big bomb, he crawled in among the ruins, at great risk to his life, and endeavoured to save a man who was buried under a pile of fallen debris.

In doing so he was imprisoned by some falling bricks, and he was only dug out with great difficulty.

THE HEROES AT HOME

SECOND A. G. WIGAN.

The following incident shows that our Scouts do not forget what they have learnt, in moments of great emergency, and that the cool-headedness and self-control that is generally acquired by a Scout, stands him in good stead in moments of strain.

An air raid was in progress, on May 25th, 1917. The Headmaster of the Grange School, Folkestone, was engaged in collecting the boys into a bomb-proof spot in the basement. One of the Scouts belonging to the School Troop, Second L. G. Wigan, chanced to be looking out of the window. Coming across the playground towards the house he saw the figure of a man swaying unsteadily as he walked, his clothes covered with blood. It was the gardener, and obviously he had been badly wounded! There was no time to hesitate. Without waiting for any one, Wigan ran out of the house, regardless of the boom and crash of the guns, the whirr of enemy aircraft, and the falling splinters of shrapnel. He was only just in time. As he reached the spot the man tottered forward, and fell heavily to the ground, unconscious. Blood was pouring from a gash across his throat.

Kneeling at his side, Wigan examined the wound, and, to his dismay, recognized that both the jugular vein and the carotid artery had been severed by a piece of bomb.

To stop the flow of blood was the one thing to be done.

Anything in the way of a tourniquet is impossible, of course, in such a case. Wigan's ambulance training had taught him that digital pressure was the only chance. The terrible appearance of the unfortunate victim, and the unnerving sounds of the air-raid failed to disturb the plucky young Scout. With coolness and precision he acted exactly as his ambulance instructor had taught him, and remained at his task until his Scoutmaster arrived.

The man's life, alas, could not be saved, but had the wound been less severe the timely assistance and presence of mind of the Scout would very probably have saved him.

"When I found him," says his Scoutmaster, "Wigan's only remark was, 'Oh, Sir, I hope I have done right; it was not easy to find the pressure point.'"

SCOUT C. FRY.

On the same occasion a bomb fell on a house in St. John's Street, Folkestone, and partly demolished it. Some Scouts were on the spot, ready to help in any way they could. There was little to be done until help should arrive.

Realizing, however, the probable terror of the

THE HEROES AT HOME

luckless inmates, unable to get out of the tottering remains of the building, Scout Fry, and another boy, determined to reach them, and at least cheer them up with comforting reassurance. Scaling some outhouses, and climbing up by means of rain pipes and gutters, the boys managed to reach the window of an attic.

Within, they found two women, terrified at their position, and shaken with the violence of the explosion. The mere sight of a Scout, with his cheery face and confidence that everything will be all right, was intensely comforting. At any moment the house might have collapsed, but the two boys, seeing that their presence was so great a consolation to the women, remained with them until they were rescued.

ESCAPED PRISONERS

During the war, many civilians and military prisoners of war escaped from the various internment camps all over the country, and in more than one case their apprehension has been due to the smartness of Scouts.

One of the first lessons in Scoutcraft is observation. A good Scout learns to use his eyes, so that some little detail about a person whom he meets in the street tells him a great deal about that person. It is possible to tell a person's occupation from their hands, their character from the way they walk or wear their hats.

It was due to this training that Scout Thomas Gibson was successful in catching two escaped prisoners, and the way he did it makes interesting reading.

While walking along a road by Stales Lodge, near Kettering, he saw two strangers approaching. Gibson's eyes were keenly on the alert, for he had heard of the escape of two prisoners from Rothwell internment camp.

Something peculiar about them seemed to tell him that these were the two German prisoners who had escaped, and he gave those two the fright of their lives.

Boldly confronting the two men, he ordered them at the point of a shot-gun to walk with him to the nearest police-station, where he handed over his captives after guarding them some time till the police superintendent arrived in his motor-car from Kettering.

I don't suppose Gibson ever thought that it would be his luck to capture the men, but by exercising his powers of observation and resource he was successful, and he was brave enough to effect their arrest in a quiet, systematic manner.

Several other Scouts have been successful in arresting escaped prisoners.

CHAPTER VII

Just—a Scout

SCOUT HEROES we have called this book, and by HEROES we have meant to indicate those whose glorious deeds have brought them a well-earned recognition. But among those of our Scouts who have served at the Front and come home to the old Troop, or have done their bit, and " gone home," there is many a *hero*—many a boy who risked or gave up his life for another, or for his ideals of loyalty and service.

Alone, unseen, he did some deed that would have made men wonder and admire. But no man will ever know that deed : no *man*, we said—it is written in the Roll of Honour that is kept in Heaven. And so we cannot write of this hidden heroism ; we can only, here, tender our thanks to those boys who went out, and are conscious that they did *their best*, cost what it might.

Then, again, there is another class of Scout Hero. Perhaps the chance of doing something " great " never came his way. He stood for hours, knee-deep in muddy water; patiently he fought a rear-guard action; for two, three, four years he was constantly cold and hungry and dirty and footsore; for weeks on end he lived in the constant realisation that at any moment a shell might burst in his bit of the trench.

No adventures ever came his way; the chance of doing some supreme good turn never presented itself. No one has called him a Hero; he is just —a Scout. But a Scout who went through the War and remained a Scout to the end is, to our mind, a Hero. To be a *Scout* in the clean, healthy, chivalrous atmosphere of a camp on the English Downs, or by the cool, green sea, is one thing; and to be a *Scout* through the long, slow months of a gruesome war, where mud, and privation and (perhaps) injustice, and low principles, and " man's inhumanity to man " are all part of the day's work—that is a different matter.

Of these innumerable Heroes, then, we cannot write. There is no good story, no good yarn, connected with their heroism. The number of times their fidelity to the 1st Scout Law, the 2nd, the 7th, the 10th, helped their mates to remain true men—this will never be known. The number of times their practice of the 3rd, the 4th, the 5th and 6th brought comfort to some well-nigh broken heart, or to some suffering animal—this will never

JUST A SCOUT

be known on earth. The number of times these Scouts smiled, because of the 8th Scout Law, and kept up the morale of the Army, no man will ever be able to recount. And so, to those who have come home, we can only say, " Thank God for you " ; and to those who have "*gone home* " —some day we shall be able to say it, too, if God so will.

And yet there is a great deal of " Scouting " at the Front that may well be told and described, and that should be of great interest to the young Scouts who were not able to go Overseas to the Great War.

In this chapter we propose to give some little pictures of the Scout, as he appeared in the War. We know his cheery face so well, as he swings along the hard, high road, with sleeves up, and bare, brown knees ; or " stalks " warily through the undergrowth ; or goes whistling down the dingy London alley ; let us, then, look at this same cheery face under the dull, rain-sodden skies of France ; by the light of the Hun's star shells ; as he performs a good turn for a mate ; as he faces death on the bloody field, or death in the still, white hospital ward.

Keeping his eye on the Kid

He was only twenty himself, the Scout who told

me this story, but he was a corporal, and had seen some stiff fighting, since he joined up.

"It's hard," he said, "to see the youngsters come out, and get hit the first day. They're as keen as mustard, and they *won't* keep their heads down. Up they pop over the parapet, just for a look round, and ping—they've got one between the eyes.

"There was one kid I had to look after. It was like this. As we were waiting at the Docks to go on board—it was my third time across—there was an old lady saying good-bye to her son. He wasn't eighteen, and her only one. She was old—grey-haired and bent. She was—well, you know. Mothers didn't ought to come to the Docks. Just as we was marching off to go on board, she came up to me and says, 'Corporal, I want you to do me a favour.' 'Yes, mother,' I says, 'anything you like.' 'It's just,' she said, 'to keep an eye on my boy, in France. He's all I have.' 'Right you are, mother,' I says. 'Will you *promise* me?' she says. So I promised.

"Well, I kept my eye on the kid. But one night I missed him. When I found him, and says, 'What's on?' he says, 'I've volunteered for a bombing stunt.' 'Look here,' I says, 'haven't I told you often enough you ain't to volunteer for *nothing*?' But it was done. So I volunteered too.

JUST—A SCOUT

' We went over the top together. It was pitch dark. There was a lot of wire and all sorts of mess about. We turned round so many times that in the end we didn't know which was our trenches and which was Jerry's. ' Do you know which are our'n ? ' said the Sergeant. ' No,' I said, ' let's have a go at these.'

" Well, we got close to 'em, and we thought we was back at our own lines. But suddenly Jerry started—*zit, zit, brrrrr, zit*, they went. It was close range and we got the wind up a bit. There was nothing for it but to retire to our trenches. The kid had got hold of my equipment, behind. ' Oh, Bill,' he says, ' Bill. . . .' ' All right,' I says, and pulls him round in front of me, and we starts back. But the next minute—*phut*, he'd stopped one.

" I got him back to our lines ; the old fireman's lift, of course.

" Now he's back in Blighty, and got his ticket. I kept my eye on the old lady's kid, all right."

" Be Prepared "

" My Scout training helped me from the day I entered the Army to the day I left it," says an officer in the R.F.A. " I went to France in 1915. There was not a man in the battery who knew how to make a bivouac. Our second night in

France we halted in a field. No covering had been provided, and it was raining. I had to get the men together and show them how to lace up the waterproof sheets and make a shelter. We had only had our ground sheets issued the day before leaving England, and we had been in huts all the time, so that we could not have practised before, if we wished. To soldiers, now, this will seem very strange. But it must be remembered this was 1915.

" In the same year we were in the Somme region. Our Colonel, knowing I was a Scout, suggested building a hut to protect the harness. I asked for material, and the Colonel replied, ' I thought a Boy Scout made a spoon out of two blades of grass. Surely you can build a hut out of what you can find.'

" There was one other Scout in the battery, so we determined not to let the Movement down. I had been an examiner for the Pioneer's Badge, and knew something about the subject. So we went and felled a few saplings and proceeded to build a hut.

" We had no nails, or rope for lashing, so we collected the binding wire off our trusses of hay, and used that. We then collected rushes from the river and thatched the whole of the hut, keeping the rushes in place by binding them together

JUST A SCOUT

between two sticks, with a sort of hairpin made of the wire. The hut was 100 feet by 10 feet and quite waterproof. Our example was copied by many.

" In Salonika I frequently got the job of map-making. At one time, when in the mountains, endeavouring to find a possible path for the guns, I had to follow the trail of a mule. This was not a mule-track, but the trail left by one or two mules only. We became enveloped in a mountain mist, lost the trail, and, as my compass had broken, we should have been lost, had it not been for the fact that Scouting had taught me to notice the direction of the wind. This does not sound much, but when one is fifteen or twenty miles in front of one's Division, it is not advisable to get lost.

"At another time I took a party of men into Kavalla Wood to fell trees for fortifications. Being used to taking Scouts out, I foolishly did not ask if any of the party could cook. They couldn't, so I had to do it myself.

" While there it occurred to me that the branches we were trimming off were being wasted, and remembering the Chief's notes on how to make charcoal, I decided to put these into practice. We turned out about four sacks of charcoal per day, without hindering the work of tree-felling."

"I joined the R.E.'s as a Private," says another officer, "in 1914. Most of the Company to which I was posted consisted of civil and mechanical engineers, but I was the only one who knew drill. The third day we did signalling. Fortunately the Troop had taught me to Semaphore and Morse, so the C.O. put me in charge of the 'awkward squad.'

"A few days afterwards some spars and lashings turned up and we were put on knot-tying and lashing; most of the Company knew all about strain and spanning, etc., but they couldn't tie a knot or make a square lashing, which the Scouts had taught me. I was a Sergeant in three months. In this way Scouting has stood me in good stead throughout the War."

"When out on Patrol work," says another Scout, "my chum was badly wounded in the arm, from which he bled profusely. I remembered my practice with the Scouts and improvised a tourniquet. The M.O. told my chum that I certainly saved his life, thanks to my Scout training.

"When I first joined up, together with two of my Scout friends, the battalion was very short of cooks. As we all three had the Cook's badge we volunteered for that duty, and for some time did practically all the cooking for our company."

JUST—A SCOUT

Tracking

"I was in charge of a small party in Paschendaele," says a Corporal of the London Regiment, "when I noticed some footprints in the snow. My Scoutmaster had been most keen on tracking, consequently I had instinctively compared the impression made by a German boot and that made by those of the British and the Allies.

"My little party separated and crept along, following the direction of the 'trail.' From the tracks the party of Bosches seemed to be about ten or twelve. The trail led towards some ruined buildings. These we skirted, but as no footprints appeared on the other side we knew they were still inside. We got to the rear of them, and crept in, and so surprised the party that my party, eight in number, were able to kill six and take eight prisoners.

"In this and many other ways Scouting has been most useful to me during my Army life."

A Leading Seaman, R.N.V.R., says: "One day when about to cut some barbed wire I noticed the impression of footprints in the mud, which were certainly German, so I glanced round to see where they led to, and saw, quite close to where I was, a German helmet and a broken box, and other odds and ends, one of which was attached to the barbed wire by a short lead. Had I cut the barbed wire before disconnecting the lead I should undoubtedly have been blown up."

To end up with we will give the beautiful story of a Scout's death in a hospital in Belgium. This boy was a true Scout,—" the first Scout in Petersfield," and the means of starting the Movement there.

The way he endeared himself to those who nursed him; his patience, courage, trust in God, and the peaceful way he " passed to higher service," should be an inspiration to all Scouts. And to those who have, perhaps, some dearly loved friend or brother, of whom they have only been able to ascertain that he " died of wounds in hospital," this little story should bring great comfort, for it shows that although among so-called " strangers," this Scout died in an atmosphere of love and tenderest care.

Those who nursed him learnt to love him in those few short days, partly for himself, it is true; but we must remember that their lives have been given up entirely to loving and tending all those who need love and care, because Christ once said, "Inasmuch as ye have done it unto one of the least of these My brethren, ye have done it unto

JUST—A SCOUT

Me." They gave their very best, because they were giving to Christ.

We will give the story exactly as it reached his mother, in the words of the English nun who nursed him, and of the doctor who attended him.

> St. Joseph's Convent,
> Blaugies,
> Hainaut,
> Belgium.

Mrs. Heriot,
Dear Madam,—

"It is with deep regret that I am writing to you to announce the death of your son, Henry Alfred Heriot of the 15th Hussars, at our Convent, at present being used as an Ambulance for soldiers wounded during the war. He was seriously wounded in the leg, in this neighbourhood, on Monday, 24th of August, 1914, in an engagement with some German troops, and was brought into our Ursuline Convent with several others of his Regiment, the same evening.

"Our doctor found that one of his legs was badly broken, causing a large wound. Happily we are two English Sisters here, so he had the satisfaction of having us near him during his sufferings. He endeared himself to us by his great patience. He spoke to me several times about his home and his family, asking me to write to you and tell you he was always thinking of you. Unluckily, as all communication was stopped, we were unable to comply with his request.

"On the Wednesday following, our doctor had a consultation with two others, and it was decided that the only means of saving his life was to amputate his leg at once. He accepted this decision most courageously, but burst into tears when asked for his home address. I spoke to him of God, and told him to offer all his sufferings to Him, and make acts of love and of sorrow for any past sin he may have committed. He said he had already done so, several times, and would continue to do so. I asked him if he had been baptised. He replied he would very much like to receive Baptism. This he received conditionally, from the hands of our Vicar.

"On the Thursday his leg was amputated by three doctors. That night our doctor's wife and I watched by him. He was so patient. There was a nameless something about him that claimed our sympathy. You will see by the letter our doctor sends how

JUST—A SCOUT

fond everyone was of him. Towards four o'clock I noticed that he breathed with difficulty, and asked him if he would like to be raised. He assented, and we re-arranged his pillow. He had grown very pale, but always replied he was not suffering much. He then extended a hand to each of us as if in sign of adieu. I gave him my Crucifix to hold. It seemed to comfort him, as he kissed it several times and laid it on the coverlet.

" Gradually his breathing grew shorter, and after ten minutes, ceased. He passed away so peacefully and gently. We all feel he has gone straight to Heaven. We then composed him for his last, long sleep. He was carried in his coffin to the cemetery at Blaugies. The following day it was found that his grave was covered with flowers. The villagers are full of sympathy for the wounded English soldiers. We have a few of his belongings—a medal and pay book, and letters in a pocket book that belonged to a chum. We will send them to you as soon as possible.

" For myself, I am glad to have had the privilege of nursing him. He has left such a good remembrance behind him, and will never be forgotten here. Once more I express my sincere sympathy to you in the loss of your dear son, and shall be pleased to answer any letters you may care to write to the above address."

(Signed) SŒUR MARIE ANDREE.
(*Ursuline.*)

" MADAM,—

" I feel it my duty to add a few words to Sister Marie Andree's letter. Your dear son came to us wounded, on August 14th. In spite of the maternal care and nursing of the Sisters who surrounded him; in spite of the efforts myself and fellow physicians made to save his life, he passed away, without suffering, the following Friday.

" Your brave little soldier had spent only a few days with us, but they were enough to attract to him all the sympathy that his gentle character and perfect breeding deserved. Be assured, Madam, that nothing has been spared to give him all the care his state required. Night and day they watched his bed. The English nun who is writing you, and my wife. spent the last night with him. All my family felt an especial affection for this dear child, who recalled my own son who is also fighting under the flag. If, after the terrible war, you would wish, Madam, to come and pray at his grave in the cemetery at Blaugies, the doctor's house is open to you with all his heart."

(Signed) P. DEVREAU, *Doctor*.

With these beautiful letters we will close this chapter on the boys whose chief claim to our respect is that they were—just SCOUTS.

CHAPTER VIII

Called to Higher Service

IT is only in moments of quiet reflection that one recalls to mind the happy times spent in the company of those who, alas, are no more, that one realises how great has been the loss to the Scout movement by the death on the battle-fields of some of its most outstanding members.

But God has been pleased to call them to Higher Service, and the stories of their noble lives will go down in our Scout history as a lasting memorial to their names.

There are many heroes who never wear a decoration, and many, no doubt, whose life story would make instructive and interesting reading. One could fill a huge volume with such stories. The Editor asks forgiveness if some who, in the opinion of his readers, should be included here, have been omitted.

**CAPTAIN THE LATE
HON. ROLAND E. PHILIPPS, M.C.**
(COMMISSIONER FOR N.E. AND E. LONDON.)

" We **are** intensely happy that at last

CALLED TO HIGHER SERVICE 219

the time is at hand when we may give to our country the highest service and sacrifice for which we have prepared ourselves."

So wrote one of the truest Scouts who ever lived. In the days of peace he had lived for service—service of his fellows for God's sake, of God in his fellows. He had given himself, heart and soul, to a great cause. And when war came, and service of a new sort became the first duty of every Englishman, he was ready to serve the new cause, with all his heart. It was not in a spirit of adventure that he went to the Front, nor imbued with a thirst for military glory. "I have no wish to appear before the world as a warrior," he wrote. "If I enjoy my soldiering, it is simply as a Scout who enjoys the job which seems to him at the moment to be the one that he is called on to perform. After the war I shall enjoy every other job a great deal more!"

It was, then, the very highest motive that inspired his life as a soldier, and no mere instinct or ambition. That such a motive produced supremely good work is testified by the words of his Colonel, written to his father, Lord St. Davids after Capt. Roland Philipps had fallen. "An irreparable loss has been suffered by the battalion in the death of your son. He was the finest natural leader of men I have ever seen, and his courage and dash and enthusiasm would have appeared fanatical were it not for the coolness and sane decision he displayed when his objective was obtained."

Here is the story of one of his adventures, told in his own words. He did not write it for publication, but in a letter to his friend, Mr. H. G. Elwes, Editor of the *Headquarters Gazette*. In giving permission for its publication, he wrote : " I do not look upon anything I write in the *Gazette* as ' an article for the press,' but just as an exchange of thoughts with friends."

How we attacked the German Lines

" One afternoon last month our Colonel told us that we were in for an attack on the German lines, and the next two days were, without any exception, the most exciting period of my life. The attack was to be at 5.45 p.m. on Thursday evening. My company, ' B,' was to be in the middle, with two companies of another battalion on the left, and our own ' C,' company on the right. The signal for the attack was to be the explosion of an enormous mine underneath a part of the German fire-trench.

" Every moment from then on was spent in arranging details, and on Wednesday night we told the men exactly what was expected of each one of

CALLED TO HIGHER SERVICE 221

them. I gave them my last talk on Thursday morning. Their spirit of fearlessness and determination was wonderful. I told them that some months ago they had joined the Army to serve their King and their Country, and now for many of them there would be the supreme opportunity of rendering service and of sacrifice. Every officer, N.C.O., and man would go in with faith, cheeriness, and a strong right arm. We would work together and each one do his best, and whatever we accomplished would not have been done in vain. Oh! I wish you could have seen those men. The atmosphere was charged with the warmth of their loyalty. I did indeed most truly love them.

"5.15 p.m.—Our first party was to consist of fifty men lightly equipped and specially chosen. I was to lead them myself. The second party of thirty-five men was to follow immediately afterwards, and to bring up picks, shovels, sandbags, and other material for consolidating the position when captured.

"The fifty were already in position by their ladders. There was time for one final word of serious instruction. I told the men that in case the mine explosion knocked in our own trench with the concussion, if there were only three men left, those three would immediately cut across and hold the German trench until the arrival of the others.

"'We will, sir.'

"'You can trust the 9th, sir.'

"'Good old "B" Company,' were some of the replies, and it was clear that every man was out for business, and that no further words were needed or would make much difference.

"5.45 p.m. Had the mine failed? Good Heavens! The whole earth began to tremble, then to shake, then to sway from side to side. Then huge fragments of earth, and wire, and trench, and men were hurled in one black volcano eighty feet into the air. Nearer they came and nearer. There was a rumbling roar, and the next thing I knew was that I had received a great blow across my face and side of the head, and that my eyes, nose, and mouth were streaming with blood. It was only afterwards that I learnt that nearly thirty of my fellows were either buried or partially disabled before they could start. But now was no time for hesitation.

"'Come on, boys,' and twenty stalwart Fusiliers were galloping with me like a pack of hounds across the open. In less than two minutes we were on the German fire-trench. It was literally teeming with the enemy. They were pouring out from their deep dug-outs wild and half stupefied

CALLED TO HIGHER SERVICE 223

by the shock of the explosion. I blazed off as hard as I could with my automatic revolver. Three shots out of four went home, but the last of the three German Tommies fired at me in the same instant as I did, and as he fell I felt a throb on my breast and blood trickling down inside my shirt.

"After that the fighting was fast and furious. Guns started firing on all sides—also trench mortars and minenwerfers. The air was thick with bullets. Groans and shouts were mingled with the spluttering and stuttering of machine guns. I dashed along to the left flank. The battalion there had failed to come up. They had lost their direction. Our left flank was in the air. Bang! Bang! Bang! A terrific counter-attack was being launched upon us with bombs.

"'Come on, the bombers. Hold them back. We will have more bombs here in a minute.'

"By Jove! how they fought, those first few bombers, but at first it is hard to get adequate supplies of bombs into action, and owing to the enemy's efforts and the exposure of our left flank man after man of them was being wounded. I began throwing bombs myself—a pretty bad hand at it, but it is a case of now or never. Six have gone, and I am getting into my stride, when thud and whack on my back, and I am lying face downwards at the bottom of the trench.

"'The Captain is gone.'

"'Gone. What do you mean?'

"'Why, I thought you was dead, sir.'

"'Dead! Why, we're only just beginning.'

"I sent two long messages to the Colonel, one by hand, and the other by the signallers, whose wire had just been laid, but might at any moment be broken. I told him that we had taken the German trench, that the men were holding on like heroes, that we were in touch on the right but not on the left, and that we were fighting hard to keep back the German bombers. That my only subaltern, a grand little fellow, had just been killed, and that we had accounted for about eighty Germans. That we were still in good form and getting along splendidly.

"After this the situation was getting critical, but even the wounded stuck to their job and kept passing the bombs along, and gradually we began to get the mastery.

"I crept along to the right and found my second in command. I asked him to go forward and keep things going. I wanted to get up some more bombs and bombers, and also, if possible, to report personally to the Colonel, as the chances were that my previous messages had never reached him.

"Finally, after ten minutes of hair-breadth

CALLED TO HIGHER SERVICE 225

escapes and alternate rising and sinking, both of body and of spirit, I reached him, but to my intense dismay he ordered me to the field ambulance. I felt like a professional football player ordered off the field by the referee in the middle of the Cup Final.

"At the moment of writing I am in hospital, but a few small bullet holes do not do much harm, and very soon I hope to be back again with my battalion. If any of my brother Scouts inquire for me, please say I am still very happy and as fit as a fiddle, and with all the strings still unbroken.

"When I went over the parapet I was wearing a Tenderfoot Badge in my buttonhole. As a Scout said to you the other day at Colchester, 'Those are the things that help.'"

GONE HOME

To a man who faced life in the spirit in which Roland Philipps faced it all was joy; hardships and difficulties had their own worth; and a soldier's death was the great privilege for which (as he wrote) "we have prepared ourselves."

Whence came this joy, this peace, this contentment? Our only answer can be to quote his own words.

On the eve of "The Great Push" his letter is headed, "A very happy bivouac before battle," and it ends, "nothing can separate us from the love of God which is in Jesus Christ our Lord—that is why I am not afraid."

And then the last letter written late at night on July 6th is headed, "A land of striving for higher things." And it ends: "Good-bye. Our supreme opportunity of serving our Country is at hand. My life has been a very happy one, and no shell or bullet can end it. I only pray that through all I may remain near to God, for in that way alone may I ever be with those I love—my friends and my boys."

It was early on the morning of the 7th that Capt. Philipps called his men together. He told them they were about to undertake a desperate adventure, but there was nothing to fear in death. A few weeks before he had spoken to them on the subject, "And God shall wipe away all tears from their eyes, and there shall be no more death." And he had written to me that the men had understood. Now, with this thought in their hearts they faced death together.

"Come on, lads, come on," he cried, as he leapt over the parapet.

"Our brigade was ordered to take the German lines and village of——on July 7th," writes Major Overton, who was acting Commandant of the battalion, "and Roland, in his usual gallant way,

CALLED TO HIGHER SERVICE 227

led his company over the parapet, and was waving his men on when I saw him hit.

" One of his men informed me afterwards that he had been killed. I cannot express in words the loss he is to me and the brigade in every way. No one could show a higher standard of courage, coolness, and devotion to duty than he did."

So died a great soldier and a great Scout ; and because it is rather as Scout than as soldier that he would wish to appear it is fitting that we should give some account of his life and his work in those days before the war called him from the life he loved, to the sterner form of service.

Here is an account written by one who was his friend,[1] and which gives a true picture of him as a Scout.

SCOUTING DAYS

" To convey an adequate impression of Roland Philipps' work amongst Scouts and Scoutmasters of North-East London is impossible within the narrow bounds of language. We cannot hope even to suggest the vigour and freshness which he brought—the influence he had—and the general sense of new life which he managed to impart to

[1] William Black, S.M., 15th N.E. London Troop, and a Commissioner during the early part of the war. He was killed on active service.

everyone he met. It was, moreover, so greatly by what he was that he helped us, that his doings, splendid in themselves, seem but a little record to us who were privileged to know his strong, pure, and altogether joyous personality. He came to us young, and practically a stranger. He found Scouting for boys carried on by all sorts and conditions of men in a hundred different and sometimes conflicting ways.

We had been running our Clubs to our own satisfaction; Scouting was an excellent extra occupation, and the ideas of Headquarters were not too seriously regarded.

When Roland Philipps came he began to make it clear that Scouting for boys had to be a great Brotherhood, strong in discipline through the honour and loyalty of its members, united as only those can be who work in common for an exalted ideal.

He emphasised from the beginning that Scouting must needs be a great spiritual force, and on the first part of the Scout's Promise—" A Scout is true to God "—he took his stand.

Whether the Troop were Anglican, Wesleyan, Roman Catholic or Jewish, he urged the need of loyalty to God, in whatever way the boys were taught to worship.

On this foundation Roland Philipps worked,

CALLED TO HIGHER SERVICE 229

taking the Scout Promise and the Scout Law as the framework of his structure. " A Scout," he would say in effect, " is not a boy in shorts and a big hat—who can cook, bandage, signal, and find his way about. He is a boy however poorly dressed, and even however inefficient in practical Scouting, who has taken the Scout Promise and is doing his best to keep the Scout Law."

In pursuance of this faith, that great spiritual and moral principles must be the foundation of Scouting, he organised that wonderful series of lectures on the ten Scout Laws held during the winter of 1912–1913. No one but Roland Philipps could have carried out such a plan. To invite a thousand boys to come from their clubs on ten Saturday nights and listen to lectures on more or less ethical subjects ; to invite well-known and busy men to face the ordeal of interesting such an army on such subjects ; to persuade Scoutmasters that their boys would really like it ; to test and bring out the discipline and loyalty which is at the heart of every real Boy Scout ; these were the tasks which he set himself to, and accomplished.

All of us who were at these lectures feel that the highest point was reached when, at the request of his Scoutmasters, he himself spoke on the tenth Scout Law, " A Scout is pure in thought, word and deed." His mother was on the platform, and well we remember his ringing words:

"Chaps, a Scout, by God's help is pure."

No one who spoke to our boys before or since made so strong an impression. His words seemed to us most truly inspired by the Spirit of God, and for the living memory of that night alone we could say that "he being dead yet speaketh."

Yet in all this exultation of thought and precept Roland Philipps was eminently practical, thoroughly efficient, and not only a lover of boys, but a real boy himself. He played and enjoyed Scout games with as much zest as the youngest boy in the Troop, and in every way he was a true Scout. If he had been ten years younger he would have been a King's Scout, as, in a higher way, he is indeed now. He learned to tie a score of knots, went through an ambulance course, was a good signaller, and would cook his meal with boys in camp, any day.

And then he found the Patrol Leader. We do not mean that there were no leaders, nor that he told us a new thing. But he made us understand the Chief Scout's ideal, and sent many of us back to begin again by reading *Scouting for Boys* afresh. He showed us that the only possible way of really running Scouts was by training them in small, self-contained groups

CALLED TO HIGHER SERVICE 231

called Patrols, each with a leader at its head who really did lead ; a boy whom the Scoutmaster trusted and who was responsible for his charge.

It was Roland Philipps who founded the first Patrol Leaders Parliament, who insisted, at our big lectures, on the boys coming quietly in patrols in charge of a leader only (and never was order better maintained). It was he who wrote that admirable exposition of the Chief Scout's ideas, " The Patrol System," and " Letters to a Patrol Leader,"[1] and inculcated responsibility, loyalty, self discipline and efficiency in this wonderful work.

The Scoutmasters, young and old, were his loved friends, his trusted comrades. He helped them, he criticised them, he even " slated " them, and was quite ruthless as to many of their pet prejudices and methods. And his men, like his boys, never left him.

Loyalty to the Chief Scout and Headquarters, in detail as well as spirit, he practised and insisted on, and it was on his initiative that Scoutmasters and A.S.M.'s on appointment took the Scout promise with their boys.

When war broke out, as Commissioner for N.E. and E. London, Roland Philipps took the control of all the public service so keenly carried

[1] Published by Messrs. C. A. Pearson, Ltd.

out by the boys in those busy districts. During that anxious time he showed himself to be a wise and strong leader, realising the needs of the situation, yet not carried away by the excitement of it.

At the end of that first month he saw that his duty was to take up arms, and leaving the work and the boys he loved, he went to serve his country. He worked and lived for his men as he had done for his boys, and he led them to victory even as he laid down his life.

Knowing him as we did, we know that with him death itself is a victory. We knew his glorious faith in God, his unfaltering confidence in the eternity of life ; that sure and certain hope that makes death for the true Scout a call to higher service. For such a one we could not sorrow as those without hope. When we gathered our boys together it was to praise God for the glorious life of their leader who had gone before. We sang that song of triumph :

> " For all Thy saints who from their labours rest,
> Who Thee by Faith before the world confessed,
> Thy Name, Lord Jesus, be for ever blest,
>   Alleluia."

To this we may add a few extracts from another account of Roland Philipps written by another

CALLED TO HIGHER SERVICE 233

friend of his—Stanley Ince—extracts which give little personal touches appealing to every Scout.

" He set himself to become one with his boys. He made his home at University House, Victoria Park Square, Bethnal Green. He was up with the paper boys in the mornings, and would start the day with a cold tub and exercises from *Scouting for Boys*. The motor-car, which he at first used, vanished after a week or two. He was asked where it was and replied laconically, 'Chucked it.' If motor 'buses were good enough for his boys they were good enough for him. Riding breeches went the same road. Senior boys who were getting sensitive about the East-enders' comments on their knees found their Commissioner receiving the same attentions with obvious enjoyment.

" ' Yah, crusty knees,' yelled the urchins.

" ' Better than a crusty temper, sonny,' said the Commissioner. ' Would *you* like to come and be a Scout ? '

" He came to regard shorts as a sort of emblem of the free and boyish spirit of Scouting and would have no other wear. He told with boyish glee of the discomfiture of an M.C. at a certain Scout function who was refusing to present him and his friend Anthony Slingsby to royalty ' dressed like that '—when the Chief Scout appeared—*in shorts !*

" The work of organising the district did not prevent Roland Philipps from maintaining close touch with individual Troops and boys. Every free night found him in one or other of the Troop Headquarters teaching a new game, demonstrating a quicker way of tying a knot, or talking to a Patrol about Scout Law. In fact he was never more exuberantly happy than at such times.

" To the boys the Commissioner was a personal friend and a Brother Scout. A new Troop was starting in a slum area and Roland explained to the ragged and unpromising youngsters the rule of the good turn. He showed them how to tie the knot in the handkerchief (very few had handkerchiefs, but he told them anything that would knot would do). Would they try for a month to keep the rule! They were dubious. Would they try if he tied *two* knots and did two good turns? Still they wavered. Would they if he did *four*? It was too much and they yelled approval. So for one month the Hon. Roland Philipps went about with a handkerchief knotted at each corner looking very disreputable. He confessed that four good turns per day took a deal of finding, but no boy kept the promise more faithfully than he did.

" He won the hearts of the boys, because he

CALLED TO HIGHER SERVICE 235

had the heart of a boy. In the summer of 1913 he was visiting a camp to inspect it. As he approached the ground he flung off his bicycle. ' I'm not going in like an inspecting General.' So bikes were put in a ditch and Commissioner and Scoutmaster stalked into camp on hands and knees. The delight of the boys was only exceeded by his own when he was spotted by a sharp-eyed Scout and dragged into camp, a prisoner. He was at once the centre of a jolly group and was heard informing a Tenderfoot, with a limp brim to his hat, that it could be starched with rice pudding and ironed with a hot brick."

The following little stories are recounted by Mr. H. G. Elwes :

" It was a showery evening in July, 1914, that a wire arrived at my Headquarters, ' Spending the night with you,—Roland,' and shortly afterwards as I looked out of the window I saw him running down the street from the station. He was in Scout uniform. Just a shirt and shorts, a hat and scarf, with no coat or luggage. 'My dear chap,' I said when I met him at the door and saw how wet he was, ' where have you been, and what are you up to ? '

" And this is the story he told. ' As Commissioner for East and North-East London, you see, it's my duty to visit any of my Troops that are in camp. So I went to see the Toynbee Hall Troop who are camping with their Scoutmaster, Dr. Lukis, at Little Baddow. Then I had to run four miles to the station to catch a train to Walton-on-the-Naze, where there's another camp. When I got there I found there was only forty-five minutes before the last train left for Colchester. The Scoutmaster said, "Will you give the boys an address?" But I said, "No, let's play a game." So we had a ripping game and then I just ran to the station in time, and here I am.'

"We were going down to Manchester one day to complete arrangements for the Scoutmasters' Conference to be held at Easter, 1914. I got to Euston Station first and secured two seats in the train. It was getting close on the time for the train to start, and I was just wondering if Roland was going to miss it, when in Scout uniform he dashed through the crowd, just in time, and on being cross-examined as to whether he had overslept himself, I extracted the following characteristic excuse for his late arrival:

" 'Well, you see, just as I got to the station a large family arrived on the way to Liverpool. A mother, I think, and a lot of children with bundles and bags. They were not the kind of party that provide tips, and the porters seemed busy elsewhere, so, of course, I took charge of the party; but one bundle came undone, and then a small child fell down and cried, and it took some time to get them comfortably into their train.'

" We were travelling on the top of a 'bus from Bethnal Green to Liverpool Street late one night, when suddenly he jumped up and waved his hand, and then gave the full salute. ' Hullo,' I said, ' who's that to ? The Commissioner for London, at least, I suppose.' ' Oh, no,' he said, ' I saw a Tenderfoot on the top of that 'bus. I do like to greet a brother Scout.'

" It was in March 1915, that I paid a visit to Aldershot. He had just been promoted Captain, and I found him brimming over with excitement.

" ' What have you done now ' ? I asked.

" ' Dined with the King and Queen,' he said, ' and they were so kind, but that's not the best news.'

" ' Well, what is it ? ' I asked again. And then he told me how he had started a Troop of Scouts in a famous Preparatory School on the previous Saturday, and how he was to examine them in the Tenderfoot Tests in a few days' time. ' I determined,' he said, ' that I would start one more school Troop before I left for the war, and if I am spared to come back on leave I shall try and start another school Troop every time.'

"And so he did.

"'I feel that preparatory schools are my special job in England during the war beyond everything else. It is no use returning to England on leave unless one means to try to be useful, is it?' he wrote some months ago.

"We were in the lift at the Cavendish Club. I had come to spend the last Sunday of his last leave with him, before he returned to the Front. The lift boy had been reading the *Gazette* for April. 'And was it really you, sir?' he said to Captain Philipps, pointing to an article, 'How we attacked the German Lines,' and Captain Philipps smiled and said, 'Yes, it really was, and would you like to see what the King gave me this week?' And he took from his pocket the Military Cross. 'Oh, sir,' cried the lift boy, 'I do want to be a Scout.'

"It was 7 a.m. that we stood together on Victoria platform. The train was crowded with officers returning to the Front. We were talking of all the things we hoped to do when the war was over. (We always talked of these when I saw him off.) 'If it is God's Will, I shall come back to the boys,' he said: 'and if it is God's Will, I shall go to work elsewhere. What does it matter? God is so good.'"

CALLED TO HIGHER SERVICE.

To face page 238.

CALLED TO HIGHER SERVICE

THE LATE CAPTAIN JAS. L. LAWRENCE

BY a SCOTTISH FRIEND.

I remember well my first interview with James Lawrence about Boy Scouts. I had asked him to form a Troop of Scouts in connection with a Boys' Club in which he was much interested. To make a long story short, he saw the opportunity of doing great work amongst the boys of Scotland, and he threw himself—heart and soul—into accomplishing this end.

He was a man who never undertook anything without careful consideration of future possibilities. In his opinion, a Scout Troop had to be run on systematic lines, and, after organising his own Troop, he devoted himself unsparingly to helping the Troops in the district.

It was clear to him that, in order to insure the permanency of the Movement, it was necessary to have the various Scout Associations linked up. He began with Midlothian, and it was largely through him that a meeting was convened to place the Troops in that county on an excellent basis. He did not stop there. His outlook was wide, and, together with the assistance of others in Scotland, he undertook the formation of a Scottish Headquarters, which has resulted in continuity of work and the establishment of the Boy Scout Movement in Scotland.

A man of simple tastes, he disliked conventionality or " show." He was fond of outdoor life, and, long before he was a " Boy Scout," he took a practical interest in schemes to enable boys to enjoy the simple life under canvas. He was never happier than when at camp; his manly figure—his sleeves rolled up in workmanlike order —was a picture that one cannot forget. He was never idle; there was always some improvement, wanted, and, with his quiet unobtrusive manner, he carried everyone with him, no matter how difficult the scheme was.

Of an unselfish nature, he was always ready to help any one in trouble, and many a time he backed up someone in difficulty. When on walking tours, or cycling, he always made a point of furthering the work of the Scout Movement. He had great faith in boys, and he certainly got the best out of them. He never " nagged " at them; he said little, but he showed, by example, what he wanted the others to do—and they did it.

In short, he was a man. To him an organised picnic was obnoxious. He liked to get away into the wilds, pick up twigs and light a fire. Then he produced a " billy," and made some tea. He did not carry luxuries on these occasions— just bread and cheese.

He was unselfish to a degree. The last time

CALLED TO HIGHER SERVICE

he was home on leave—as I was saying good-bye to him—I remarked that we might meet in France. His reply showed the unselfishness of the man. " I hope not ; I shouldn't like to see you there." He was willing to give up his own life, and did not want anyone to share his dangers.

MAURICE PARTRIDGE GAMON

(SCOUTMASTER WELLINGTON TROOP.
KILLED IN ACTION, JULY, 1916.)

Maurice Gamon loved children, and was never so happy as when surrounded by young people. For seven years he devoted his energies to Sunday-school work in East London ; but he found—as so many others have done—that the great difficulty was to hold the boys.

When his attention was drawn to Scouting, and he read the handbook, he realised that here was the solution of the problem. But unfortunately those who controlled the Sunday-school with which he was connected were hard to convince. And, as he once said, " he who would introduce any innovation into a Sunday-school requires not only the patience of Job, but the courage and confidence of David as well ! "

It was not until after nearly a year of " quiet but persistent agitation " that he at last received permission to make an "experimental" start. Thus the first meeting of the Wellington Troop was held in a tiny mission room in South-East London in November, 1909.

The boys were most enthusiastic, and the little Troop won many honours, yet, while the Scoutmaster teacher gave up all his leisure-time to secure for his Scouts a taste of open-air life and healthy exercise without which the Sunday-school can but produce a "namby-pamby type of character," his fellow-teachers held aloof, for they thought that behind the scheme of Scouting lurked the Bogey—Militarism.

In spite of constant discouragement the Troop held on for two years. But, when the school authorities refused the Scouts the use of the schoolroom for *the half of one evening* per week, the Wellington Troop were perforce obliged to seek a fresh home. The offer of splendid Headquarters at Christ Church, Westminster Bridge Road, was gratefully accepted; and there, as is well known to most of our readers, the Wellington Troop received every help and encouragement, and is now one of the most successful Troops in the South London district.

* * * * *

At the outbreak of war, Maurice Gamon was in camp with his Troop, but he immediately

CALLED TO HIGHER SERVICE 243

returned to town and went to the H.A.C., where he had served for several years as a gun driver. A few weeks later he received his commission in the Lancashire Fusiliers, and went to Hull. He stayed there for nearly six months, and went to the Front at Christmas, 1914.

The whole-hearted enthusiasm with which he had carried on Scouting with his boys in England stood him in good stead in the far sterner work with the "boys" at the Front. And the very full diary he kept of his doings, and sent home regularly, to be read to his Scouts, shows how finely he put into practice, when the great test came, those principles which he had set forth so delightfully in his little book, *The Spirit of Scouting*.

"This is certainly the greatest game I have ever played," he wrote in a vivid account of life in a Belgian cottage close to the German lines. He adds how a touch of home was added by the photos of his Scouts which stood on the mantelshelf; and how—while sentries kept watch outside, and bullets struck the cottage walls—he imagined himself in his small flat again, with his boys sitting round the fire on a Sunday night.

The Lancashire Fusiliers fought at the second battle of Ypres, where Captain Gamon was badly gassed. He was invalided home; and during his convalescence he occupied his time by getting married and making plans for the future welfare of his Troop. In six weeks, though still suffering from the effects of the gas, he was sent back to Flanders.

His next home-coming was in the same year, when he was slightly wounded; and on his final visit to England, when he had a week's leave, he saw his four-months'-old son for the first time.

He was killed in the Great Advance on July 1st, gallantly leading his men.

Shortly before his death he wrote:

" Out here, where many a Scoutmaster must soon be contemplating the coming days, knowing full well the price that England's victory will entail, no thought brings greater comfort than the certain recollection that if we are laid aside our Troops will carry on. The Scout spirit cannot die. And though some of us may win the Scout sign, ' Gone Home,' on Active Service, the Boy Scouts will keep smiling and push along."

THE PASSING OF OSWALD WILLIAMS

Another very gallant Scout carried his Scouting ideals into a brighter world by laying down his life in France. I speak of Oswald

CALLED TO HIGHER SERVICE 245

Williams. These lines were written in order that his work in Wales might be permanently recorded in the newspaper that he loved above all others—the *Headquarters Gazette*. For two years and more before the war broke out he had been devoting his time to the work of organising the Scouts in the Welsh towns and villages, as well as in Hereford and Gloucester, and in his own native county of Monmouthshire.

In Wales he had every kind of difficulty to contend with—political, sectarian, and geographical. Yet he overcame them all by constantly journeying to all parts of the Principality, and by showing a deep appreciation of work already done and an obstinate faith in the certainty of greater work being carried out in the future. By his unfailing optimism and dogged determination, he managed to stir even the most distant village and the most lethargic town to the inspiration of Scout ideals and the thrill of Scouting practices. There is no man, dead or living, who has done more than he to advance the progress of the Scout Movement in Wales.

If he won his way by tact and sympathy, it is equally true that he carried all before him by his faith in the reality of the Scout Promise, and in the value of Scout training as an educational and moral factor in the life of the nation. He identified Scouting with his Christianity, and his Christianity was that of a very devout and loyal Roman Catholic.

" The finest example and the finest teaching a man can give to his boys are not by talking but by the life he leads." These were the words of Oswald Williams at the Manchester Conference—words to which an added meaning has been given by his own life of service and of sacrifice.

LIEUTENANT STERN

BY E. H. KLOOT (Scoutmaster 7th Stepney Troop).

Second-Lieutenant Leonard Stern, B.A., Cantab., was the elder son of the Rev. J. F. Stern, minister of the East London Synagogue. He was educated at the University College School ; and on leaving school in 1910 proceeded to Cambridge as an exhibitioner in classics at Magdalene College. In 1913 he graduated B.A. with first-class honours in the Classical Tripos of that year, and in the following year he gained second-class honours in the History Tripos. He won his college football colours in 1912, and played in the college team against Magdalene College, Oxford. On leaving Cambridge he joined me as a Scoutmaster, and helped to make the 7th Stepney one of the best Troops in East London.

We were in camp when war was declared, but

CALLED TO HIGHER SERVICE 247

after consultation with the Commissioner, the late Hon. Roland Philipps, and the late Dr. Lukis, we decided not to strike camp until August 9th, by which time arrangements were made to utilise the East London Troops to the best advantage. I shall never forget the energy which Stern and the late Dr. Lukis put into the work of organising the District. I believe on many nights in each week they did not go to bed at all!

Enlisting in the 2/13th (Kensington) Battalion of the London Regiment, with other East London Scouts, Stern was immediately given a non-commissioned rank. It is typical of him that shortly after his enlistment, when a man whom he knew, and who had seen service in South Africa, enlisted in the ranks, he at once resigned his stripes so that this man might be appointed sergeant in his place. Stern speedily rose again to the rank of sergeant, and at the urgent desire of those who knew his worth, he applied for a commission and left for the Front on March 17th.

In notifying his death, Major Stafford wrote: " He met his death leading his men in the true British way. . . . Although he had only been with us a short time, he had already won the esteem of his brother officers, and gave great promise as an officer. He was put in charge of the bombers, and showed great zeal and initiative in his work."

The Scout Movement has lost a valuable and genuine worker in Leonard H. Stern. He followed Dr. Lukis, from Toynbee Hall to an unknown spot in mother earth far too quickly. I myself have lost a spiritual brother. The troops of the District have lost an example of a true Scout, who will not be replaced for many a day. The boys of my own Troop have lost a comrade and teacher who has helped to mould their lives for the better, and through them Leonard Stern's spirit will live for the betterment of humanity in the future.

LIEUTENANT N. V. HOLDEN

(MANCHESTER ASSOCIATION)

"Norman V. Holden, a Lieutenant in the Lancashire Fusiliers, died from wounds received in action whilst fighting with his regiment on the Gallipoli Peninsula."

Such ran the official announcement, but behind the bald statement is hidden the record of a singularly noble life. Although only twenty-five years of age, Lieut. Holden has achieved distinction, and his early death, whilst a loss amongst the host of his friends, becomes a victory for himself.

He was the son of the Rev. W. Holden, St. James' Church, Moston, Manchester, and his early education was received at Monsall. Afterwards he

CALLED TO HIGHER SERVICE

passed to the Manchester Grammar School, thence to St. John's College, Cambridge, where he took his B.A. degree.

The success accruing to the Manchester Association of Boy Scouts is very largely the result of his foresight and administration. He was an autocrat, but also a friend. He did not hesitate to seek advice, as many secretaries in other parts of the country can testify, and he was quick to seize upon any *good* idea. His life was outwardly apparently uneventful, but the sphere of his influence widened from year to year. Scouting was only one of his many interests, and unlike most men who take part in several things at one time, he was successful in all of them. Such men do not need when the end comes to make excuse for having lived.

One who knew him well recently said : "He was faithful in his home ; faithful in his studies ; faithful in his pursuit of ideals."

On two occasions he refused to be made a Scout Commissioner, preferring to work as Secretary where he believed he could do his best work.

LIEUTENANT. ANTHONY E. K. SLINGSBY

(IMPERIAL HEADQUARTERS STAFF)

The death in action on the Western Front on July 14th, 1915, of Lieut. Anthony Slingsby removed one of the most lovable characters it has ever been the writer's good fortune to meet.

It was on going down from Oxford that he began to take an interest in the Scout Movement; and it is no exaggeration to say that no one in the Craven district wielded so much influence for good among the boys. His connection with the Scouts dated from 1908, and his interest never waned. He became a District Scout Commissioner, and later was attached to Headquarters Staff.

The Territorial manœuvres at Marske in July, 1914, were the first he attended as a Territorial officer. They were interrupted by the call for mobilisation. Lieut. Slingsby went out with the 6th Duke of Wellington's Regiment to France, where he earned the reputation of a truly gallant soldier. As Roland Philipps—a dear friend of his—wrote of him, in the *Headquarters Gazette* for August, 1915:

> "To him the tie of human friendship overcame all distinctions of age, sex, or class. In a London Club no one would know more than he about his fellow members, but he would be equally well acquainted with the family affairs of the hall porter or the lift boy. Wherever he went he managed to create a large circle of intimate acquaintances that would include bishops, railway porters,

CALLED TO HIGHER SERVICE 251

'Varsity athletes, chauffeurs, members of Parliament, and charwomen ! He never forgot people he had once met.

" If he had an exceptionally large number of friends it was because he himself was a friend to all, and nobody was ever more of a brother Scout to the boys and men in the Scout Movement. . . . Those of us who loved him and trusted him can feel that his friendship was never a greater or more beautiful thing to us than it is to-day—when for him the last stream has been crossed and the final victory won."

One of his men, associated with him intimately in Scouting and active service, describes Anthony Slingsby as a Scout of the first order—unselfish, noble, steadfast, his untiring energy being devoted to the welfare of his boys. His one idea in joining the Territorials was to interest others in the Scout Movement, and it originated in this fashion :

A certain Brigadier-General, who was interested in the Movement, refused to take an active part therein. Anthony Slingsby thereupon suggested that he would take a commission in the General's brigade if the Brigadier would be Commissioner for a certain district. The sporting offer was accepted in the same sporting spirit.

Anthony Slingsby at this time had six or seven

troops in various localities. They were an efficient lot, and the Commissioner's method of working them in his absence was based on the Patrol Leaders' Court of Honour. This Court tried all offending members, no Scoutmasters or A. S. M.s being present. The success of the Court was demonstrated by the large number of troops which adopted the scheme. Anthony Slingsby became Assistant Organising Secretary for the North of England in 1912. He was also connected with the Child Emigration Society and his influence amongst the boys is testified to by the fact that out of about 250 boys who were sent to the Colonies only one failed to do himself credit.

As a Territorial officer Anthony Slingsby was a true Scout and a born leader of men. A typical incident may be related. On one occasion (in August, 1914) the Colonel called upon the battalion to volunteer *en masse*. The men were taken by surprise, and only 150 responded (though hundreds did so afterwards). Out of the 150, the signallers, of whom Anthony was in command, volunteered in a body, with one exception.

The first night in France saw him sleeping with his section in the open air. A week later the battalion went into action. Lieut. Slingsby distinguished himself by laying connection wires to

CALLED TO HIGHER SERVICE 253

all companies, thus enabling the C.O. to keep in communication with his battalion. Another test of his leadership may be cited. When volunteers were asked for, every man of his section turned out, though only two were needed.

Lieut. Slingsby never failed to visit his section in the trenches. He was always on the alert to alleviate their discomforts. In the battle of Festubert in May, 1915, he moved about patrolling wires utterly regardless of danger. He had so thoroughly organised the communications that not one of the companies was out of touch with Headquarters.

Towards the end of May the battalion trekked to Ypres—a long and rough journey. Not a single man fell out, though many were dead beat. Anthony Slingsby's wonderful influence and example held them together. He himself carried rifle, kit, etc. During his all too brief service in the fighting line he never forgot he was a Scout. He was beloved by his men, and his memory will long remain a fragrant treasure among the "boys," whose welfare was ever in his thoughts.

Colonel Ulick de Burgh, C.B., Commissioner for Rovers, and formerly Deputy Chief Commissioner, contributes the following about Anthony Slingsby :

It is not easy to write about Anthony Slingsby because he was unique. In certain phases of life I probably knew more about him than others of his many friends. I knew him under all sorts of conditions during the last two years of his life at Exeter College, Oxford, at work and at play, in undergraduate circles in their rooms, in the J.C.R.—and later when he left Oxford, during, and up to the time of the close of his army life, he was often in my house.

In all these situations he was unique. His cheerfulness, in spite of the great drawback of his deafness (brought on by high diving), was wonderful; yet I often saw him under conditions of deep depression. He was prepared to befriend and defend anybody in trouble; he was also prepared to fight anybody in authority on a question of principle. In both situations he was absolutely reckless.

He seemed to me to be one of the most popular men I ever knew, but he never courted popularity. Being a sportsman to the core, he often could beat men at their own game, and was not to be trifled with. He would take on anybody, from a Divine to a costermonger, in argument, and hold his own.

He had all the "good things of life" within his reach, and held them in contempt where he

CALLED TO HIGHER SERVICE 255

could, by giving time, influence or money, help a poor lad. I have known him part with things of value very dear to him, to devote the money to the cause of his older Scouts. He was recklessly untidy, yet sternly efficient ; hard to move when he had made up his mind, even when, as he found later, he was wrong. He had strong convictions, and differed with me, at least once, very seriously. It hurt him badly, but I was obliged to maintain my ground. This never interfered with the very deep friendship.

He was one of the most religious men I have ever met—all his reading, life, and conversation with me testified to that ; yet he never " talked religion." He did more, he lived it in all the paths of a self-denying, self-sacrificing love for his fellows. To the day of his death he kept up writing to me from the trenches, in Flanders. In that last letter before he was shot helping a soldier Scout, he wrote, " This is Hell ! yet I have never all my life felt so absolutely at rest, with God and man, as I do now."

With a keen sense of humour he detected and mercilessly chaffed all pomposity and sham. With an undeviating love he helped scores of youngsters to run straight, and plucked many brands from the fire, to put self-respect and higher hopes into their hearts. He believed in the ideals of the Scout training as the illustration of what a Christian gentleman might become, and he gave his life, from Oxford days to that of the fatal trench, to doing good as he found it ready to his hand to do. Though wiry he was not strong in health. I never thought his a " good life " or could picture him as growing elderly—nor do I think he desired it.

This is a feeble sketch, in a few rough lines, of a very young man who honoured me with his friendship ; who was a true Scout ; and who is as likely as any man I have known " to shine as the stars for ever and ever " when all comes to be revealed.

ABBREVIATIONS

Scout.

C.C.	County Commissioner.
A.C.C.	Assistant County Commissioner.
D.C.	District Commissioner.
A.D.C.	Assistant District Commissioner.
D.S.M.	District Scoutmaster.
S.M.	Scoutmaster.
A.S.M.	Assistant Scoutmaster.
Chpln.	Chaplain.
P.L.	Patrol Leader.
K.S.	King's Scout.
Sec.	Secretary.

Military and Naval.

Gen.	General.
Mjr. Gen.	Major General.
Mjr.	Major.
Capt.	Captain.
Lt.	Lieutenant.
2/Lt.	Second Lieutenant.
R.S.M.	Regimental Sergeant Major.
C.S.M.	Company Sergeant Major.
Q.M.S.	Quartermaster Sergeant.
S/Sgt.	Staff Sergeant.
Sgt.	Sergeant.
Cpl.	Corporal.
L/cpl.	Lance Corporal.
Pte.	Private.
Gnr.	Gunner.
Spr.	Sapper.
A.B.	Able Seaman.

VICTORIA CROSS

CATES, GEORGE EDWARD. A.S.M., Wimbledon. 2nd Lt., Rifle Bde.

Whilst engaged in deepening a trench he found a buried bomb. He pressed it back with his foot, but it exploded, killing him.

(See full account on page 41.)

CORNWELL, JOHN TRAVERS. Scout, St. Mary's Mission (Manor Park). Boy 1st Class, H.M.S. *Chester*.

For devotion to duty. He remained standing at his gun though mortally wounded, with ten of the gun's crew lying dead around him.

(See full account on page 128.)

258 THE SCOUTS' BOOK OF HEROES

CRAIG, JOHN MANSON. Scout, 5th Perthshire. 2/Lt., R. Scots Fus.

   On three occasions he behaved in a conspicuously brave manner. He went out under a hail of bullets to bring in the wounded.

   (See full account on page 48.)

CRUICKSHANK, ROBERT EDWARD. Scout, 53rd Nth. London. L.-Cpl., London Scottish.

   He made three attempts to take an important message, but was forced to give up, having been severely wounded.

   (See full account on page 46.)

DEAN, DONALD. Scout, 1st Sittingbourne. Lt., R.W. Kents.

   Most conspicuous bravery, skilful command and devotion to duty during the period September 24–26, 1918.

   (See full account on page 61.)

DIMMER, Scout Worker, Southend. Lt.-Col., R. Berks.

   For gallantry in an attack on November 12, 1914. He kept a machine gun trained on the enemy and continued to fire despite the fact that he was severely wounded.

   (See full account on page 51.)

HAINE, REGINALD. P.L., Petersham. Lt., H.A.C.

   For gallantry in leading an attack, showing a splendid example which inspired his men to continue their efforts.

   (See full account on page 42.)

HALLOWES, ROBERT PRICE. Instr., St. Peter's, Port Talbot. Lt., 4th Middlesex.

   Conspicuous bravery and devotion to duty. He set a magnificent example to his men.

   Also awarded the M.C.

   (See full account on page 63.)

LAIDLAW, DANIEL. A.S.M., 1st Alnwick. Piper, K.O.S.B.

   For gallantry at Loos. He played his comrades into action.

   (See full account on page 36.)

MCKEAN, GEORGE B. S.M., Robertson Pres. Troop, Alberta. Capt., Canadians.

   For conspicuous bravery in an attack.

   (See full account on page 54.)

C.M.G.—D.S.O.

TOYE, ALFRED MAURICE. P.L., 2nd Aldershot. Major, 2nd Middlesex.
> For exceptional bravery at a bridgehead. With his men he stuck to a post, and though repulsed three times succeeded in holding it until reinforcements arrived.
> (See full account on page 44.)

C.M.G.

ANDERSON, REV. F. J. S.M., Shorncliffe. Chpln.
BURN, E. F. MURDOCK. D.C., Sth. Notts. Mjr.-Gen., 1st Mounted Div.
> Also twice Mentioned.

JEFFREYS, H. B. C.C. Mjr.-Gen.

DISTINGUISHED SERVICE ORDER

BETTS, J. D.S.M., 1st Aldershot. Major, A.G.S.
CHILD, SIR S. H. A.C.C. Bgd.-Gen., Ter. Art.
DANE, J. A. 16th Hunts. Major, R.F.A.
> N.E. of Ypres on October 3rd, 1917, he at once went through a barrage and after half-hour's work with the help of three others succeeded in rescuing an officer.

GORDON, W. A. A.C., Thornbury and Dursley. Col., Worcester.
GUINNESS, REV. WYNDHAM, S.M. 2nd Curragh Troop, C.F.
> (See full account on page 64.)

INOSBY, J. E. S.M., 2nd Folkestone. Lt., R.A.F.
LAMONTRE. Sec., 14th Hampstead. 2/Lt., Gren. Gds.
LEONARD, REV. M. P. G. S.M., 15th Manchester. C.F., King's Own Lancaster.
LEWIS, D. A. P.L., 2nd Swansea Valley. Capt., R.W.F.

MEYNELL, F. H. D.C. Major, Ter. Art. Staff Batt.

MOSBY, J. G. A.S.M., 1st Norwich. Lt., R.A.F.
Successfully bringing home machine fifteen miles after being badly wounded and his pilot killed.
(See full account on page 159.)

THOMPSON, H. G. D.C. Major, R.F.A.

TURNER, E. C. A.C., Thornbury and Dursley. Glos. Yeo.

WEBSTER, E. C. Scout, 2nd Heacham. 2/Lt., London.
Successful reconnoitring and gallant leading.

WHITSON, H. P.L., Glasgow. Lt., H.L.I.

WIGGIN, W. H. D.C., Alvechurch. Lt.-Col., Worc. Yeo.

WILLIAMS, Rev. C. L. S.M., Shorncliffe. C.F.

WILSON, F. Inst., 9th Walthamstow. Lt., 7th Essex.
Rescuing two brother officers who were wounded, under heavy shell fire.

WOOD, T. P.L., 1st Hirst. A.B., H.M.S.

MILITARY CROSS

ABBOTT, G. WYMAN. S.M., 8th Hunts. Capt., 7th R. Warwicks.
And Italian Cross.

ANDERSON, C. B. A.S.M., 3rd Bromley. 20th County of London.
With Palms. Also Croix de Guerre with Palms.

ANDREWS, J. O. A.S.M., 135th Manchester. Major, R.A.F.
Also D.S.O. with Bar, and Medal from the King of Montenegro.

ANGUS, G. S.M., 45th Newcastle. Major, Stf. Durham Heavy Bde.

MILITARY CROSS

APPLEYARD, JOHN E. A.S.M, 55th Herne Hill. Lt., R.E.
> At a critical moment taking over and holding a gap in the line till other troops could be brought up.

ATKINS, I. A.S.M., 1st Oakengates. Lt.

AUNNELEY, W. H. P.L., 1st High Barnet. T. 2/Lt., Essex.
> Conspicuous gallantry and devotion to duty during an enemy attack.

BAILEY, ALEC HORSMAN-. S.M., Foxholes. Lt.-Col., R.F.A.

BAILEY, GUY HORSMAN-. S M., Foxholes. Major, R.H.A.

BALL, C. A.S.M., 7th Chelsea. Capt., M.G.C.

BARBER, E. W. A.S.M., 1st Great and Little Cornards. Lt., Suff. Yeo.
> In an attack on a village he brought his guns into action within 300 yards of the enemy. By excellent covering fire he held on without escort and so gave the infantry time to reorganise and attack. He rescued one of his wounded men.

BARLOW-POOLE, REV. G. D. Chpln., 5th Clapham, Holy Trinity. Major.

LORD BARNARD, CHRISTOPHER WILLIAM. S.M., Staindrop. Capt., West. and Cumb. Yeo.

BELL, W. P.L., 1st Bangor. Capt., R.I.R.

BERNE, H. C. P.L. Ld. Beresford's Own Troop. Lt., Leinster and R.A.F.

BLACKMORE, F. P.L., 3rd Ware. Lt., Herts.

BLAIR, REV. D. A.S.M., 3rd East Linton. Capt., Chpln.

BLAIR, E. A.S.M., 1st Glasgow. Lt., A.H.

BOND, G. H. S.M., 2nd Wellington. Lt., York and Lancs.
> Taking charge in advance when senior officers were killed.

BRADBEER, B. J. V. A.S.M., 1st Melton Constable. Capt., 1st Tank Batt.
> Also Mention.

BRASSINGTON, E. Scout, 1st Melford. Lt., M.G.C.
  Holding an advanced position for four days under heavy fire.
BREALY, SAMUEL. A.S.M., 6th Willesden. Lt., M.G.C.
  He obtained valuable information under intense machine gun and shell fire.
BRODIE, C. G. C.C. Major, R.E.
BROMLEY, H. Second, 1st Hinckley. 2/Lt., Lesters.
BROOKS, HENRY J. A.S.M., 2nd Odiham, Odiham Town. Major, Manchester.
  And Italian Croix de Guerre.
BROWN, JOSEPH. S.M., 1st Barrington. Capt., N.F.'s.
  Also M.M. and Bar.
BROWNE, HAROLD ST. JOHN. Hon. Sec., Seriatun, Major, 4th Northants.
BRYAN, F. S. Com., 1st Hindley. Capt., 21st Middlesex.
BRYSON, H. P. P.L., 2nd Armagh. 2/Lt., Tank Corps.
  Also Croix de Guerre.
BUJNONSKI, A. A.S.M., 1st Glasgow. Lt.
BURN, M. Scout, 1st Hexham. Lt., Tank Corps.
  And M.M.
BURROWS, H. R. P.L., Weeton. Capt., 8th Batt. W. Yorks Leeds Rifles, T.F.
  Also Croix de Guerre with Palms and Mentioned.
BUTLER, A. ILLINGWORTH. Blue Coat School, Reading. Capt., R.A
  This officer fought his section in the open, engaging enemy infantry and tanks until they got within fifty yards, scoring direct hit at this distance. He rallied the infantry and only withdrew the last moment, having himself to drive in a gun team when the driver was killed.
  (See full account on page 67.)
CHAD, T. P.L., West Chiltington. Capt., 2nd Royal Sussex.
  And Bar. Also Mentioned.
CHURCHILL, E. F. S.M., Warren. Capt., R.E.

MILITARY CROSS 263

CLARKSON, A. B. S.M., 2nd Keighley. Col., 6th Duke of Wellington West Riding.
Also D.S.O.

CLAY, B. P.L., 1st Hexham. Capt., 6th North. Fus.

CLEVELAND, REV. F. W. Chpln., 1st Porthill. T.C.F., 1/6th N. Staffs.

COE, EDWARD H. S.M., 1st Norwich. Lt., R.E.

COLTAR, E. V. Scout, 1st Kingston.

COMPTON, ROBERT. A.S.M., 9th Epping Forest. Lt., Manchester.

CONCANNON, M. P. A.S.M., 1st and 2nd Golders Green, Capt., R.F.A.

CONSTABLE, GUY SELFTON. S.M., 1st Arundel. Major, 4th Batt. Royal Sussex.

COPESTAKE, V. P.L., 4th Derwent. 2/Lt., Notts and Derby.

COTTRILL, T. A.S.M., 1st Fallowfield. 2/Lt., R.E.

CRAWSHAU, C. H. S.M., 103rd Manchester. Major, K.O.S.B.
Also Bar and D.S.O.

CRISFORD, K. S.M., Upper Norwood. Chpln.

CROSBY, JACK. P.L., 152nd Nth. Ldn. Capt., London Irish.

CULVER, JOE. A.S.M., 1st East Ham. 2/Lt.
Also M.M.

DANMERS, REV. G. C. Dis. Sec., Leiston.
Also Bar.

DAVIDSON, D. P.L., Leeson Park. Capt., R. Innis. Fus.
Also Croix de Guerre.

DAVIS, L. P.L., 4th Walthamstow. Capt.

DAVIS, P. P.L., 2nd St. Pancras. Lt., R.E.
And Bar.

DAWES, R. V. A.S.M., 2nd Bridgnorth. Capt., R.G.A.

DEAN, A. C. S.M., 6th Manchester. Capt., R.F.

DeBRUYKER, H. P.L., St. Stanislas Troop. Sgt.

DE COCDU, EDMUND. P.L., St. Stanislas Troop. Pte.
Also M.M.

DENNING, C. P.L., 4th Dover. Capt., R.A.F.
Brought down two enemy machines. He captured pilot and observer and put out fire which they had made by lighting their machines.

DICKINSON, A. P.L., Hallam. Lt., 62nd Infty. Bde.
And Bar.

DOWDEN, H. J. P.L., 14th Greenwich. 2/Lt., R.F.A.

DUNNETT, W. E. Scout, 1st Croften Park. Capt., R.F.A.
Also M.M.

DUNNET, W. P.L., 5th Brockley. Lt., L.R.B.
Also M.M.

DUNWORTH, P. J. S.M., St. Phillip's, W. Sussex. Capt., Innis. Fus.

EDWARDS, J. A.S.M., 1st Dundee. Major, R.F.A.
With Two Bars. Also D.S.O.

ELLIS, S. P.L., Bideford. Capt., R. Fus.

ELLISON, C. E. M. Scout, Sandroyd Schl. Capt., Grenadier Gds.

FAWCETT, ARTHUR. Instr., 12th Cheltenham. Capt., 9th Glos.

FAWCETT, HERBERT. S.M., 1st Cullercoats. Lt., D.L.I.

FISCHEL, STANLEY. Scout, 1st College (Beccles). 2/Lt., R.G.A.

FISH, FRANK. A.S.M., 66th Nth. London. Lt., R. Fus.

FISHER, A. S.M., 2nd Skipton. Lt., K.R.R.

FITZWILLIAMS, K. L. S.M., Denchworth. Major, R.H.A.

FLETT, G. A.S.M., Grantown. Capt. 6th Seaforth Hdrs.

FONDIE, S. F. S.M., 2nd and 3rd Elgin. Lt.

MILITARY CROSS 265

FORSTER, F. G. O. A.S.M., 1st Alpertors. Major, Army Ordance Corps.

FRASER, L. Scout, 1st Elgin. Capt., Seaforths.
Also D.S.O.

FRY, FREDK. W. Scout, 7th Cheltenham. 2/Lt., Glos.

GELL, E. A. S. S.M., Shorncliffe. Lt.-Col., R. Fus.
Also D.S.O.

GREENHILL, C. A.S.M., 113th Glasgow. T. 2/Lt., Worcesters.
Devotion to duty during a raid upon enemy trenches. Finding his party suddenly attacked by a machine gun he attacked it with bombs, putting it out of action and saving his company from many casualties.

GILES, ERIC. A.S.M., 135th Manchester. Lt., R.F.A.
Extinguishing fires near ammunition dump and reading signals of enemy.

GOLDING, C. Scout, 1st Haberdashers Troop. H.A.C.

GOODBURN, ROBERT. S.M., 89th Liverpool. Major, Yorks and Lancaster.

GRAHAM, D. A. H. P.L., 1st Glasgow. Capt., S.R.

GRANT, D. F. S.M., 1st Reading. Major, R.F.A.

GRANTHAM, D. R. A.S.M., 3rd Dorking. Lt., R.E.

GRIFFITH, M. A.S.M., 10th Bromley. Lt., R.F.A.

HAGNE, F. Second, 2nd Beds. (Original). Capt., 1st Bedford.

HALL, E. L. Second, 1st Bexley Heath. Lt.

HAMILTON, H. C. S.M., 63rd Nth. London. Lt., Lon. Scot.

HANNA, DAVID W. S.M., 7th Fulham. Lt., R. Fus.
For rescuing a corporal of his section lying on No Man's Land, whilst wounded himself.

HARDY, E. P.L., 4th Derwent. 2/Lt., M.G.C.

HAZEL, R. H. S.M., 1st East Grinstead. Lt., R.E.

HELBY, T. E. H. P.L., 2nd Armagh. Major, R.F.A.

HENDERSON, W. G. Scout, 1st Elgin. Lt., Seaforths.

HENDREY, FRANK. P.L., 1st Farnham. 2/Lt.
Also D.C.M.

HICKMAN, JOHN. Scout, St. George's, Southall. Lt., R.G.A.

HILL, W. C. 10th Belfast. Lt., R.I.R.

HILLS, OSWALD M. Scout, 1st Upton. 2/Lt., 10th Cheshires.
Gallantry in an attack.

HILTON, J. C. C.M., 1st St. Mark's, Newtown. Lt.-Com., R.N.D.
Special service. And Bar.

HINTON, W. G. A.S.M., 1st North Somerset. Capt., 1st Devon.

HIRST, L. J. Scout, 4th Bancrofts School. 2/Lt., R.E.

HITTON, J. CURVON. P.L., 1st Wigan. Lt.-Com., R.N.D.
With Bar.

HOGG, W. P.L., 1st Bangor. Lt., R.I.R.

HOLCOMBE, S. A.S.M., 51st Sth. Ldn. Lt., 11th County of London.
Special duty after being gassed in getting a dangerous position. Granted by Gen. Plumer.

HORSCROFT, STEPHEN (JACK). P.L., Wateringbury. 2/Lt., R.A.F.
Kept his mortars in action under a heavy fire until every round was fired, causing the enemy heavy casualties.

HOUGH, P. T. S.M., 1st Goldthorpe. Capt., R.E.
Also Mentioned in Despatches.

HOWARD, A. H. S. Chm., Thornbury and Dursley. Major, Glos. Yeo.

HOY, CAMBEL. Scout, 1st Newbiggen. Lt., R.A.F.

HUCKER, J. R. P.L., 4th Bancrofts School. Capt., 13th E. Surrey.

HULBERT. S.M., Longford. Major, Wilts.

MILITARY CROSS 267

HUTCHINGS, WILLIAM HUGH, B.A. A.S.M., 3rd Westcliff. Chpln., R.A. Chpln.'s Dept.

HUTTON, W. H. A.S.M., Kineton. Capt., R.F.A.

INGRAMS, F. Ex. P.L., 1st Purley and Coulsdon. 2/Lt., 9th East Surrey.

JAMES, D. T. S.M., 1st Stirling. Lt., A.S.C.

JEPSON, DOCTOR W. B. A.S.M., St. John's Deptford. Capt., R.A.M.C.
Attending and removing wounded under severe fire.

JEROME. Second, St. Stephen's, Hounslow. Lt., R. Fus.

JOHNSON, FRANK. A.S.M., St. Mary, Islington. Lt.-R.F.A.

JOHNSON, W. H. A.S.M., 123rd Manchester. R. Warwicks.

JOHNSTONE, J. I. P.L., 1st Hatcham. Capt., K.O.S.B.

JONES, D. S. H. A.S.M., 1st Manc. Gram. Schl. Capt.

JONES, F. E. S.M., 61st and 62nd N. Lon. Lt., 1/4th Ox. and Bucks.

JONES, F. M. HARVEY. A.S.M., St. Peter's, Bexhill. 2/Lt., 3rd Worc.
He showed courage and initiative when in charge of his platoon during an attack, capturing two machine guns. He fearlessly patrolled to the front, securing valuable information concerning an impending counter-attack.

JONES, JAMES CETHIN B.A. A.S.M., 3rd Westcliff. Chpln., R.A. Chplns Dept.

JONES, REV. T. W. A. Chpln., 2nd Kingsley Park.

KEELING, HERBERT. A.S.M., Capt., Hants.

KILLENDER, S. P.L., 33rd Liverpool. 2/Lt., King's Liverpool.

KING, C. NOEL. S.M., 9th Wisbech. A/Capt., R.G.A.

KING, L. A.S.M., 1st Sidcup. Lt.

KNOTT, LOUIS C. S.M., 13th Windsor. Capt. and Adjt., 1/6th Glos.

268 THE SCOUTS' BOOK OF HEROES

LAVARS, VICTOR. P.L., 1st Ryde (Parish Church). Lt., Berkshire.

LAW, R. A. F. G. P.L., 4th Dover (Woolton Court). Lt., Wiltshire.
   Also Bar and Twice Mentioned.

LEGGATT, W. T.L., 9th Greenwich. Capt., R.A.F.

LLOYD, S. S.M., 123rd Manchester. Lt., R.N.D., R.E.
   With Bar.

LOCKHART, L. Scout, 1st Sidcup. 2/Lt.
   Extinguishing burning munition dump. And Bar.

LOCKHART, S. Scout, 27th Liverpool. Lt., 5th King's.

LORD, W. P.L., 9th Greenwich. Capt.
   Also M.M.

LUMMIS, WILLIAM MURRELL. S.M., 2nd Aldershot. Capt., 2nd Suffolk.

LYNCH, J. P. A.S.M., 33rd Liverpool. Lt., R.F.A.

McCALMAN, REV. H. S. S.M., 1st Sittingbourne. Chpln., R.F.A.

McCUDDEN, J. Scout, 1st Sheppey. Capt. R.A.F.

MacINTYRE, A. C. S.M., Bonawe. Major, 1/5th Seaforths.
   Also Croix de Guerre.

MACKIE, W. GORDON. A.S.M., Billingslunt. Lt., Duke of Wellington.
   Gallantry under close machine gun, rushing posts, securing maps and papers from wounded and dead enemy in front of lines, etc. Severely wounded, losing an eye.

MACKINTOSH, I. Scout, Grantown. Capt., 1st Cameron Hdrs.

McLARLAM, J. Second, 1st Heacham. Lt., A. and S Hdrs.

McQUAKER, T. P.L., 1st Glasgow. Capt., H.L.I.

MANLEY, P. Scout, 1st Sheppey. Lt.

MARGETSON, E. A.S.M., 14th Hampstead. 1/Lt., Artist Rifles.

MILITARY CROSS 269

Carrying despatches from end of signalling wire, when some had broken, to battery under heavy shell fire.

MARRYLEES, S. B. A.S.M., 11th Western. Capt., 4th A. and S. Hdrs.

MASON, F. C. S.M., Farnborough. Lt., Duke of Cornwall's Light Infty.

MASON, I. J. P.L., 1st Kingstown. Capt., 4th R. Sussex.

MAYHALL, E. G. A.S.M., 6th Manchester. 2/Lt., Cheshire.

MILLIKEN, J. Scout, 1st Bangor. Lt., R.I.R.

MITCHELL, W. E. P.L., 1st Bangor. Lt.

MOISE, E. VICTOR. A.S.M., Walmer. Capt., R.E.

MOLYNEUX, H. P.L., 1st Reigate. Capt., 3rd Hampshire.

MOOR, J. S.M., 1st Conset Tech. Inst. 2/Lt., Durham Light Infty.

With two N.C.O.'s and two Lewis guns he attacked a strong German post in Bourlon Chateau, enfilading it and so enabling a brigade of our men previously held up to reach their objective.

MORGAN, REV. A. T. S.M., St. Mary, Islington. Chpln., 12th Division.

MOSS, G. L. Instr., 7th Sth. Dublin. Capt, R.A.F.

MOSSCROP, A. A.S.M., 6th Manchester. 2/Lt., K.O.R.L.

MOULT, R. F. P.L., Stapleford and Sandiacre. Lt., Sher. For.

Recommended.

NEALE, M. A.S.M., 1st Bristol. Major, Army Ordnance Corps.

NEAME, GEOFFREY. A.S.M., 5th Faversham. Major, R.F.A.

NICHOLLS, A. L. Scout, Lt., A.S.C.

NIGHTINGALE, H. C. Scout, 1st Chelsea. 2/Lt., London.

OGDEN, GORDON. A.S.M., 18th Croydon, Sanderstead. 2/Lt., R.F.A.

OSMOND, W. P.L., 1st Salisbury. Lt., A.I.F.

PALMER, PERCY. S.M., 1st Mkt. Harborough. 2/Lt., R.A.F.

PARHAM, Rev. A. G. S.M., 2nd Oxford. Chpln., 2nd Sth. Mid. Mtd. Bde.
> Attending to wounded until last ship had left. (Gallipoli.)

PARKHAM, Rev. A. G. S.M., 3rd Bromley. Oxford and Bucks.

PARRY, E. S. L. A.S.M., 4th Harrow. Major, R.F.A.

PATTENSON, A. Scout, 1st Southend-on-Sea. Lt., East Surrey.

PEARSALL, H. G. A.S.M., 5th Batley. Major, Tank Corps.

PEARSON, Rev. L. T. Chpln., 12th Cheltenham. Chpln.

PEDLOW. Scout, 1st Ballymena. Capt., Royal Dublin Fusiliers.

PEPIATT, L. E. A.S.M., 12th Epping Forest. Capt., London.
> And Bar.

PEPPIATT, K. O. A.S.M., 12th Epping Forest. Capt., London.
> And Bar.

PHILLIMORE, Rev. S. H., M.A. Prsdt., 93rd Liverpool Chpln., Grenadier Guards.
> And Bar.

PHILLIPS, G. C. D. A.S.M., 3rd Chiswick. Capt., R.E.

PLATTEN. P.L., 15th Norwich. 2/Lt., Norfolk.
> Led his platoon through heavy shell fire. Though wounded gained his objective and strengthened the position before going to the dressing station.

PLUCKROSE, R. G. Scout, 4th Bancrofts School. Lt., Oxford and Bucks Light Infantry.

PLUMPTRE, Rev. BASIL. Chpln., 20th Sth. Ldn. Capt. 1/22nd London.

MILITARY CROSS 271

POLGLAZE, WILLIAM ARNOLD. A.S.M., Polkerris. A/Mjr., 103rd Brigade, R.F.A.
Also Mentioned.

POOLE, RICHARD. P.L., 3rd Wallasey (Emmanuel). Lt., 12th Cheshire.

POWELL, L. S.M., Artington. Capt., R.F.A.

PRINCE, T. S.P.L., 12th Epping Forest. Capt.
Also Order of Croix of Belgium, and Croix de Guerre and Mons Star.

RAMWELL, JACK. Scout, 1st Wigan. Lt., R.N.D.

RAZZELL, A. M. P.L., The Bostalls, 2nd. 2/Lt., R.W.K.

REDGRAVE, C. R. A.S.M., 57th Nth. London. Major, M.G.C.

REID, REV. C. Chpln., 1st Glasgow.

RHYS, THOMAS. A.S.M., 1st Welwyn. Capt., 5th Cheshire.

RIDDELL, G. B. S.M., 2nd Chester. Capt., North. Fus.

ROBERTS, E. M. A.S.M., 3rd Bethnal Green. Capt., North. Fus.
He went over the top after the attack and explored a German tunnel in No Man's Land.

ROBERTSON, M. R. S.M., Chailey and Newick. Capt., 12th Essex.

ROSS, HADDOW. A.S.M., 14th Falkirk. Major, R.F.A.
When his battery was heavily shelled and all the personnel of the guns except five men were either killed or wounded, he took charge and maintained two and sometimes three of the guns in action until the arrival of reinforcements. In order to do this he acted as layer at one gun and superintended the work of the whole at the same time.

ROYLE, R. H. S.M., St. Silas The Martyr, Manchester. Major, 11th Manchester.

RUMP, FRANK. Hackford House. Canadians.

SACKETT, H. Scout, 1st Ramsgate. R.A.F.

SASSE, GEOFFREY G. A.S.M., 55th Herne Hill. Lt., M.G.C.
And Promotion.

SAUNDERS, H. C. Scout, 1st Reigate. Lt., Queen's R.W.S.

SHEARER. 4th Stirling. Lt., Canadians.

SHEPHERD, C. H. A.S., Sandroyd Schl. Major, M.G.C.

SLADE, E. H. A.S.M., 5th Brockley. Capt., L.R.N.
Also M.M. and 1914 Star.

SMITH, FRANK C. A.S.M., 1st Hammersmith. Capt. and Ajdt., K.R.R.

SMITH, S. A. P.L., 1st Bexley Heath. Capt.

SNOWDEN, H. T. S.M., 4th Malvern Link. Capt., 1/5th Glos.
(See full account on page 72.)

SOUTHERN, NORMAN. A.S.M., 1st Newbiggin. Act. Major, R.F.A.
Also French War Cross.

SOUTHWOOD, STEWART. P.L., 1st Gravesend. Capt., D.L.I.

STEELE, H. A.S.M., 1st Hexham. Capt., North Fus.
And Bar.

STEWARD, A. J. A.S.M., 2nd Bridgnorth. Capt., R.G.A.
Also Bar.

STEWART, W. R. S.M., Stoke-by-Nayland. Lt.-Col., Rifle Bde.
Also D.S.O. and Mention in Despatches.

STOCKDALE, JOHN. A.S.M., Hackington. Lt., D.L.I.
When a number of men were liable to be cut off, he with great initiative led his company in a counter-attack, delaying the enemy sufficiently to allow the front line to withdraw unmolested.

STUART, W. B. Instr., 1st Ballymena. Capt., R.I.R.

STUNNER, C. R. Scout, 7th Croydon. Lt., R.F.A.
When a direct hit was made on a team belonging to another battery and all the drivers were wounded this officer went to their assistance in full view of the enemy and succeeded in releasing the surviving horses, while the wounded drivers were helped to a place of comparative safety.

MILITARY CROSS 273

SUTTON, W. G. Scout. 2/Lt., R.G.A.

SYMES, GEORGE W. P.L., 1st Bridport. Capt., M.G.C.
Capturing a Hun officer and thirty men single-handed in a German trench. And Bar.

TAYLOR, JOHN. A.S.M., 113th Glasgow. 2/Lt., R. Scots.
When our attack was held up by wire he led a bombing attack from a flank with great dash, which enabled the supporting parties to capture 400 yards of trenches and 200 prisoners.

TEBBOTT, A. Scout, 1st Finedon. Pte., Northants.

TELFER, REV. W. S.M., 9th Sth. Ldn. Mjr. C.F., 14th Div., H.Q.

TEN-BROOKE, B. Scout, 2nd Beds. Lt., 6th Dorset.

THOMAS, L. C. Scout, 1st Farnham. Capt., East Surrey.
Also Bar. (See account on page 69.)

THOMPSON, DOUGLAS. P.L, 1st Morpeth. Capt., D.L.I.
Also D.S.O., and Croix de Guerre.

THORNE, JOHN ERNEST. P.L., 7th Hook. Lt., Royal Sussex.

THORPE, ROBERT. A.S.M., 135th Manchester. Lt.. North. Fus.

TINKLER, L. M. S.M., 72nd Liverpool. Capt., Yorkshire.

TURNER, REGINALD. S.M., 2nd Chesterfield. Major, 1st Tank Batt.

UNDERHAY, CYRIL T. Instr., 153rd N. Ldn. Capt., 11th Batt. Ldn.
And Mentioned.

VALLANCEY, F. G. A. P.L., 1st Haberdashers Troop. Capt., 15th Batt. R.Fus.
And Croix de Guerre.

VICKERS, FREDERICK C. A.S.M., 2nd Kingsley Park. Northants.

WAIDE, E. F. P.L., 14th Liverpool. Lt.

S

WALDERSGRAVE, Rev. S. C. S.M., 92nd Liverpool. Chpln.

WALKEY, F. J. Chpln. Lt.-Col.

WALSH, R. P. S.M., 9th Dublin. Lt.-Col., R.E.

WARDROPE, J. Scout, 16th Falkirk. Lt., Seaforths.

WARRAN, ERNEST. Scout, Tavistock. Lt., Duke of Cornwall L.I.

WATSON, S. R. P.L., 4th Harrow. Lt., Sher. For.

WINN, J. P.L., 25th Portsmouth. 2/Lt., Hants.

WISELY, G. L. K. S.M., 1st Orpington. Major, R.F.A.

WOOD, S. F. H. Scout, 1st Wigan. 2/Lt., M.G.C.

WRIGHT, S. G. P.L., 2nd Sidcup. 2/Lt., R.W.K.

YOUNG, ERIC. Coalville. Capt., Glos.

YOUNG, G. Scout, 1st Burton-on-Trent. 2/Lt., North Staffs.

DISTINGUISHED FLYING CROSS

ALIIBAN, DOUGLAS. Scout, 2nd Chesterfield. Pilot, R.A.F.

Conspicuous bravery in fighting enemy machines and bombing Turkish positions in Palestine General's Forces.

BALLANTYNE, G. A.S.M., 1st Streatham Common. Lt., R.A.F.

Bringing down enemy aircraft. Carrying on when wounded.

DAVIES, D. P.L., 4th Harrow. Capt., R.A.F.

DEW, D. A. P.L., 4th Harrow. Lt., R.A.F.

EDWARDS, C. Scout, 1st St. Albans. Flt. Sub-Lt., R.N.A.S.

In a raid he landed on an aerodrome and swept the hangars with his machine guns before rising.

DISTINGUISHED FLYING CROSS

FROME, NORMAN. P.L., 18th Bristol. Lt., R.A.F.
Bombed bridge in Germany, and on his return journey fought with Richtofen's Circus, bringing two enemy machines down.

HALSTED, T. N. Scout, 1st Reigate. Capt., R.A.F.
Also D.S.C.

HOLLIGAN, P. T. P.L., 1st Withington. Lt., R.A.F.
Low bombing, five Huns destroyed.

HOLLINGHURST, LESLIE NORMAN. A.S.M., 1st Ilford. Capt. and Flt.-Com., R.A.F.

JAMISON, R. A.S.M., 25th Belfast. R.A.F.

LOWE, C. L. Scout, 2nd Bridgnorth. 2/Lt., R.A.F.

McEVAY, C. Scout, 1st Haberdashers. Capt., R.A.F.

MANTH, ANTHONY J. P.L., 17th Epping Forest. 2/Lt. Sea Patrol Ægean.
Led his flight for two and a half hours in a successful raid on Constantinople. Formation attacked by hostile scouts, but by clever airmanship he destroyed two enemy machines without incurring loss to his flight.

TUTTE, ALEC.˙ Scout, 19th St. Marks. Obsvr., R.A.F.
Pilot fainted and observer climbed to his seat and restored consciousness. Before reaching ground pilot again fainted and was again restored sufficiently to land without damage. (See full account on page 167.)

WALLS, W. Y. S.M., Bridge of Allan. Capt., R.A.F.
Brilliant observation work.

WARNER, J. W. A.S.M., 10th Harrogate. Lt., R.A.F.
Officially credited with destroying eight enemy machines and shooting three down out of control. See full account on page 171.

DISTINGUISHED FLYING MEDAL

DEELEY, CYRIL RUPERT. R.N.A.S. Scout, Birmingham Association.
(See full account on page 174.)

FLETCHER, RONALD M. Scout, 9th Beds.   2/Lt. R.A.F.
  Bringing down seven Hun planes.
MIDDLETON, W. J. A.S.M., 2nd Epping Forest.   Sgt. Obsvr., R.A.F.
  Good bombing and carrying on duty under exceptional circumstances.
  (See full account on page 163.)

AIR MEDAL

CRISP, HARRY. A.C.M., 2nd Tewkesbury.   3rd Air Mch., R.A.F.

DISTINGUISHED CONDUCT MEDAL

ALLEN, T. A.S.M., 1st Hirst.   Cpl., R.E.
  Also M.M.
ALLSOP, WILLIE. Scout, 8th Worksop.   Pte., Sher. Forest.
ARTHUR, RICHARD. P.L., 1st Glynneath.   A/C.S.M., 4th S.W.B.
  Also M.M. and Mention in Despatches.
ATKINSON, ALBERT J. P.L., 1st Hebburn.   Bdr., A78, B.R.F.A.
BAGGS, R. H. A.S.M., 1st Kensington.   Sgt., R.A.M.C.
BALSOM, CYRIL. S.P.L., 1st St. Thomas.   L.-Cpl., R.A.M.C.
BEECH, NORMAN. Scout, 1st Harrogate.   2/Lt., W. Yorkshire.
BEEDIE, G. P.L., Bervie.   Cpl., 2nd M.S.F.
BENTLEY, A. E. P.L., Cheshunt and Waltham Cross.   2/Lt., Beds.
  (See full account on page 112.)

DISTINGUISHED CONDUCT MEDAL

BLAIR. 1st Glasgow. Pte., R.H.
   Also Croix de Guerre.
BOYCE, G. P.L., 7th Sth. Dublin. Sgt., Sth. Irish Horse.
BRACEWELL, FRED. Scout, Barnoldswick. Pte., Duke of Wellington.
BREWER. Scout, St. George's, Southall. Pte.
BRIDGES, E. Scout, 5th Epping Forest. Cpl., 2nd Essex.
BROOKES, F. G. Second, 1st Thornbury. Sgt., 7th Batt. London.
   Taking a German stronghold and beating off two German attacks after all officers were killed or wounded. Carrying messages through heavy machine gun and shell fire. Also M.M.
BROWN, JAS. Scout, 1st Stirling. Pte., S.A.I.
BROWN. P.L., 4th Sidcup. Pte., Buffs.
BULL, HERBERT C. Scout, The Bostalls 2nd. Pte., R. Fus.
   (See full account on page 116.)
BUNCLARK, A. V. Scout, 13th Peek Frean's Own. Sgt., 22nd Con. of Lon.
   And Bar to French Decoration.
BURLONG, PERCY. Second, 1st Braintree. Cpl., 9th Essex.
   Also M.M.
CALVERT, GEO. Scout, 1st Cullingworth. Sgt., Duke of Wellington W. Rid.
   Also M.M.
CHILD, F. J. Scout, Pulborough. Cpl., T. M. B.
CHILDS, J. W. Scout, 1st Todmorden. Pte., Lancs. Fus.
   Also mentioned.
CHIVIES, JACK. Scout, 19th Soton. Newton Abbey. Pte., Middlesex.
CLAMMER, R. C. Scout, 1st Stepney (Toynbee). Sgt., 1/4th London.
   Also M.M.

CLAMP, J. Scout, Coalville.   Cpl., K.R.R.
   Also M.M.
COLE, L. V. P.L.   Sgt., R.E.
COLLIER, W. O. Scout, 1st Haberdashers Troop.
COOPER, H. P.L., Hallam.   R.F.A.
CRAINER, L. A.S.M.,   Pte., Engineers.
   Also Extra Bar.
CROOKES, JAMES. P.L., 1st Bolton.   Cpl., W.R.D.R.E.
   Also M.M. and Bar.
CRUTCHLEY, W. Second.   Spr., R.E.
DAVIES, ARTHUR. P.L., Moorside I.M.   Pte., Manchester.
DENTON, A. H. Scout, 14th Derby.   5th Notts and Derby.
DENTON, P. Second, 1st Cowes.   Gnr., R.F.A.
DIPPER, C. P.L., 1st Daventry.   C.S.M., 8th North Fus.
DOLEMAN, F. P.L., 10th and 11th Oldham.   Sgt., Manchester.
   And Bar.
GARRET, HARRY. Instr., Barnoldswick.   Sgt., Duke of Wellington.
GLEDHILL, HAROLD. Scout, 1st Altofts.   C.S.M., 1/4th K.O.Y.L.I.
GRAUBNER, H. Scout, 19th Oxford.   Sgt., 5th Ox. and Bucks L.I.
GRIFFITHS, K. P.L., 2nd Newport.   Bdr., R.F.A.
   Also Croix de Guerre.
HALL, NEVILLE. Scout, 1st Kings Norton.   Pte., R.E.
HARDING, W. P.L., 1st Goldthorpe.   Pte., Worcester.
   Also Croix de Guerre.
HARTSHORN, E. P. A.S.M., 6th Manchester.   Lt., 8th Gurkha Rfls.

DISTINGUISHED CONDUCT MEDAL 279

HENNESEY, MAURICE. Scout, 1st Anglesey. Sgt., R.W.F.

HILDRETH, ALFRED GENNIS. A.S.M., 1st Holmewood. C.S.M., Sher. Forest.
> When in command of raiding party successfully entering enemy trenches and inflicting numerous casualties and skilfully drawing in his wounded.

HINKS, JACK. P.L., 3rd Faversham. Pte., Canadians.

HOBBS, FREDERICK. Scout, 19th Soton, Newton Abbey. Sgt., R. Artillery.

HOMERSHAW, F. Scout, 1st Elgin. Sgt., I.F.
> Captured farm and Pill Box. Swam canal for reinforcements. Also M.M. and Bar.

HOOPER, F. K.S., 1st Dewsbury. 2/Lt., K.O.Y.L.I. (Signallers).

HUXLEY. S.M., 1st Barrow. Sgt., R.E.

JAMES, T. E. A.S.M., Sproughton. Pte., R.F.A.
> Also M.S.M. and M.M.

JONES, VICTOR. S.M., 8th Gloucester. Sgt., 5th Glos.

KEEN, W. J. A.S.M., 5th Epping Forest. Pte., 1/7th Essex.

KEMP, PERCY. Scout, 1st Ludgershall. Pte., Devons.

KING, E. W. A.S.M., 1st Salisbury. Sgt., R.E.

LAURENCE, CHARLES. A.S.M., 1st Alpeton. Cpl., R. Irish Fus.

LIGHTFOOT, JOHN. Scout, Tunstall. Pte., I.M. Nth. Staffs.
> Also M.M.

LOMAX, F. P.L., 10th and 11th Oldham. Cpl., R.A.M.C.

LOWE, NORMAN. P.L., 3rd Longton. Sgt., 12th R. Fus.
> Also mentioned.

McCARTHER, J. P.L., 99th Bannatyne's Own. Cpl., 7th H.L.I.
> Also M.M.

THE SCOUTS' BOOK OF HEROES

MARCHANT, J. Scout, 2nd Sidcup. Pte., R. Fus.

MARTIN, WILLIAM. Scout, Levknor. Sig., Cheshire.

MASSEY, ROBERT. Scout. L.-Cpl., M.G.C.

When supply of bombs had run out he mounted his gun on a parapet under heavy fire and engaged the enemy at thirty yards distant until the gun was put out of order, but not until a fresh supply of bombs arrived. Also R.S.S.M.

(See full account on page 110.)

MATCHETT, F. Scout, 27th Liverpool. Sgt., Innis. Fus.

MATHER, T. F. P.L., 5th Manchester. Sgt., 1/7th Batt. Manchester.

MURRAY, ERNEST FRANCIS HUME. Instr. Capt., H.A.C.

And Commission.

NEWPORT, HARVEY. A.S.M., 115th Manchester. Cpl., 16th R.W. Fus.

NEWTON, J. Second, Grasmore Works. Pte., Sher. Forest.

NILSON, A. E. A.S.M., 1st Llanidloes. Lt., 1/7th R.W. Fus.

Also Cross of St. George.

PAYNTER. St. Stephen's, Hounslow. F.. R.Q.M., R.A.

PEEK, F. P.L., 1st Aldeburgh. Sgt., R.G.A.

PIGGOTT, NEVILLE. Scout, Leiston.

Also Serbian Cross.

PIKE, P. K.S., Virginia Water. Cpl.

POEPER, PERCY. T. Foot., Mayfield and Clifton. Pte., Sher. Forest.

POPPLEWELL, E. Scout, Nth. Fryston and Sth. Milford. Pte., R.M.A.

Also Belgian Croix de Guerre.

PRENTICE, EDWIN. Scout, 1st Kingsley Park.

PULLAR, W. Scout, 1st Forres. 2/Lt., Seaforth Hghrs.

RAMAGE, L. Scout, 3rd East Linton. L.-Cpl., R. Scots.

RANSOM, J. L. P.L., 2nd Bridgnorth. Pte., London R.

DISTINGUISHED CONDUCT MEDAL 281

RAYNOR, J. W. S.M., 1st Hollinwood. Sgt., Gor. Highlanders.
REED, FRED. P.L., 1st Bedlington. Sig., H.M.S. *Jupiter* 2.
REID, W. M. Scout, Fauldhouse. L.-Cpl., 7/8th O.S.B.
RICHARDS, F. Scout, 1st Croften Park. R.F.C.
RIDGWAY, J. P.L., 1st Chislehurst. Sgt., W. Kents.
RIGBY, W. A. S.M., 27th Northern. 2/Lt., 5th Scot. Rfls.
ROSMOND, J. Scout, 15th N. Devon. Cpl., Berks.
RUFFELL, ARTHUR E. P.L., Maldon. Sgt., A.S.C. (Camel Corps) from 1/5th Essex.
> Repeated journeys under heavy shell fire and machine gun fire to establish communication and bring in wounded. Palestine.

RYDER, J. L. Cpl., 3rd Tunstall. Gnr., R.F.A.
Also M.M.
SAUNDERS, GEORGE. P.L., 15th Bristol St. Martin's. Pte., 4th Glos.
SAVAGE, JACK. S.M., 10th and 11th Oldham.
SELL, LEONARD. A.S.M., 3rd Ware. Cpl., R.A.S.C.
Also M.M.
SHARP, LEO. A.S.M. Sgt., R.E.
SHEPPARD, F. W. A.S.M., Lady Jersey's Own Troop. C.S.M. Queen's Westminsters.
Also two Bars.
SLOAN, ROBERT. P.L., Bramber and Beeding. Pte., R. Sussex.
SMITH, R. Scout, 1st Southend-on-Sea. Trpr., C. of Lon. I. Yeo.
SMITH, R. WRAY. Hon. S.M., 1st Pelan. Sgt., R.A.M.C.
> Devotion to duty whilst voluntarily acting as guide to party of Infantry which had been wrongly directed. Attending to and evacuating wounded under heavy bombardment. Evacuating wounded and Aid Post complete after being left as a volunteer in charge when unit retired during the March retreat of our Forces. Also Military Medal and Bar to Military Medal.

SMITH, SIDNEY ALLEN. A.S.M., 7th Hernhill. Sgt., R.A.M.C.
   And Russian Order of St. George.
SPENCER, C. Scout, 3rd Royal Eltham. Sgt., R. Fus.
STANLEY, T. B. S.M., Stocksbridge. Trpr., Aust. L.H.
STEWART, J. Scout, 1st Lossiemouth. Sgt., 6th Seaforth Highlanders.
STONE, F. Scout, Duke of Somerset's Own Troop. Sgt., 4th Hants L.I.
THORNTON. Scout, St. Stephen's, Hounslow. Pte.
THURGOOD, VICTOR. Second, 8th St. Pancras. Pte., 3rd London R.F.
TREGALE, LEONARD. Second, Pte., 7th Devon.
TURNLEY, W. E. A.S.M., 8th Liverpool. Sgt., Aust. Forces.
VINCENT, G. E. P.L., 2nd Hampstead. Pte., Lon. Irish.
WALKER, W. Scout, 106th Manchester. Pte., L.N. Lancs.
WALL, SIDNEY. Barcombe.
WARD, H. PHILLIP. T.L., 5th Ipswich. Sgt., 3rd Batt. Aust. Imp. Forces.
   Also M.M.
WEST, CHARLES F. Scout, 1st Arundel. Sgt., Royal Sussex.
WEST, FRANK. P.L., 66th Manchester. Pte., Lancs. Fus.
WESTBURY, E. A. P.L., Grasmore Works. L.-Cpl. Glos.
WHIPP, H. Scout, 13th Peek Frean's Own. Pte., R.W. Surrey.
WHITING, J. A.S.M., 6th Swansea Valley. Sgt., Wiltshire.
WHITTINGTON, BOB. Effingham. Sgt., 3rd Worcesters.
   Also twice mentioned.

MILITARY MEDAL

WILBOUR, ALBERT. Second, 1st Hinckley. Sgt., Lesters.

WILBY, FRED. Scout, 4th Chatham. Pte.

WILCOX, R. P. S.M., 10th and 11th Oldham. N.C.O., W. Riding.
  Also M.M. and Bar.

WILLIAMS, J. Scout, 13th Peek Frean's Own Troop. Sgt., Scot. Rfls.

WILSON, ALEXANDER. S.M., 29th Newcastle. Sgt., R.E.

WOOLEY, THOMAS. Scout, 27th Oldham. Pte., 16th Service Batt.

WORSFOLD, HAROLD. Scout, 1st Ludgershall. Pte., Devons.

DISTINGUISHED SERVICE CROSS

STRINGER, ERIC. P.L., 1st Kingston. Lt., R.A.F.

MILITARY MEDAL

ADAM, A. P.L., 2nd Cork. Pte., R.A.S.C.

ADDERLEY, PERCY. Instr., 1st Porthill. Sgt., Gren. Gds.

ADLAM, A. C. P.L., Duke of Somerset's Own. Sgt., Scots Gds.

ADSON, FREDERICK. P.L., 15th Hunts. Cpl., 5th Northants.
  And one Bar.

ALLAN, A. P.L., 1st Chertsey. Cpl., Essex.

ALLEN, F. J. P.L., 16th Newbury. Cpl., R. Berks.

ALLEN, STANLEY. Scout, 1st Penwortham. Sgt., Lancs. Fus.

284 THE SCOUTS' BOOK OF HEROES

ANDERSON, F. Scout, St. Edmunds. 2nd Northants.

ANDERSON, W. Scout, 109th Eastern Dis. Pte., 1/7th H.L.I.

ANSELL, C. P.L., Cheshunt and Waltham Cross. Pte.

ANSELL, H. A.S.M., 1st Brighton. Rifle Bde.

ARCHER, LEONARD. P.L., 5th Clapham. Sgt., Scots Gds.

ARCHER, E. Scout, Brackley. Sgt., Northants.
  Also Croix de Guerre. Carrying despatches to French Army during the great retreat.

ARNOLD, HUBERT. S. Scout, 3rd Sheppey. Sgt., R.E.
  Blowing up bridge during retreat. Organising " Mono Rail " to front.

ASHBY, C. E. Second, The Onesters. Lt., Beds.
  Also three times Mentioned.

ASPINALL, J. S.M., 1st Leigh. Pte., Border.

AVERILL, EDWARD. Scout, 2nd Tunstall. Spr., R.E.
  Laying a telephone wire and after it was cut bringing back a message by hand.

AYRES, GEORGE. P.L., Barwick and Stanhoe. Cpl., 8th Norfolks.
  Signalling service at the taking of Regina Fort.

ATKINS, ERNEST. A.S.M., 2nd Deal and Walmer. Sgt., R.E.
  And Bar.

BACKHOFF, H. A. W. P.L., 3rd Fulham. Sgt., 12th London (Rangers).

BAGLEY, ALBERT E. P.L., 4th Wallsend. Pte., North. Fus.

BAILEY, GOWON. P.L., 5th Sheppey. Cpl., R.F.A.

BAILEY, L. P.L., 2nd Leyton. Sgt., Aust. Forces.

BAKER, W. L. P.L., 1st Finedon. Pte., R.A.F.

BANITT, GEORGE. P.L., 5th N. London. Gnr., Artillery.

MILITARY MEDAL 285

BANKS, HENRY WALL. Scout, Penrith 2nd. L.-Cpl., 5th Border.

BANNISTER, TOM. P.L., 66th Manchester. Pte., R.A.M.C.

BARHAM, E. F. A.S.M., 33rd West London. Pte., East Surrey.

BARHAM, L. P.L., 4th Walthamstow. Pte.

BARKER, LORD. Instr., 1st Ashton. Cpl., 2/9th Manchester.

BARLOW, A. Scout, 8th Croydon (Christ Church). Sig., 4th Queen's R.W.S.

BARLOW, HARROLD. P.L., 1st Mkt., Harborough. Pte., R.A.M.C.

BARRATT, WILSON. Scout, 1st Spilsby. L.-Cpl., S. Staffords.

Also Mention.

BATCHELOR, WALTER. P.L., Tring, S. Peter and S. Paul. Cpl., M.G.C.

BATES, GEORGE. Scout, Kineton. R.F.A.

BATTLE, LANCE. P.L., 1st Eye. Bdr., R.F.A.

BEAUMONT, A. E. D. Second, 9th Epping Forest. R.F.A.

BEAUMONT, FRANCIS. S.M., 156th N. London. Leading Aircraftsman, R.A.F.

Remaining in the air for forty-eight hours, dropping 279 bombs over Mannheim and district and bravery on all occasions.

BECKETT, E. E. S.M., Foleshill. 2/Cpl., R.E.

BECKETT, W. M. P.L., 1st Formby. Pte., King's (Liverpool).

BELL, JOHN. A.S.M., 1st Bedlington. 2/Lt., North. Fus.

BELSHAM, W. G. P.L., 1st Walsall. Pte., 9th Batt. Essex.

Capturing machine gun and four Germans and gaining important information.

BEYNON, FRED. P.L., 19th St. Mark's. Cpl., Warwicks.

BIGLEY, PERCY. Scout, Irthlingborough. Pte.

BIGLEY, REGINALD. P.L., 4th Rochdale. Cpl., R.W. Fus.

BINGHAM, O. P.L., 1st East Grinstead. Lt., Canadian Infty.

BINSTEAD, HAROLD G. Scout, 1st South Mimms. Pte., 1st Essex.

BLANCHFLOWER, VICTOR. Scout, 1st Swaffham. Cpl., 21st London Rfls.
Volunteered to carry despatches, five who went before having been killed.

BODDY, V. P.L., 20th West London. 51st London Division.

BOND, WILFRED. P.L., Hambleden. Pte., Ox. and Bucks.

BOOKER. P.L., 1st Orpington. Cpl., Scot. Rifles.

BOOTHBY, ALBERT. Scout.

BOYD, BRIAN. P.L., 10th Belfast. 2/Lt., V.C.V.

BRACE, HARRY. Band Instr., 12th Cheltenham. Pte., R.E.

BRADSHAW, CLAUDE. Scout, Coalville. Sgt.

BREED, STEPHEN. Scout, 1st Foots Cray. L.-Cpl., R.W.K.

BREEZE, J. W. P.L., Tunstall. L.-Cpl., R.E.

BRENNAND, H. N. P.L., St. Peter's, Blackburn. Gnr., R.F.A.

BRETT, E. A.S.M., 2nd Chelsea (St. Luke's). Cpl., East Surrey.

BRETT, HARRY. P.L., Mortheam. Cpl., 1st Lincolns.

BRIERLEY, C. Scout, 127th Manchester. L.-Cpl., 6th Manchester.

BROOKES, J. A.S.M., 1st Hairfoot. Cpl., West Yorks.

MILITARY MEDAL 287

BROOKS, J. S.M., 183rd Manchester. Cpl., R.G.A.
After having been buried and stripped of clothing by an explosion he volunteered to fire remaining ammunition if he could get another gun, as position was serious owing to enemy advancing; this was done and he was successful.

BROSTER, HAROLD. Scout, 1st Upton. Pte., R.A M.C.

BROWN, C. R. A.S.M., 10th Poplar. L.-Cpl., R.W.K.

BROWN, HAROLD. Amb. Instr., 110th Liverpool. Sgt., R.A.M.C.
Administering anæsthetic under shell fire in front line trenches.

BROWNHILL, A. S.M., Croft Hall, 1st Sheffield. 2/Lt., R.F.C.

BROWNHILL, A. E. Scout, Hallam. Lt., R.A.M.C. and R.F.A.
And Bar.

BULLEN, E. G. P.L., 1st Guildford. Cadet, 12th Hants.

BURNELL, C. Scout, 1st Caterham. Pte.

BUTLER, ALBERT. P.L., 6th East London. Pte., Cold. Gds.

CALDICOTT, WILLIAM. Scout, 1st Kings Norton. Pte., R. Warwicks.

CALLEY, E. Scout, 4th St. Albans. Pte., 2nd R. Sussex.
For being one of the first to cross Sambre Canal and helping to flare the first bridge. For getting a disused Lewis gun into action on the retreating enemy and taking messages under fire.

CAMP, FREDERICK. P.L., 13th Holborn. Rfln., K.R.R.

CAPON, W. Turner's Hill. Pte., 7th London.

CARTER, THOMAS. P.L., 1st Preston (Y.M.C.A.) Pte., Lanc. Fus.

CASE, WM. P.L., 1st Hindley. Pte., K.O.R.I.

CASTLE, R. Second, 3rd Ware. Cpl., Herts.

CATCHPOLE, C. Scout, 1st College (Beccles Town). 2/Lt., 7th Suffolk.

CAVELL, CLIFFORD. A.S.M., St. Mary, Islington. Sgt., Hampshire.

THE SCOUTS' BOOK OF HEROES

CHAMBERLAIN, HARRY. Scout. Pte., 18th Hussars).

CHANTRELL, BERNARD. Scout, Irthlingborough. Pte., 6th Northants.

CHELL, ALBERT. Scout, Mayfield and Clifton. Sgt., Sher. For.

CHESHER, WILLIAM. Scout, 1st South Mimms. Dvr., R.F.A.
Attending to three of his mates and dressing their wounds under heavy fire, then getting them under cover.

CHILDS, RAYMOND. P.L., Amport Monxton. Cpl., 1st Herts.

CHRISTMAS, H. C. Scout, 1st Richmond. Pte., 7th City of London.
For saving wounded officers and men under heavy shell, machine gun and rifle fire.

CLARK, JOHN EDWARD. S.M., St. Mary's, Kettering. Pte., R. Fus.

CLARKE, A. P.L., 2nd Epping Forest. Pte., Lon. Rifle Bde.

CLARKE, A. C. B. A.S.M., 1st Frodsham. Sgt., 9th Cheshire.

CLARKSON, J. Scout, 1st Colne (Mayor's Own). Pte., M.G.C.

CLEAL, SAMUEL. P.L., 1st Tolworth. C.Q.M.S., 6th R. Berks.

COAN, THOMAS. S.M., 121st Manchester. Q.M.S., 1/3rd E. Lancs., Fld. Amb.

COCKER, J. A.S.M., 4th South London, St. Katharine's. Sgt., K.R.R.

COLLINS, A. A.S.M., Lady Jersey's Own Troop. Sgt., 8th Royal Fusiliers.

COLLINS, L. C. P.L., 1st Hatcham. L.-Cpl., L.R.B.

COLLIS, ROY NEVILLE. P.L., 13th Windsor. Sgt., R.E.

COODALL, A. Scout, 9th Epping Forest. Pte., Lon. Rifle Bde.

MILITARY MEDAL 289

COOK, A. P.L., 2nd St. Pancras. Capt., R.F.A.

COOK, ALFRED. Scout, 3rd Chatham. Cpl., M.G.C.

COOK, E. P.L., 1st South London. Gnr., R.G.A.

COOK, G. A.S.M., 12th Woolstan. C.S.M.

COOKE, F. Scout, 1st East Grinstead. L.-Cpl., R.E.

COOPER, GEORGE. Scout, 24th Children's Home. Pte.

COOPER, GEORGE M. M. Second, 55th Herne Hill. Pte., Q.R.W. Surreys.
> Awarded posthumously for deflecting a bomb thrown at his officer. He died of the wounds sustained.

CONELLY, GEORGE. Second, 72nd Sth. Ldn. L.-Cpl., 1/24th Queen's.
> And Bar.

CONNOR, NORMAN. Scout, Garelockhead. Sgt., H.L.I.
> With Bar.

COPP, REGINALD J. Scout, Nos. 1 and 2, Barnstaple. 2/Lt., M.G.C.

CORBETT, HAROLD. A.S.M., 20th Barnsley. Sgt. 2/4th York and Lancs.
> Stretcher-bearer. Collecting wounded and saving life under very heavy shell and rifle fire. And Bar.

CORNELL, CHARLES. 1st Goodmayes.

CORNELL, R. Scout, 9th Guildford. Cpl., R.N.D.
> Throwing live bomb out of trench. Rescuing wounded under heavy shell fire. Also Croix de Guerre.

COWANS, W. Instr., 45th Newcastle. Sgt., R.A.M.C.
> Also Bar.

COWELL, HERBERT. Scout, Accrington Borough. Pte.

COWEN, W. P.L., 2nd Whitehaven. Cpl., Border.

COWIE, DONALD. P.L., 1st Upton. Cpl., 1/10th Scot. King's Liverpool.

COTTON, W. ARTHUR. P.L., St. Edmund's. L.-Cpl., R.A.M.C.

COX, GEORGE. A.S.M., 18th Camelon. L.-Cpl., 7th A. and S. Hgrs.

T

COX, PHILLIP. P.L., 1st Dartford. Pte., R.A.M.C.

CRAGG, RICHARD. Scout, 5th Ipswich. Pte., 1st Suffolk.

CRAMP, GEORGE. Scout, 1st Battle. Sgt., R.F.A.

CREASE, EDWARD H. P.L., 18th Bristol. Pte., Lord Strathcona's Horse.

CROWE, G. P.L., 2nd Epping Forest. Sgt., R.F.A.

CROWTHER, A. W. Scout, Shorncliffe. Gnr., R.A.M.C.

CUNNINGHAM, P. P.L., 1st Stonehaven. Sgt., Tank Corps.
> Rescuing crew of supply tank which had been set on fire. Rescuing tanks under aerial bombardment. Also Diploma.

DALE, RICHARD. Scout, Camelford. Pte., Worcester.

DANDO, WILFRED. A.C.M., 62nd Bristol. Sgt., 6th Glos.

DAVENPORT, N. S. Scout, 7th Brunswick. Pte.

DAVIES, J. S. A.S.M., 1st Baglan. Pte., 1/5th Glos.
> With a corporal he got across the Sambre at Oise Canal under fire, towing a Lewis gun on a raft and saved a bridge. The Germans had blown up two bridges across the canal already.

DAVIES, T. V. Scout, 4th Bancrofts Schl. L.-Cpl., 3rd Essex.

DAVIES, J. P.L., 1st Pendlebury. Pte., R.F.A.

DAVIS, F. W. A.S.M., The Onesters. Pte., 2nd R. Dublin Fus.
> Also Mention and winner of the Guinchy Diamond.

DAY, JOE. P.L., 1st Newmarket.

DAY, STANLEY S. P.L., 2nd Kingsley Park. R.A.M.C.

DENNIS, JACK. Scout, 5th Clapham, Holy Trinity. Pte., R.A.M.C.

DENYER, P. P.L., 1st Cambridge. Sgt., 1/1st Bn. Cambridge.

DICKSON, H. A.S.M., 13th Peek Frean's Own Troop. Sgt., 12th East Surrey.

MILITARY MEDAL 291

DOBB, ARTHUR. P.L., 3rd Southport. Bdr., R.F.A.

DOBSON, HERBERT. P.L., 4th .Lancaster. Sgt., 5th Batt. K.O.R.L.

DOODY, FRED. Second, 1st Holmewood. L.-Cpl., Sher. For.
Also Bar.

DORGAN, J. S.M., 1st Hirst. Sgt., North. Fus.

DOWNING, ALEX. Second, 10th Harrogate. 2/Lt., 7th Leicesters.

DOWNING, FREDERICK. P.L., 27th Derby. Pte., R.A.S.C.

DREW, EDWARD. S.M., Whenountt. Cpl., R.E.

DRONFIELD, H. Second, 1st Staveley Town, Now—Courts Own, Staveley. Pte., Scot. Rifles.
Taking charge of convoy at a critical moment and getting ammunition up into the front line at Ypres.

DUCK, R. L. P.L., 4th Bancrofts Schl. Pte., Lon. Scot,
See full account on page 99.

DUNCAN, D. S.M., 29th Grahams Road. Sgt.-Mjr., 2nd A. and S. Hdrs.
Also Mentioned.

EARLE, JAMES. Sec. Com., 2nd Warrington. Sgt., 2nd Rifle Bde.

EDGE, THOMAS. A.S.M., 2nd Tunstall. R.F.A.

ELLENY, REGINALD. Scout, 1st Lyndhurst. Gnr., R.F.A.
Carrying on communication as runner, during retreat from Kemmel.

ELLIOT, FREDK. Scout, 8th Beckenham. Sgt.

ELLIS, CLIFFORD. T.L., 1st Faversham. 2/Lt., Indian Cav.

ELLSON, W. A.S.M., 1st Finedon. Pte., R.N.V.R.

EMMETT, R. P.L. L.-Cpl., Duke of Wellington's.

ENO, HENRY. P.L., Williton. Pte., S.L.I.

ESPUI, JACK. 1st Banoratham. Pte.

ETHERIDGE, LEWIS. A.S.M., 5th N. London. Sgt., R.G.A.

ETHERINGTON, SYDNEY. Scout, Petersham. L.-Cpl., E. Surrey.

EVANS, N. S. S.M., 1st Normanton. L.-Cpl., R.A.M.C.

EVERED, P. H. A.S.M., 28th West London. Sgt., 2nd R.F.T.F.

FARNWORTH, JAMES. Scout, Barnoldswick. Pte.

FARNWORTH, WILLIAM. Scout, 1st Pendlebury. Pte., Lancs. Fus.

FIELD, S. P.L., Steyning. Pte., R. Surreys.

FIELDING, H. Scout, 10th and 11th Oldham. Pte.

FITCHIE, ERNEST. A.S.M., 1st Preston (Y.M.C.A.). Gnr., R.F.A.

FLETCHER, ERNEST A. P.L., 13th Windsor. Spr., R.E.

FLETCHER, WILLIAM. Scout, 1st Harrogate. Pte., R. Fus.

FOTGAN, JOHN. Scout, 4th Stirling. Pte., A. and S. Hdrs.

FRASER, R. Scout, 1st Forres. Bdr., R.F.A.

FREEMAN, T. Scout, 1st Saxmundham. L.-Cpl., 4th Batt. Suffolks.

FROST, B. Barwick and Stanhoe. Cpl., 8th Norfolks.

FOWLE, VICTOR. P.L., Petersham. Lt.

FULTON, G. W. Scout, 1st Forres. Cpl., Seaforth.

GACON, C. P.L., 1st Bournemouth. Pte.

GARNETT, ARTHUR. P.L., Kineton. Sgt.

GARRETT, WILLIAM. P.L., Sundridge. Pte., Queen's Own.

GEORGE, WILLIAM. Scout, Holy Trinity, Blackburn. Pte., East Lancs.

MILITARY MEDAL 293

GIRDLER, ARTHUR. Scout, 12th Odiham. Sgt., R.W. Surrey.
Held his position for eighty-six hours with eight other men, though isolated from his unit. Himself in charge. And Bar.

GITTINGS, J. Scout, Broseley. K.S.L.I.

GODDARD, FRANK. P.L., 4th N.B. (Hanney). Pte., 51st Batt. Canadian.

GOLDER, M. Instr., 1st Chertsey. Sgt.-Mjr.

GOODWIN, G. W. P.L., 13th Croydon. Sig., 1st Queen's R.W.S.

GOODWIN, J. R. P.L., 1st Stepney (Toynbee). L.-Cpl., 1/13th London.

GOUGH, FRANK. Scout, 3rd St. Albans. Pte., Herts.

GRANGER, CLARENCE. Scout, 1st Sutton-in-Craven. Sgt., 1/6th Duke of Wellington, W. Rid.

GRANT, L. Scout, 1st Forres. Cpl., Canadians.

GRAVER, N. Scout, 2nd Chorlton-c.-Hardy. Pte., R.A.M.C.

GREEN, ERNEST THOMAS. A.S.M., Watlington. Sgt., 17th R. Fus.

GREEN, MARK. Scout, 1st Uttoxeter. Pte., 6th Nth. Staffs.

GREEN, STANLEY. A.S.M., 18th Nth. Poplar. Pioneer, R.E.

GREENGRASS, D. Scout, 1st Chislehurst. Sgt., W. Kents.

GREGORY, C. Scout, 23rd West London. Rfln., 12th London (Rangers).

GUESS. P.L., 1st Leighton Buzzard. 2/Lt.

GUYMER, T. W. P.L., 22nd Norwich. Sig., 2nd Batt. R. Sussex.

HALL, H. S.P.L., 2nd Kingston Sea-Scouts. R.S.M., Seaforth Highlanders.
And Bar.
See full account on page 75.

294 THE SCOUTS' BOOK OF HEROES

HAMLIN, WILLIAM. P.L., 3rd Guernsey. Sig. Bdr., R.F.A.
    He went over the top with the French-Canadians with the first wave, kept up communication throughout the day by telephone and flags and lamp in the evenings. Remained with dying officer throughout the night under very heavy shell fire, cross machine gun fire and an awful snowstorm; was found next morning in a state of exhaustion.

HAMMOND, W. H. S.M., 1st Mkt. Harborough. Cpl., Act. Sgt., 1st Northamptons.

HANKINS, A. P.L., 2nd Sidcup. Cpl., K.R.R.

HANNOCK, A. Scout, 10th and 11th Oldham. Pte., 1/10th Manchester.

HARDING, WILLIAM. P.L., 11th Manchester. Sig., 22nd Manchester.

HARLEY, GEORGE. A.S.M., Offley. Cpl., R.E.
    Bridging the river Lys under fire. After forty hours' continuous work he was left in command of all that remained of the original working party.

HARLEY, WM. Scout, 53rd Manchester. Cpl., Manchester.

HARRIS, JAMES. Scout, 1st Bisley. Pte., R. Fus.

HARRIS, JOHN. P.L., 4th N.B. (Hanney). Lt., Queen's R.W. Surrey.
    And Bar.

HARRISON, H. P.L., 2nd Herne Bay. Pte., Buffs.

HARRISON, JAMES PERCY. S.M., Duston. Cpl., R.A.M.C.

HARROP, ERNEST. P.L., 29th Newcastle. Gnr., R.F.A.

HARTLEY, ROBERT. P.L., 2nd St. Pancras. Pte., R.E.

HARWOOD, J. Scout, St. Phillip's, W. Sussex. Sgt., 4th R. Sussex.

HASTINGS, ALFRID HOWARD. A.S.M., 1st Eastbourne. Cpl., Canadian Scottish.

HATCHER, WILLIAM. Scout, 1st St. Pancras. Sgt., R.F.A.

MILITARY MEDAL

HAYES, THOMAS. 2nd Class, 1st Harden. Cpl., 9th Duke of Wellington, W. Rid.

HEADEACH, M. C. P. P.S.M., 2nd Harrow. Sgt., York and Lancs.

HEADLAND. Scout, 10th St. Pancras.
And Croix de Guerre.

HEIGHLEY, S. V. Scout, 27th Liverpool. L.-Cpl.

HENDERSON, J. S.M., Cross Lanes. L.-Cpl., 10th Duke of Wellington.

HENDRY, R. D. Scout, 2nd Beds. Cpl., 18th Canadians.
Mentioned and recommended for D.C.M.

HENLEY, H. H. A.S.M., 9th Dublin. 2/Lt., R.I.R.

HERRING, A. J. M. P.L., 151st Nth. London. Pte., R.A.S.C.
Driving his ambulance into Gugny three times after it was evacuated by our troops, bringing out many wounded, thus saving them from capture.

HEYCOCK, W. J. Scout Bugler, 1st Aberavon. Gnr., 1st R.H.A.
Also French M.M.

HEYS, WALTER. Scout, 1st Todmorden. Pte., Duke of Wellington.

HICKMAN, B. Scout, 1st Daventry. L.-Cpl., M.G.C.

HICKS, W. Instr., 2nd Skipton. Cpl., 1/6th Duke of Wellington.

HIER, SIDNEY. P.L. Gnr., R.G.A.

HIGGS, E. C. P.L., 2nd St. Albans. L.-Cpl., 1st Beds.

HIGHTON, HAROLD. Scout, 1st Hindley. Pte., Buffs.

HILL, FRED T. P.L., Maldon. Sgt., 1/24th Lon. Regt.

HILLS, LESLIE G. S.M., Lt., R.A.F.

HINCKS, S. P.L., 1st Hinckley. Pte., Leicester Regt,

HIRD, J. Scout, 1st Colne (Mayor's Own). Pte., East Lancs.

HOAR, F. P.L., 2nd Boxmoor. Cpl., 2nd Welsh.

HOCKLEY, G. Scout, Long Cross. Cpl., Queen's W. Surrey.

HODGKINSON, ARTHUR. P.L., Barnoldswick. Cpl. Duke of Wellingtons.

HOLLAND, HERBERT. P.L., 20th West London. R.F.A.
(See full account on page 103.)

HOLMES, HAROLD. A.S.M., 20th Newbury. Pte., R.E.

HOOPER, THOMAS. P.L., 1st Lea. Cpl., L.N. Lanc.

HORN, R. H. W. P.L., 1st Cranbrook. Cpl., Buffs.
(See full account on page 105.)

HORNAL, J. A.S.M., 23rd West London. C.S.M., 12th London (Rangers).

HOSE, JACK. Scout, 1st Southend-on-Sea. Pioneer, R.E.

HOULDEN, AMOS. 1st Banoratham. Sgt., 1st Northants.

HOUSTON, R. Second, 1st Newtownards. Sgt., R.I.R.

HOWARTH, FRANK. A.S.M., Silver Street Wesleyan. Sgt., 11th Batt. Manchester.

HOWARTH, JOSEPH. S.M., 5th Rossendale. Sig., R.F.A.

HOWELL, A. F. A.S.M., St. Matthias, Poplar. Sgt., 1/17th Batt. London.

HOWITT, ARTHUR. Scout, Seventh Cheltenham. S.M., 2/5th Glos.

HUDSON, C. A. P.L., Nether Thong. Sig., D. of Wellington, W. Riding.

HUGHES, F. G. P.L., 114th Manchester. Cpl., R. Fus.
Erecting a bridge over a river under very heavy fire.
(See full account on page 124.)

HUIE, R. P.L., 4th Gateshead, Christ Church. Pte.

HULBERT, E. K.S., 1st Richmond. Cpl., R.A.S.C.

HUNT, A. KENNEDY. Scout, 3rd Plymouth. Sgt., 10th R. Fus.

HUNT, J. Scout, 1st Hamsterly Colliery. Pte., D.L.I.

HUNTER, JOHN. Scout, Pelton Fell. Sgt., D.L.I.

HUNTLEY,, J. Second, 1st Dunbar. Cpl., R.E.

MILITARY MEDAL

INEE, A. P.L., 1st Hirst. Sgt.

INNES, J. A.S.M., Leamington. Pte., 8th Black Watch.

IMPSON, HERBERT A. A.S.M.., 1st Swaffham. Capt., Norfolk.
Also Croix de Guerre, O.B.E., and Twice Mentioned.

JACKSON, A. R. A.S.M., 20th West London. Cpl. Sig., Rifle Bde.
(See full account on page 79.)

JACKSON, T. S.M., 199th Manchester. Spr., R.E.

JAKES, PERCY. A.S.M., 5th Soke (Castor). 2/Lt., 1st Queens.

JAMES, E. P.L., 1st Llandrindod. Sgt., 1st Herefords.

JAMES, FRANK O. 1st Rochdale. 5/6th Batt. R. Scots.

JAMIESON, GEORGE. P.L., Hawkhurst. Sgt., 9th Northants.

JARDINE, THOMAS. P.L., First Hebburn. Lt., 2nd Batt. North.
Awarded a Commission.

JARVIS, R. A. Second, 1st Conisboro. Sgt., York and Lancs.
Also Belgian Croix de Guerre.

JEANS, C. Scout, 1st Bexley Heath. Gnr., R.G.A.

JENKINS, IVOR. A.S.M., 1st Neath. L.-Cpl., 15th Welsh Regt.

JENNER, DOUGLAS. A.S.M., 3rd Erith. Sgt., 7th East Kent.
Keeping telephone and communication. Repairing wires under fire six days and nights.

JENNINGS, G. K. S.M., 4th Kingston. C.S.M., East Surrey.

JEPSON, W. Scout. 143rd Manchester. L.-Cpl., 20th Manchester.

JONES, C. 9th Bromley. L.-Cpl., R.W.K.

JONES, D. Scout, 1st Llandrindod. S/Sgt., R.A.M.C.

JONES, FRANK. P.L., Broseley.   Cpl., K.S.L.I.
JONES, JOSEPH JOHN. A.C.M., 1st Goodmayes.   Sig., 1st Ldn. Scott.
JONES, S. ERNEST. A.S.M., 1st Kensington.   Sgt., A. and S. Hdrs.
JORDAN, G. P.L., 8th Croydon (Christ Church). L.-Cpl., K.O.Y.L.I.
JUGGINS, THOMAS. P.L., 1st Oakridge.   Cpl., 8th Glos.
(See full account on page 95.)
KAY, ROBIN. P.L., 1st Glasgow.   Cpl.
KEARON, DOUGLAS G. Scout, 55th Liverpool.   Pte., Buffs.
KELLY, JNO. A.S.M., 53rd Manchester.   2/Lt., Res. of Officers.
KEMP, ROBERT. K.S., 10th St. Pancras.
KEMP, S. J. P.L., 2nd St. Pancras.   Sgt., R.E.
(See full account on page 127.)
KENNERLEY, FRANK. A.S.M., 1st Hale.   Pte., R.A.M.C.
KERSHAW, J. K. P.L., Crossley School.   Sgt., 2/7th King's Liverpool.
KIDD, HUGH. Second, Littlebury.   Sgt., Essex Regt.
KING, A. V. P.L., 6th Holborn.   Spr., R.E.
KIRK, DENYS. Second, Blue-Coat School.   Cpl., R. Fus.
LAKE, CYRIL. Scout, 4th Chichester.   L.-Cpl., R.G.A.
LAND, WILLIAM. P.L., Cromford.   L.-Cpl., Sher. For.
LANE, CHARLES. P.L., Bramcote.   L.-Cpl., 17th Lanc. Fus.
Rescuing his officer and sixteen men wounded by heavy barrage fire. Applying first aid—sending for ambulance—and then carrying on without them to a successful conclusion.
LATIMER, G. A.S.M., St. Edmund's Troop.   Sgt., 4th Northants.
LAWRANCE, CHARLES. P.L., 1st South Mimms.   Sgt., 1/4th York and Lancs.

MILITARY MEDAL 299

LAWRENCE, ALBERT. A.S.M., 1st Shepperton. Sgt., R.G.A.

LAWRENCE, FREDERICK C. Scout, Highclere. Rfln., K.R.R.
(See full account on page 93.)

LAWRENCE, H. A.S.M., 6th West Ham. Pte., Middlesex.

LAWRENCE, H. P.L., Nether Thong. L.-Cpl., R.G.A.

LAWRENSON, W. Scout, 1st Penwortham. Sgt., L. North Lancs.

LEACH, S. Scout, Ormesby. L.-Cpl., Norfolks.

LEBBON, EDWARD. Ldr., Thetford Town. Sgt., 1st Batt. Norfolk.

LEE, F. Scout, 1st Wormley. Sgt., Beds.

LEE, H. Scout, 5th Batley. Sig., H.L.I.

LESLIE, R. A.S.M., 8th Walthamstow. Sig., 6th London.

LEWIN, F. L. P.L., 8th Poplar. Sgt., R. Fus.
And Bar.

LIDDIARD, S. P.L., 2nd Willesden. L.-Cpl., Rifle Bde.

LINDLEY, C. Scout, 1st Woodlands. Pte., R.F.A.

LINSCOTT, C. W. A.S.M., 4th South London, St. Katharine's. Pte., R.A.M.C.

LINSDELL, REGINALD. Scout, 1st Kingsley Park.
Gallantry in rearguard action during retreat, taking charge of company and being fertile in ideas which were adopted.

LLOYD, R. P.L., Leeson Park. Sgt., R. Innis. Fus.
Also Parchment.

LOVEWELL, C. A.S.M., 15th Norwich. Cpl., Suffolk.

LOWNDES, WILLIAM. A.S.M., 1st Bollington. Pte., Cheshire.

LYNN, JAMES. P.L., 1st Bedlington. 2/Lt., East Yorks.

LYTLE, S. E. P.L., 1st Formby. L.-Cpl., Tank Corps.

THE SCOUTS' BOOK OF HEROES

McCALPINE, C. P.L., 2nd N.T. Ards. Pte., R.E.

MACHIN, J. P.L., 1st Normanton. Cpl., K.O.Y.L.I.

McKIBBIN, A. J. Second, Shorncliffe. Gnr., R.F.A.

MAIDEN, BERT. P.L., 1st Willaston. Pte., M.G.C.

MARGRAVE, PERCY. S.M., 10th Manchester. Sgt., R.A.M.C.

MARSHALL, ARTHUR. Instr., 1st Todmorden. Pte., Gren. Gds.

> Volunteered to cross open ground under very heavy shell fire to obtain connection with the 21st Division. They met a German Patrol lying out and after a bombing fight they captured four of the enemy, obtained touch with the 21st and returned with their prisoners.

MASON, T. W. R. A.S.M., 71st Sth. Ldn. (Brixton Y.M.C.A.). Gym. Instr., R.A.F.

MASON, WILLIAM. P.L., 5th N. London. Sig., Duke of Cornwall L.I.

MATTHEWS, ARTHUR. P.L. Sgt. C. Ser. Rifles.

MATTHEWS, H. S.M., 47th N.E. London. L.-Cpl., 10th Essex.

MATTHEWS, W. A.S.M., 1st Taibach. Cpl., 1/5th Devons.

> And Bar.

MILNE, JOHN. Scout, 1st Rochdale. Pte., Manchester Pals.

MINHINNICK, WILLIAM. A.S.M., Tavistock. Pte., 5th Devons.

MOODIE, R. Scout, 16th Falkirk. Dvr., R.A.S.C.

MORAN, PETER. Scout. Sgt., West Riding.

MORETON, S. C. P.L., 2nd Beds. (Original). Pte., R.A.M.C.

MORGAN, H. S. P.L., Prendergast. Gnr., R.G.A.

MORGAN, NOEL. P.L., 27th Liverpool. Sgt., 2nd W. Lancs. Fld. Amb.

> And Bar.

MILITARY MEDAL 301

MORPHEW, GEORGE. Scout, 1st Slough, St. Paul's. Pte., R.A.M.C.

MORRISH, E. P.L., 1st Bexley Heath. Rfln., L.R.B.
Platoon runner. " Never failed in his mission."

MOYES, JOHN. Scout, 1st Stirling. Pte., R.E.

MUNRO, G. Scout, 1st Lossiemouth. Sgt., Seaforth Highlanders.

NASH, EDWARD. P.L., 6th Rochester. Sig. Cpl., Canadian Mtd. Rifles.

NASH, GEORGE H. A.S.M., St. Matthias, B.G. Sgt., 7th Buffs.
Holding advance post against counter-attacks when officers had become casualties.

NEALER, H. A. P.L., 13th Peek Frean's Own Troop. Sgt., 8th E. Surrey.

NEW, E. P.L., 20th West London. R.F.

NEWTON, J. S.M., 1st Rugeley. Capt., N. Staffs.
Also Croix de Guerre.

NICHOLL, PERCY. P.L., 12th Brighton. Pte., R. Sussex.
Also Bar.

NILSON, J. Scout, 6th Stirling. Pte., 7th A. and S.H.

NOBLE, FRANK. P.L., 1st Ryton. Pte., D.L.I.

NORRIS, BERT. Scout, 1st Bridport. Cpl., 1/5th Devon.

NORRIS, W. F. Scout, 13th Peek Frean's Own Troop. Capt., R.G.A.
And Bar. Twice Mentioned in Despatches.

NUTTER, JAMES H. Late S.M., 1st Evenwood. Sgt., R.A.M.C.

OGDEN, FRANCIS. Scout, 53rd Manchester. Pte., King's Liverpool.

O'SHAUGNESSEY, C. Scout, 4th Waterloo. Bdr., R.F.A.
And Croix de Guerre.

PAGET, WILLIAM. Second, 23rd Cheltenham. Bdr., R.F.A.

PALMORE, JOSEPH. Second, 3rd Seven Kings. Sgt., Scot. Infty.
  Also D.C.M.

PARKER, CLIFFORD. Scout, 1st Swinton. L.-Cpl., E. Yorks.

PARKER, H. E. P.L., 16th Bristol. L.-Cpl., 6th Glos.

PARKER, RAYMOND. Scout, 1st College (Beccles Town). Pte.

PARKER, WM. A.S.M., 3rd Oldham. Cpl., 1/10th Manchesters.

PARSONS, E. Second, 1st Cowes. Rfln., 1/8th Hants.

PASSMORE, P. G. A.S.M., Bideford. Trpr., R. Nth. Devon Hus.

PATERSON, R. W. A.S.M., 6th Wakefield. Sgt., K.O.Y.L.I.

PAYNE, CECIL. Scout, 1st Newmarket. Pte., Suffolks.

PEACEY, HAROLD. Scout, 7th Cheltenham. Dvr., R.F.A.

PEARCE, H. S. S.M., 2nd Leytonstone. L.-Cpl., Queen's R.W. Surrey.

PEARSON, LEN. P.L., 1st Goodmayes. 20th County of London.

PECKHAM, J. Scout, Milford-on-Sea. Dvr., R.F.A.

PERRY, H. N. Scout, Oxfordshire Pioneer. Sgt., Gren. Gds.

PETTOCK. Scout, 1st Newmarket. Suffolks.

PHEAI, HAROLD. A.S.M., 2nd Bathwick. Sgt., R.F.A.
  Also Mentioned.

PHILLIPS, ARTHUR. P.L., 2nd Whitley. Sgt., Northumberlands.

PHILLIPS, DICK. Scout, Goldhanger. Pte. Pub. Schls. Batt.
  (See full account on page 91.)

MILITARY MEDAL 303

PHILLIPS, ERNEST. Scout, Eastdean. Sgt., Rifle Bde.
PHILLIPS, HERBERT. P.L., 11th West Ham. Sgt., 4th Middlesex.
PHILLIPS, R. Second, 1st Newtownards. Spr., R.E.
POND, G. Scout, 1st Newmarket. Cambridgeshires.
PLATT, GEO. A.S.M., 110th Manchester. Pte., R.N.D.
PLIMMER, EDWARD. Scout, 1st Mollinwood. Pte., R.A.M.C.
PLUNKETT, H. S.M., 10th N. London. Sgt., London.
POLLEY, FREDERICK CHARLES. Scout, 5th Colchester. Cpl., Tank Corps.
POOLEY, G. R. A.S.M., 48th N.E. London. Cpl., Yeomanry.
POST, ALBERT. P.L., 57th and 58th Lambeth.
POWELL, HORACE. P.L., 5th N. London. Spr., R.E.
PRATER, H. E. Shorncliffe. Pioneer, R.E.
PRESTON, W. J. A.S.M., Newbold Verdon. King's Sgt., L.N. Lanc.
> Also Croix de Guerre.

PRICE, JNO. P.L., 53rd Manchester. Sgt., R.E.
PROSPER, PETER. A.S.M., 4th Whyteleafe. Spr., R.E.
PUDDICK, P. P.L., Albury. Sgt., Wilts.
> Also Promotion.

QUELCH, L. Scout, Oxford. Pte., R.F.A.
QUELCH, LIONEL. 2nd, Beech Hill. Pte., 1/4th Wilts.
QUINN, P. Scout, 7th and 8th Stirling. Pte., A. and S. Hdrs.
QUINTON, DICK. Scout, 2nd Littlehampton. Pte., R. Sussex.
RAINBOW, FRANK. A.S.M., Harbury. Sgt., R.A.M.C.
> Sent all his men into a shelter trench during heavy shelling and went out himself to fetch in any stragglers. And Bar.

RAMM, GEOFFREY. P.L., 1st Cawston. Cpl., 9th Norfolks.

RAMSEY, T. Second, 41st Glasgow. Cpl., R.F.A.

RATCLIFFE, J. Scout, 2nd Dukinfield. Pte., 2/9th Manchester.

RAYNOR, WILLIAM. A.S.M., 1st Hollinwood. Sgt., Manchester.

READ, PHILIP. P.L., 23rd All Saints, Bournemouth. Sgt., Hants.

READ, W. J. S.M., 1st Sidcup. 2/Lt., R. Fus.

REECE, J. 22nd East Ham. Pte., R. Berks.

REED, G. A.S.M., 1st Lea. Lt., Tank Corps.
First King's Scout in Lancashire.

REES, PERCY. S.M. Sgt., Welsh.

REES, PERCY. A.S.M., 1st Loughor. Cpl., H.A.C.
Saving the ammunition from a gun-carriage which was on fire.

REEVES, B. A. Scout, 2nd and 3rd Farnboro. Pte., Suffolks.

REMNANT, CHARLES W. A.S.M., Eastdean. Sgt., 7th R. Sussex.

RICHARDSON, ARTHUR ERNEST. Scout, Abington. Cpl., 9th Cheshires.

RICKETTS, HARRY. A.S.M., 7th Bristol. Sgt., 6th Glosters.

RIDDLE, HARROLD. P.L., 1st Ryton. Sgt., D.L.I.

RIDLEY, EDMUND. Scout, 1st Bedlington. L.-Cpl., N.Fus.

ROBERTS, EDWARD. T.L., Rossett. Pte., Worcesters.

ROBINSON, J. P.L., 1st Lichfield. Cpl., Black Watch.

ROBINSON, J. P.L., Whitwick. Cpl., 5th Leicesters.

ROBINSON, J. R. S.M., 1st Doncaster. Cpl., 2/4th Lon. Scot.

ROTHWELL, H. Instr.

RUDLINTON, F. P.L., 1st Burton-on-Trent. Sgt., R.A.M.C.

MILITARY MEDAL 305

RULLY, GEORGE. Scout, 53rd Manchester. Pte., D.C.L.I.

RUMSAY, W. Scout, 1st Addiscombe. Spr., R.E.

RUSSELL, SIDNEY. Scout, 7th Bristol. Cpl., M.G.C.

RUTTER, W. RALPH. S.M., 7th Willesden. L.-Cpl., 1st Batt. Kensingtons.

SACHETT, A. Scout, 1st Ramsgate. Cpl., R.A.F.

SAINSBURY, R. Second, 26th Bristol. Pte., R.A.M.C.

SAMMONS, HENRY. P.L., 1st Bisley. Pte., 1/7th Middlesex.

SAMPSON, W. Scout, 1st Brighton. R.A.M.C.

SAVILL, WILFRED. P.L., 1st Brentwood Public Service Trpr., Essex Yeo.

SAWFORD, SAM. P.L., 24th Beds. Sgt., Beds.

SAYER, WILLIAM E. A.S.M., 51st Bristol. L.-Cpl. A. and S. Highlanders.

SCHEUMIER, C. P.L., 2nd Leyton. R. Fus.

SCHOLS, ALBERT H. P.L., 32nd Oldham. Pte., Cheshire.

SCHOOLER, J. Second, 1st Dunbar. Trpr., Scots Greys.

SCIWENER, HORACE. Scout, 3rd Boxmoor. Pte., Beds.

SCOTHORN, T. P.L., 1st Highfields. Pte., York and Lancs.

SCOTT, JOSEPH. P.L., 2nd Hampstead. Pte., R.W.K.
Twice recommended.

SCOTT, J. A.S.M., 1st Bothal. L.-Cpl., N. Fus.

SEAGER, J. Scout, 9th Greenwich. L.-Cpl., Lancers.

SETTERFIELD, T. Scout, 1st Ramsgate. Cpl., Buffs.

SEWARD, BERT. S.M., 10th Hammersmith. Cpl., R.A.M.C.

SEWARD, G. Scout, 4th Hunts. Sgt., Bucks.
And Bar.

SHARP, WALLACE. P.L., 6th East London. Cpl., 1st King's Own R. Lancs.

Locating enemy camp at great personal risk.

SHAUGHNESSY, THOMAS. Scout, 53rd Manchester. Cpl., M.G.C.

SHAW, G. P.L., 1st Forres. L.-Cpl., R.A.M.C. and Middlesex.

SILVEY, CHARLES. Scout, Hermitage. L.-Cpl., Q.V.R.

SIMPSON, E. Scout, 1st Wakefield. Cpl., 2/4th K.O.Y.L.I.

Went forward himself and cut his way through a dense belt of wire, went back and brought up his section under heavy fire. He then went out and bandaged his platoon officer who was lying badly wounded.

(See full account on page 88.)

SISSON, H. Scout, 2nd Dukinfield. Pte., R.A.M.C.

SIVYER, H. S.M., 11th Bromley. R. Sussex.

SKELTON, WILLIAM. S.M., 1st Thrapton. Pte., 7th Northants.

SHEPHARD, R. Scout, 12th N. London. Sig., 3rd London R.E. (T.).

SKINNER, ARTHUR EDWARD. Scout, 7th Hook Pte., 11th Hants.

SLAUGHTER, ARTHUR. P.L., 1st, 2nd, 3rd and 4th Spalding. Sgt., Q.R.R.

SMITH, A. P.L., St. Neots. Sgt., R. Warwicks.

And Bar.

SMITH, BRIGG. Scout, 1st Cullingworth. Cpl., Duke of Wellington W. Rid.

SMITH, C. W. A.S.M., 1st, 2nd, 3rd, 4th Spalding. Sgt., R.A.M.C.

SMITH, EDWARD VICTOR. A.S.M., 18th Newcastle. Pte., R.A.M.C.

SMITH, GEORGE E. A.S.M., 1st Porthill. Cpl., D.L.I.

MILITARY MEDAL

SMITH, HARRY. P.L., 1st Penwortham. Sgt.-Mjr., R.F.A.

SMITH, REGINALD. A.S.M., 28th West London. Cpl., 1/6th Duke of Wellington L.I.

SMITH, ROBERT. P.L., 1st Hammersmith. Bdr., R.F.A.

SMITH, S. J. S.M., 24th Norwich. Sgt.-Sig., 8th Batt. Norfolk.

SMITH, W. P.L., 1st Iver. Sgt.

SMYTHE, GROSVENOR-. Scout, 1st Manchester Grammar Schl. Cpl.

SMYTHE, HENRY HERBERT. Scout, Highclere. Sig., Rfle. Bde.

> Volunteering to carry message under heavy shell fire, and together with a sergeant searching for and finding the remainder of the company when it was cut off, thus making a connection.

SOANES, ARTHUR. P.L., Lubenham. Gnr., R.F.A.

> Helping in a wounded comrade, and keeping up telephonic communications between infantry and artillery under heavy shell fire.

SOLOMON, F. Scout, 2nd and 3rd Farnboro. Pte., R.W.K.

And Bar.

SPARROW, ALEXANDER. P.L., Thetford Town. L.-Cpl., 6th Beds.

> Went out at night and put out machine gunners and brought back gun which had wrought considerable destruction.

SPEED, HARRY. Scout, 1st St. Pancras. Cpl., 19th County of London.

SPENCER, A. S.M., Oxfordshire Pioneer. Sgt., M.G.C.

SPIRET, G. P.L., 1st Bagshot. C.S.M., Queen's R.W. Surrey.

STOCKER, HAROLD. A.S.M., 1st Exeter. Pte., R.A.M.C.

STOKES, STANLEY D. Sea-Scout, 2nd Deal and Walmer. Cpl., R. Sussex.

SWEENEY, C. Scout, 2nd Ware. Cpl., Beds.

SWINSON, A. A.S.M., 4th Hammersmith. Sig.

TABOR, B. Scout, 2nd Cambridge. L.-Cpl., Cambridgeshire.

TAMS, JAMES. P.L., 1st Hanley. Sig., R.F.A.
> As telephonist to the forward observing officer he laid the line from the cable to the forward O.P. in the enemy's second line, passing twice through the enemy's heavy barrage.

TARRANT, E. Scout, 1st Addiscombe. Pte., 19th County of London.

TAYLOR, MARK. P.L., Accrington Borough. Sig., R.E.

TAYLOR, RICHARD. K.S. 1/5th W. Rid.

TAXLEY, JOHN ROBERT. P.L., 1st Sporle-in-Palgrave. Cpl., 9th Duke of Wellington.
> Swimming a canal backwards and forwards under fire to carry instructions to his regimental C.O. as a runner.

TEAGERS, CECIL. Second, 1st Guernsey. Pte., 1st Service Batt., R. Guernsey L.I.

THOMAS, H. 1st Alderbury. Pte., R.A.M.C.

THOMPSON, BENJAMIN. P.L., 13th Windsor. Dmr., 11th Suffolk.

THOMPSON, P. Scout, 1st Knottingley. Q.M.S., M.G.C.

THOMPSON, WILLIAM. Scout, 4th Lancaster. Pte., 5th Batt. K.O.R. Lancs.

THORPE-TRACY, R. A.S.M., 4th East Ham. 2/Lt., 1st London.

THORPE, WALTER. P.L., 1st New Mills. Sgt., Rifle Bde.

THURGOOD, HERBERT. P.L., Standon. Cpl., 2nd Beds.

TILBURY, A. P.L., Chilworth. Spr., R.E.
> And Bar.

TILBURY, JOSEPH. P.L., Hambleden. Cpl., Ox. and Bucks.
> And Bar.

MILITARY MEDAL

TILSED, C. Scout, 1st Poole Sea Scouts. Dvr., R.F.A.
TOMPKINS, LEONARD. P.L., 1st Teddington. Rfln., Lon. Rifle Bde.
TOMLINSON, FRED. A.S.M., 1st Penwortham. Lt., Palatine Battery.
TOOGOOD, N. C. Scout, 1st Harrogate. 2/Lt., Aust. Infty.
TOWLER, J. Scout, 1st Colne (Mayor's Own). Cpl., King's Own Lanc.
TOWERS, ARTHUR. P.L., 4th Lancaster. Sgt., 5th Batt. K.O.R.
TOWN, F. P.L., 1st Coventry. Capt., Tanks.
TOWNSEND, HARRY. S.M., 1st Witney. Gnr., R.F.A.
TRAXTON, THOMAS CHEVERTON. Scout. Gnr., R.F.A.
TROUBRIDGE, E. Scout, 2nd and 3rd Farnboro. Pte., Hampshire.
TURNER, A. J. S.M., 16th Bristol. Pte., R.A.M.C.
TURNER, J. W. Scout, 1st Hamsterly Colliery. Sgt., D.L.I.
TURNER, LESLIE. P.L., 1st Wells. 2/Lt.
TURNER, S. P.L., Sutton at Hone. 2/Lt., R.W.K.
TUTTON, F. J. S.M., 1st Gravesend. 2/Lt., R. Berks.
TWIG, F. P.L., 2nd Chorlton-c.-Hardy. L.-Cpl., Manchester.
UNDERWOOD, BERNARD. Scout, 3rd Sheppey. 2/Lt. Sher. For.
VAUGHAN, A. Scout, 1st Normanton. Sgt., K.O.Y.L.I.
VENABLES, GEORGE. A.S.M., 1st Bolton. L.-Cpl., W.R.D.R.E.
VENN, WILLIAM. Second, No. 1 and 2 Barnstaple. Lt., R.E.
VOYSDEN, G. 10th Belfast. Pte., R.I.R.
WAGSTAFF, C. Scout, Oxford. Pte., Ox. and Bucks, L.I.

WAGSTAFF, LESLIE RALPH. S.M., 3rd Wimbledon. Lt., 8th K.O.L.I.
> Also Croix de Guerre.

WALKER, J. H. A.S.M., 2nd Riddings. Sgt., R.F.A.

WALKER, ROBERT. Scout, Accrington Borough. Gnr., M.G.C.

WALKER, S. P.L., 1st Southend-on-Sea. Pte., Duke of Cornwall's L.I.

WALKER, WILLIAM. P.L., 1st Sacriston. Cpl., 8th D.L.I.

WALLIS, GEO. P.L., 1st Slough, St. Paul's. Dvr., R.F.A.
> And Bar.

WALLIS, PERCY. S.S., 3rd Sheppey. 2/Lt., R.W.K.

WARD, E. G. C. S.M., 6th St. Albans. Sgt., 2/15th Batt. Ldn.
> He found himself with most of his platoon in advance of our line and hung on to his post despite the efforts of the enemy to bomb him out. By his example the party held on till dark when they were ordered back to conform with the line.

WARD, R. Second, 2nd Ross. Pte., Manchester.

WARD, W. Scout, 1st Aldeburgh. Cpl., 4th Suffolks.
> With three other men kept the enemy back, saving the French and the lives of his company.

WARE, G. J. P.L., 1st Berw. Sgt., 2nd Batt. Welsh Regt.

WARREN, D. L. Scout, 1st Leigh-on-Sea. Pte., M.G.C.

WARING, THOMAS. Second, 6th Longton. Cpl., 2nd Lancs. Fus.

WATERHOUSE, CLIFFORD. Scout, 1st New Mills Pte., Sher. For.

WATSON, MORNINGTON. P.L., 1st Cockfield. Sgt., M.G.C.

WATSON, R. Scout, Ormesby. Pte., Norfolks.

WATSON, R. B. A.S.M., 1st Daventry. Cpl., R.A.F.

WAY, HARRY. A.S.M., 1st Windsor. L.-Cpl., 1st Bucks Batt. Q.B.L.I.

MILITARY MEDAL

WAY, STANLEY. A.S.M., 1st Windsor. Cpl., 8th Batt. Tank Corps.
WELBURN, J. A.S.M., Mytholmroyd. Pte., Queen's Own York. Dragoons.
WELHAM, C. Scout, 1st Saxmundham. Pte., R.A.M.C.
WELLS, JOHN GEORGE. P.L., 26th Gateshead. L.-Cpl., R.A.M.C.
  (See full account on page 82.)
WESTBROOK, FREDERICK. P.L., Westdean. Sgt., R. Sussex.
WESTON, LEWIS HUGH P.L. Sig., R.F.A.
WHITMORE, M. E. P.L., 13th Peek Frean's Own. Pte., 22nd County of Lon.
WHITTAKER, T. H. P.L., 1st Stafford. Cpl., 2nd Lincolns.
WHITTLE, R. P.L., 1st Penwortham. Pte., 48th Canadians.
WHITWICK, R. C. P.L., Whitwick. L.-Cpl., 5th Leicesters.
WILBY, FRED. Scout, 4th Chatham. Pte., R.W.K.
WILDERSPIN, H. P.L., 4th Hunts. Sgt., London.
WILKS, S. A.S.M., Brackley. L.-Cpl., Ox. and Bucks.
WILLIAM, THOMAS CROW. Scout, 1st Anglesey. Pte.. R.W. Fus.
WILLIAMS, D. Scout, Llanrwst. Sgt., 1st R.W. Fus,
WILLIAMS, E. B. P.L., 26th West London. Lt., R.F.A.
WILLIAMS, R. Scout, 2nd Chorlton-c.-Hardy. L.-Cpl., Manchester.
WILLIAMS, S. T. P.L., 1st Berkhamsted. Pte., R. Berks.
WILLIAMSON, J. W. S.M., 49th B.P. Sgt., 7th King's Liverpool.
WILLMOTT, W. Scout, 20th West London. R. Fus.
  Also Croix de Guerre.
WILSON, C. Scout, 1st Lossiemouth. Cpl., 7th Seaforth Highlanders.
  Also Croix de Guerre.

WIMPORY, HARRY. Instr., 12th N. London. Spr., R.E.
And Bar.

WINDYBANK, FREDRICK. Scout, Witley. Pte., R.A.M.C.

WINGROVE, JOHN. Scout, 6th Wimbledon. Pte., 12th County of Lon. Rifles.
(See full account on page 86.)

WINSHIP, J. Scout, Nth. Fryston and Sth. Milford. Cpl., W. Yorks.

WIXEY, W. A. Instr., 8th Gloucester. Pte., Ox. and Bucks L.I.

WOLSTENHOLME, J. K. P.L., 1st Broadheath. Cpl. R.E.

WOOD, F. W. Scout, 2nd Conisborough. Sgt. Cadet, Y. and L.

At the risk of his life he went out to the help of seven men who were cut off from the main body and brought them in although they were wounded.

WOOD, HARRY. P.L., 1st Orpington. Pte., R.W.K.
WOODROW, WALTER. 1st Groombridge. R. Sussex.
WOODS, WILLIAM. P.L., Old Woking. L.-Cpl., R. Sussex.

At night he took a machine gun out alone and cleared sixteen of the enemy away from the front of our position.

WOODWARD, WALTER. 1st Groombridge. R. Sussex.
WRAY, ROBERT. Scout, Preston. Cpl., Beds.
WRIGHT, G. Instr., 17th Newcastle. Sgt., R.A.M.C.
WRIGHT, JACK A. P.L., 1st Spilsby. 2/Lt., M.G.C.
And Bar.
WRIGHT, NORMAN L. P.L., 1st Ashton. Pte.
YOUGS, REGINALD. Scout, 1st West Lynn. Sgt.

MERITORIOUS SERVICE MEDAL

ALLITT, WILLIAM. Scout, Leadenham. Sgt., Headquarters Staff, 11th Div., A.S.C.

BARCLAY, J. H. A.S.M., 44th Liverpool. R.O.N.S., 9th Seaforth Highlanders.

BENSTEAD, H. G. A.S.M., 1st Chinley. Sig. Sgt., 1/6th Sher. For.

BLYTH, R. L. S.M., 4th Elwick Road. Sgt.-Mjr., R.A.M.C.

CARTWRIGHT, J. P.L., Ripley. Lt., R.A.F.

COWLEY, ALLAN. A.S.M., 1st Douglas. Cpl., West Yorks.

DAVIES, EDWARD. Scout, 1st Gresford. Sgt., 4th R.W.F.

DUCKWORTH, DAVID. A.S.M., St. Thomas's, Blackburn. Sgt., R.F.A.

EVERSHED, PERCY. A.S.M., Preston. Sgt., Royal Sussex.

FOSTER, W. A. S.M., 25th Hammersmith. St.-Sgt.-Mjr., New Zealand Medical Corps.
Twice mentioned.

KEENE, J. T. A.S.M., 1st Chinley. R.S.M., Rifle Brigade.

LONG, FREDERICK J. Scout, 1st South Mimms. L.-Cpl., 2/4th Yorks and Lancs.

MADDOCK, R. D. A.S.M., 1st Newtownards. Spr., Sig. Co., R.E.

MILL, RICHARD E. A.S.M., 1st Neath. Sgt., Welsh.

O'NIEL, S. A.S.M., 1st Lemington. Sgt., K.O.Y.L.I.

PARROTT, H. P.L. St.-Sgt., R.A.S.C.
Also Mention.

PURSEHOUSE, W. H. A.S.M., Grammar School (Eye). Pte., E. Kents.

RANDLES, GEORGE. A.S.M., 1st Gresford. Sgt., Debyshire Yeo.
RANDLES, J. H. P.L., 1st Gresford. Sgt., R.W.F.
SALMON, WALTER H. S.M., Down Hall. R.-Sgt.-Mjr., R.F.A.
STOKES, H. Second, 1st Poole Sea Scouts. Sgt. (Sgnls.), R.G.A.
UPTON, E. A. S.M., 5th Clapham. R.Q.M.S., K.R.R.C.
WELLS, JOHN. Scout, 1st St. Pancras. Pte., Rifle Brde.
WILLIAMS, W. Scout, 1st Aberavon. Cpl., Q.R.H.A.

MERITORIOUS CONDUCT MEDAL

PETTER, E. D. P.L., 6th Chichester. Sgt., R.H.A.

DISTINGUISHED SERVICE MEDAL

HALE, REG. P.L., 152nd Nth. Ldn. Lt., R. Marines.
 North Sea patrolling work. Aboard armed liner auxiliary vessel. (Prior to promotion.)
HARRISON, E. A. S.M., 1st Doncaster. P.O., R.N.A.S.
HASTINGS, G. Scout, 2nd and 3rd Farnboro. H.N.M.
HATHWAY, CYRIL DANIEL. Scout, 10th Sea Scouts. Wireless Op. 2nd Cls. P.O. Destroyer, Dov. Pat.
LAYCOCK, S. K.S., 10th Harrogate. 2/Lt., R.A.F.
RALPH, H. S.M., 1st Iver. Sgt., R.F.A.
SKILTON, J. P.L., 2nd and 3rd Farnboro. Cpl., Canadians.
 Also Belgian Decoration.

R.H.S.M.—PROMOTION

THOMPSON, JOSEPH. Scout, 1st Ipswich Sea Scouts. A.B. and Torpedo man. H.M.S. *Tiger*.
WILTINS, R. P.L., 4th East Ham. Sgnl., R.N.V.R.
WORTHINGTON, FRANK. S.M., 160th Manchester. Spr., R.E.

ROYAL HUMANE SOCIETY MEDAL

HICK, B. P.L., 8th Liverpool. Chief P.O., R.N.V.R.
Saving life at sea.
LAMB, CHARLES. P.L., 2nd Penrith. Sgln. R.N., H.M.S. *Queen Elizabeth*.
Saving life at sea.
SHAW, SIDNEY. A.S.M., Stapleford and Sandiacre. A.C.C., M.T.
Life saving from drowning in France.

PROMOTION ON THE FIELD

BROOKS, P. M. A.S.M., 15th Battersea. Lt.
CECHS, H. S. A.S.M., 1st Ipswich. Lt., R. Fus.
HARROP, DANIEL. S.M., 53rd Manchester. Capt., L.N. Lancs.
HELMORE, STANLEY. A.S.M., St. Davids. 2/Lt., R.A.F.
McCARTHEY, A. St. Fagans. Lt., S.W.B.
PINNOCK, S. D. T.L., 5th Ipswich. Lt., 2nd Suffolks.

FOREIGN DECORATIONS GAINED BY SCOUTS

AFRICAN MEDAL

HARRISON, FRED. Scout, 1st Hollinwood. Pte., R.A.S.C.

CROIX DE GUERRE (BELGIAN)

CHAMBERS, ROBERT. Scout. Cpl., 15th Hants.

CLARKE, REGINALD. P.L., 23rd All Saints. St.-Sgt., R.A.M.C.

COCKERELL. P.L., St. Stephen's, Hounslow. Lt., R.A.F.
Also two Belgian Decorations.

DAY, J. J. Scout, 1st Chinley. L.-Cpl., R. Scots Fus.

HAMMER, C. P.L., 4th Walthamstow. Cpl.

HOLLAND, FRED. P.L., Cromford. L.-Cpl., Sher. For.

HOWORTH, THOMAS EGBERT. S.M., 1st Ashton. Major, 1/9th Manchester.

MERRYLEES, A. R. S.M., 11th Western. Major, 7th Gordon Highlanders.

CROIX DE GUERRE (FRANCE)

BONFOY, RALPH. A.D.C., 1st Gresford. Tr. Red X. With Palm.

BOOTHMAN, J. W. P.L., 4th Harrow. Conducteur, French Red Cross.
Bravery in driving car when attacked by enemy, also effecting repairs after being badly wounded. Broke through opposition and German machines and regained our own lines.

FOREIGN DECORATIONS

BURKELEY, R. G. WILLIAM-. Late S.M., 1st Anglesey. Major, Welsh Gds.

CHALK, T. Scout, 4th Hammersmith. Pte.

CLARKE, EDGAR. Scout, Norton Canon. Pte., 1st Hereford.

FARGUHAR, G. Scout, 1st Lossiemouth. Cpl., 6th Seaforth Highlanders.

FENTON, WILLIAM. Scout, 4th Ilford. 2/Lt., R.A.F.

FLOWERDEW-LAWSON, Miss NORMA. S.M., Walton. Red X. Amb. Dvr.

Also Belgian Order of St. Elizabeth.

FOSTER, E. W. P.L., 11th Woolwich. Capt., R.F.A.

GIDLEY, ROBERT. Scout, 3rd Chiswick. Dvr., French Red Cross.

See full account on page 121.

GREGORY, W. A.S.M., 2nd Epping Forest. Trmptr., Essex Yeo.

HARE, FRANK. Hon. S.M., 66th Nth. London. Lt., H.M. T.B.D. *Manly*.

JONES, F. P.L., 10th Poplar. Pte., S.L.I.

LOVELESS, A. P.L., 3rd Royal Eltham. Sgt., R. Fus.

MACEY, R. S.P.L., 1st Streatham Common. Lt., R.A.F.

MITCHELL, HAROLD. Scout. Spr., R.E.

MONICE, CYRIL S. KIDDAL-. Scout, 1st Tarporley. Capt., Middlesex.

With Gold Palm.

MORDAUNT, Miss WINIFRED. S.M., Walton. Red X. Amb. Dvr.

NEWLING, C. P.L., 2nd Leytonstone. Cpl., 7th Middlesex.

NICHOLAS, C. H. S.M., 1st Springfield. Major, R.A.F.

NORRIS, D. C. A.S.M., 1st Hatcham. Capt., R.A.M.C.

PETTIGREW, J. Scout, 3rd East Linton. Sgt., Royal Scots.

THE SCOUTS' BOOK OF HEROES

RICHES, H. Scout, 2nd Jarrow Presbyterian. Dvr., R.F.A.

STEPHENS, HAROLD N. S.M., 7th Hook. Lt., Motor Amb. Convoy.
And Four Bars.

WEBB, HAROLD. A.S.M., Culworth. Sgt.-Mjr., Oxford and Bucks Light Infantry.

CROCE DI GUERRA

HAMILTON, Rev. W. R. D.S., Sth. Notts. Lt.
Also Fatica di Gusma.

PATTERSON, J. 1st Glasgow. R.A.F.

GREEK MEDAL OF MILITARY MERIT

COLLER, FRANK. P.L., 5th Clapham. Ldg. Mac. and Obs., R.N.A.S.

MEDAILLE MILITAIRE

BELSHAW, CHARLES HERBERT. S.M., 3rd Atherton. C.S.M., 4th Ox. and Bucks L.I.

BLAKE, A. Second, 33rd St. Margaret's. 2/Lt., R.A.F.
Also Belgian Croix de Guerre.

BOWERS, FRED. Scout, Titchfield. Bdr., R.F.A.

LOWRIE, W. E. P.L., 7th N. London. Lt., R.A.F.
Maintaining communication by wireless under heavy bombardment from land and air.

OGDEN, LEES. Scout, 10th and 11th Oldham.

REFFELL, ALLAN. P.L., Shere. Flt.-Sgt., R.A.F.

SERBIAN ORDER OF ST. SAVA AND CROSS OF SERBIAN RED CROSS

CAHEN, LOUIS. S.M., 7th Hook. S.R.F.

FOREIGN DECORATIONS

SERBIAN GOLD MEDAL
BARRETT, LEONARD. A.S.M., 4th N.B. (Hanney). Cpl., M.G.C.

SERBIAN MEDAL
BATES, STUART. A.S.M., 66th Nth. London. Capt., Middlesex.
Also St. Michael and St. George.
LARDNER, HENRY JOHN. 1st Goodmayes.

ST. ANNE'S MEDAL (RUSSIAN ORDER)
WALTERS, A. E. P.L., 26th Bristol. Sgln., R.N.V.R.

ITALIAN FLYING CROSS
COTTLE, J. A.S.M., 3rd Plymouth. Lt., R.A.F.

ITALIAN BRONZE MEDAL
MACHIN, WILLIAM. Scout, Badshot Lea. Sgt., R A.F.

ITALIAN WAR MEDAL
ELLIS, P. W. R. P.L., 3rd Epping Forest. Middy, R.N.R.
FENN, C. Scout, 1st Alvechurch. Dvr., R.H.A.
HORRIS, J. P.L., 6th West Ham. Pte., M.G.C.
WALL, W. Second, Grasmore Works. Sgt., Sher. For.

ITALIAN SILVER MEDAL
SKINNER, A. N. 1st Salisbury. Lt., R.F.A.

MEDAL OF ST. GEORGE

BRIDGER, H. P.L., 7th Croydon. Sgt., M.G.C.
CHECKLEY. S.M., 5th Worth. Armoured Car.
  Also Medal of St. Stanislau.

RUSSIAN SILVER MEDAL ORDER OF ST. STANISLAU

COULTON, ALBERT. Instr., 3rd Atherton. Pte., Naval Sick Berth Res., H.M.S. *Jupiter*.
FARNINGHAM, J. A. A.S.M., Bervie. W.O., M. M.G.C.
  Also Order of St. George.